ROBERT BURNS: SELECTIONS

THE LIBRARY OF LITERATURE

UNDER THE GENERAL EDITORSHIP OF

JOHN HENRY RALEIGH AND IAN WATT

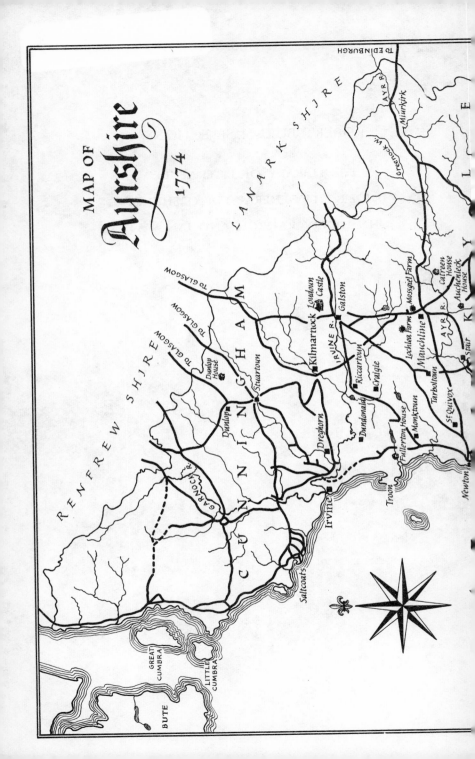

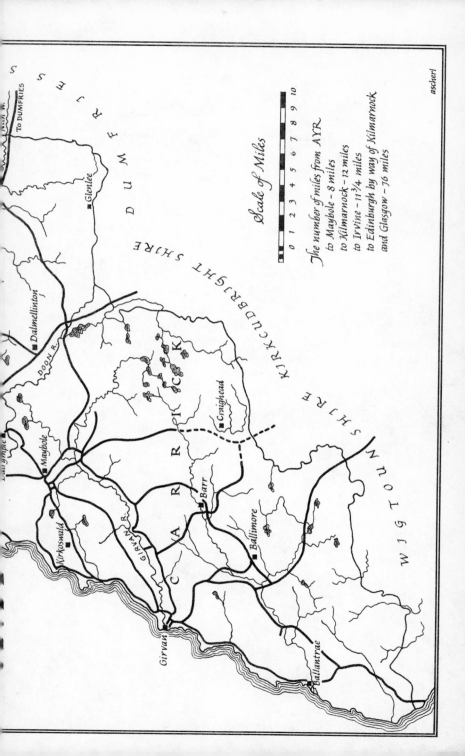

Scale of Miles

0 1 2 3 4 5 6 7 8 9 10.

The number of miles from AYR
to Maybole – 8 miles
to Kilmarnock – 12 miles
to Irvine – 11¾ miles
to Edinburgh by way of Kilmarnock
and Glasgow – 76 miles

ascherl

DUMFRIES

KIRKCUDBRIGHT SHIRE

WIGTON SHIRE

C A R R I C K

To DUMFRIES

Glenlee

Dalmellinton

DOON R.

Maybole

Dalrymple

Kirkoswald

GIRVAN R.

Craighead

Barr

Ballimore

Girvan

Ballantrae

Robert Burns:
SELECTIONS

Edited with an Introduction
and Annotations by
JOHN C. WESTON
University of Massachusetts

THE BOBBS-MERRILL COMPANY, INC.
A Subsidiary of Howard W. Sams & Co., Inc.
INDIANAPOLIS · NEW YORK

Contents

Introduction

THE LIFE OF ROBERT BURNS

Robert Burns, the first son of a poor gardener and an illiterate mother, was born on January 25, 1759, in Alloway, a few miles south of Ayr, a seaport town in southwest Scotland. His father, William Burnes (Robert changed the ending of his name later), belonged to the cotter class, which Burns later idealized in "The Cotter's Saturday Night." His brave but unsuccessful struggle for financial stability and his moderate Calvinist principles made lasting impressions on his son's more rebellious and passionate mind. Eventually there were six more children.

The family turned to full-time farming in Burns's seventh year when his father leased seventy acres nearby, the first of three such farms which kept the family grievously poor by the combination of rocky and impoverished soil and high rents. At this time Burns had already been attending a one-room village school taught by a bright and devoted young man, John Murdock, who was employed privately by a group of neighbors. Murdock managed, during Burns's three years of regular attendance, to introduce him to a vast and very mixed assortment of English literature, mainly the genteel eighteenth-century variety. Once Burns had learned to read and write and to do arithmetic, which was the purpose of sending him to school, his regular education was very spotty: alternate weeks with his brother Gilbert in the summer of his fourteenth year; a few weeks studying French with Murdock during his fifteenth; a short period when he was sixteen studying surveying, away from home for the first time, in Kirkoswald across the River Doon in the district of Carrick. But this was only part of Burns's education, for at home his father supervised courses of reading in geography, history, devotional and theological literature, and practical arithmetic. Besides the Presbyterian duty of Bible study, Burns seems to have read indiscriminately all the books he could borrow from neighbors. His study time was intermittantly snatched from the competing demands of long and arduous labor, even as a boy, on the family farm.

In Burns's eighteenth year the family moved about twelve miles to the northwest. There at Lochlie Farm between the villages of Tarbolton and Mauchline, Burns's sociable nature, frustrated up to this time by almost complete isolation, flourished. He helped form the social-debating-reading Tarbolton Bachelors' Club of intellectuals and roisterers, became an active Freemason, and formed scores of friendships and liasons with local young women. Except for an abortive attempt in 1781 to enter the flaxdressing business in Irvine, a seaport town twelve miles north of Ayr, he remained in central Ayrshire working on the family farm until the publication of his *Poems* had made him famous. Even after his father died in 1784, heavily in debt and on the very brink of ruin, he and his brother Gilbert stayed in the area by leasing the farm at nearby Mossgiel, which put Burns even closer to the activities of Mauchline. His early verse, particularly the epistles, shows that he knew all the local people and the gossip about them.

One reason for Burns's local fame was his habit of writing poetry, which probably began to circulate in manuscript in about 1782. From his fourteenth year he had been writing some good song lyrics in Scots vernacular and a few heavy moral and sentimental pieces in standard English, but his production was sparse and uneven. It was not until his early twenties when he had on his own initiative discovered the Scottish vernacular poets of the eighteenth century, particularly Allan Ramsay, that he began writing good non-lyric poetry, and it was not until he had discovered the best of all these vernacular poets, Robert Fergusson, in 1784 or 1785, that he began suddenly to produce his poetry of lasting appeal, all in Scots. By 1783 he had become self-conscious enough about his poetry to copy it, as well as remarks about it and about his poetic development, into a commonplace book, but it was not until he was twenty-six that he began to write his finest poems. Thus Burns's poetic maturity came relatively late in his short life.

The years 1785 and 1786 were not only the period in which Burns wrote almost all of his memorable non-lyric poetry, but they were also those of storm and stress. He paid a fine to the kirk and underwent public penance there for fornication, when his first daughter was born in May of 1785 to a former servant in his household, Elizabeth Paton. This was the first of perhaps nine illegitimate children Burns fathered during his lifetime, four of whom (two sets of twins) were born to his future wife Jean Armour and all of whom Burns either helped to support or raised with his family.

He endured the same punishment later for his affair with Jean, and he was thrown into an almost hysterical state of mind when he thought Jean had betrayed him by an apparent compliance with her father's renunciation of Burns as a future son-in-law. For a time he actually hid to avoid imprisonment resulting from a writ which it was rumored Jean's father had issued against him calling for the support of Jean's unborn child.

He had still another love affair with a servant girl visiting in Ayrshire, Mary Campbell, the Highland Mary of the song, who died, evidently in giving birth to Burns's child. As a desperate solution to what seemed the wreck of his life, he made repeated plans during the first three-quarters of 1786 to emigrate to Jamaica, even to the extent of booking passage several times.

But since the early spring of that year, he had also been busy putting together a volume of his poetry. Published with the help of his friends in the nearby town of Kilmarnock at the end of July, it set in motion the events which secured Burns for Scotland, temporarily eased his financial difficulties, and made him famous. *Poems Chiefly in the Scottish Dialect* was soon sold out and became an immediate success among all classes, not only in southwest Scotland but in Edinburgh, where at the end of November Burns went to arrange for a second edition. By the end of the year the most influential Scottish critic, Henry Mackenzie, had praised the *Poems* in print, and Burns's prospective Edinburgh publisher, William Creech, had issued subscription bills for a new enlarged edition.

From this time until the middle of 1788, a period of about a year and a half, Burns's life is associated with Edinburgh. Although he saw the new edition through the press and published in April 1787, he kept returning to Edinburgh, first, because he had to try to collect money owed him by his difficult publisher; second, because (at first, at least) he found the city with its social clubs, its song, its dance, and its cultural life stimulating; but mainly because he simply did not know what way of life to adopt in order to make a living, which he very early found neither his poetry nor his wealthy new friends could provide.

He was soon introduced into the best social and intellectual circles of Scottish society, which were impressed by the force of his conversation and the dignity of his unpolished manner but which could never accept him fully because of his class, his rumored indiscretions and debaucheries, and his refusal to toady. He probably enjoyed more the society of printers, publishers, schoolmasters, booksellers, and clerks of the flourishing nocturnal club-life in the old closes of the ancient city.

With some of the money from the new edition and the leisure of his indecision, he went on four separate tours of Scotland with friends, collecting songs, studying Scottish history, and (since all Scotland knew of him by this time) being entertained in farms and country houses by acquaintances whose "fierce hospitality" he always regretted the morning after. Toward the end of 1787, he met in Edinburgh an amorous but repressed and deserted wife, Agnes M'Lehose, with whom he indulged a warm but evidently chaste relationship and exchanged a great mass of inflated and genteel love letters later known as the Clarinda-Sylvander correspondence from the Arcadian names they used in their letters. Because of the insurmountable barrier of his peasant origin, Burns never managed to have a sexual affair with a lady of the upper classes, although he was on the most intimate terms otherwise with quite a few; he therefore during this period found his sexual gratification in casual relations with servant girls he picked up on the streets.

Since Burns wrote no poems of the first rank during his stay in Edinburgh, the main benefit literature derives from it is his friendship with James Johnson, an uneducated engraver and enthusiastic collector and publisher of Scots song, whose series of volumes, *The Scots Musical Museum,* quickened Burns's interest and occupied him as editor and principal contributor for the rest of his life.

Choosing what alone seemed possible as a means of survival, Burns finally decided to return to farming. He rented a piece of pretty but poor land at Ellisland in Dumfriesshire in March of 1788, and about the same time married Jean Armour. She had just given birth to their second set of twins, who died within a month. The rest of his life was a desperate struggle as a husband and father to support an increasing family. He turned tax collector in September of 1789 and gave up his farm as a bad job two years later to move six miles into the city of Dumfries.

After Britain went to war with revolutionary France, Burns's known radical sympathies made his government job so insecure that he felt himself forced by the economic tyranny of family responsibility to conform publicly to the official anti-French line. Indulging his irrepressible need for social life, Burns drank often and sometimes deep, but that he was always a drunkard and during his final years in Dumfries, a sot, is a moralistic myth fostered largely by his biographers of the last century: Burns never was a hard-drinker because his constitution could not endure much alcohol. He was undoubtedly unfaithful to Jean, a woman of great loyalty and understanding, if of absolutely no culture, although the scale of his adultery has been exaggerated. After his marriage, his only recorded bastard child (born to a barmaid of a tavern in Dumfries) was magnanimously taken by Jean into the household to be raised with her own children.

During these years in Ellisland and Dumfries, he devoted his literary activities mainly to collecting and writing songs. But he continued to write non-lyric poetry, almost none of which attained to the quality of that which he composed during the last two years in Ayrshire. Except for his songs, he was determined to employ literary types not used or little used in his earlier pieces, so as, he wrote, "to secure my old friend, Novelty, on my side, by the kind of my performances." [1] He tried moral

---

[1] *Letters,* I, 379.

epistles and satires in the manner of Alexander Pope, political ballads, serious elegies, prologues for the theater, and only once, the folk tale, "Tam o' Shanter." But "Tam o' Shanter" and the large body of songs amply refute those who posit a creative decline to parallel a reputed moral one, simply because Burns chose not to continue in his earlier vein.

Burns remained in Dumfries, an officer in the arduous duties of the Excise, until on July 21, 1796, he died from a recurrent heart condition probably brought on by overwork as a child on his father's farm. Soon after his death, Maria Riddell, for the last five years his best female friend among the upper classes, wrote an impression of his character. One passage testifies to his social accomplishments in these years: "None certainly ever outshown Burns in the charms—the sorcery I would almost call it—of fascinating conversation; the spontaneous eloquence of social argument, or the unstudied poignancy of brilliant repartee."[2]

If Burns's poetry has been neglected—as it largely has—because of interest in the poet, Burns, in a way, brought this treatment on himself. All his poems are autobiographical. Incapable of dramatic detachment, mythopoecis, or allegory, he worked with his own world. Into everything he wrote, he projected intensely and vigorously, himself, his surroundings, his personality, as a means to make his poetry more attractive, just as a skillful politician exploits himself to sell his policies. And his personality was, and through his poetry continues to be, powerful and appealing.

Most of the complexities in Burns's character resulted from two general struggles within him: one economic-social, the other religious. First, his educated and enlightened tastes and aspirations tended to ally him to the upper classes, but his lower-class origin and sympathies persisted and always rebelled against the genteel world. Second, his strong love of pleasure warred against the rigourous precepts of Calvinism learned in his youth and never completely shaken off. He saw himself as a part of a Scottish national revival but felt himself debarred from Scottish

---

[2] CW, IV, 521.

high society; he stood with the aristocrats in religious matters but against them in matters of social justice. Like an aristocrat, he imbibed the most heady ideas of the Enlightenment but he remained a peasant in many of the values and tastes learned in his childhood. He was a Scottish nationalist, although he was only tolerated or ignored by the rulers of Scotland, whom he despised. He was proud of his friends among the gentry and nobility but often saw some of them for what they were and hated some of them inwardly. He loved the pleasures of the senses and of art and repeatedly defended social deviates, but he struggled to the end of his life for decent Calvinist respectability. He was promiscuous but expressed his detestation of promiscuity. He denounced the aristocratic classical tradition in poetry but often tried to write within its confines. He was a radical democrat by passionate conviction forced into tame patriotic conformity by his sober concern for his family's survival. His sensitive pride resulted from his knowledge of the disparity between his own genius and the mediocre people around him, only privileged by the fortuitous circumstance of birth.

HISTORICAL AND POLITICAL BACKGROUND

In Burns's day, as well as today, Scotland was divided into the Highlands and the Lowlands. The Highlands lie to the west of an imaginary line extending to the north of Inverness and southeast from there to Edinburgh above the Firth of Clyde, including the islands of the Outer and the Inner Hebrides; all the rest to the east and south is the Lowlands. The people in the Highlands spoke (and to a lesser extent still speak) a Celtic language unrelated to English, called Erse or Scottish Gaelic; those of the Lowlands, Scots, a language which, like English, descends from Anglo Saxon, in this case from the Northumbrian variation of it. Burns spoke an Ayrshire dialect of Scots and wrote his poems in the literary language of Scots. The Highlanders were divided into clans which in Burns's day still retained some force, even though the English had attempted to break them up after the Uprising of 1745; the

Lowlanders had no such political divisions. Highlanders were to some extent Catholic and generally Jacobite, that is, conservative monarchists devoted to the old Stuart line descended from James VI of Scotland (James I of England). Lowlanders were Presbyterian and "Whigs," that is, extreme Protestants friendly to the Parliamentary opposition to the Stuart kings, and friendly to the Whig Settlement, which, following the deposition of James II of England, established the balance between King and Parliament in favor of the latter. Burns, always a Scottish nationalist, often identified Highland Jacobitism with Scottish independence (see Songs 26–28), thus curiously seeming to ally his abiding democratic beliefs with the reactionary Scottish faction; but such contradictions resulted from the absence in Burns's day of any established political group in Scotland of a genuinely radical persuasion.

Scotland had in 1707 lost the last vestige of her political independence by the Act of Union with England, which abolished the Scottish Parliament in the capital city of Edinburgh and provided for Scottish peers and members to be sent to the English Parliament in London. Although Scotland kept its own legal system and the management of its state religion, it was, as it is today, governed by people appointed by the prime minister in London. In Burns's day Scotland was virtually ruled by Henry Dundas, the "Grand Vizier" or "uncrowned king" of Scotland, who controlled all the patronage and most of the elections, which, because of the very limited suffrage, were susceptible of influence. Burns's politics, shading from a James Fox kind of Whiggism to radical anti-Hanoverianism, put him outside the confines of the respectable and profitable Scottish political organization. He openly attacked Dundas's nephew Robert (see "The Dean of the Faculty") and generally hated the name of Dundas. Through Whig friends of influence he acquired his minor Excise appointments in spite of his politics. And when his occasional public outbreaks of French revolutionary zeal caused concern during the repressive years following the outbreak of war with France, he only managed to keep his job by the intervention of his friends and by his own nominal political conformity. His friends probably could not have done much more for him. But a nod from

Dundas, which not surprisingly never came, would have relieved him of the crushing burden of his poverty.

Although Scotland had lost its political independence, she still retained something of an indigenous culture in spite of the English ways of the upper classes and of the Edinburgh literati. The folk and literary Scottish culture survived as an alternative to the dominant English current in Scottish life. Burns was occasionally tempted (as Sir Walter Scott always was) to deck out Scots culture in genteel English colors to please those who could do most for him. Although all the lower classes spoke broad Scots and most of the educated would permit themselves on appropriate occasions to lapse into it, Burns's upper-class friends looked condescendingly and often distastefully upon his Scots poetry as quaint, "natural," or even vulgar. The modish Scottish poets like Thomas Blacklock and James Beattie wrote pure English. David Hume asked English friends to read his manuscripts to excise all Scotticisms. Broad Scots was snobbishly considered a sign of inferior class. Burns's fine English prose was a product of the dominant Anglicizing tendency of the century, but this same impulse paradoxically ruined much of his poetry. All his best poetry resulted from the strength of the Scots sub-culture.

RELIGIOUS BACKGROUND

The Presbyterian Scottish Kirk ruled over almost all of the one and a quarter million people of Scotland at mid-century; the Scottish Episcopalians, mainly among the nobles and lairds (hereditary landowners), and the Roman Catholics in the Highlands were less than ten percent of the population and were barely tolerated groups. The General Assembly, the highest body of the Scottish Kirk, met once a year to make laws and hear cases. Below the Assembly spread a pyramid of ecclesiastical courts of decreasing geographical jurisdiction: the synod, the presbytery, and finally the kirk session. This last, composed of the minister of the parish, the elders, and the heritors of the local kirk, controlled the moral and religious behavior of the parishioners by inquiry into practices, and by imposition of fines and other punishments.

Most of the people and a large part of the parish ministers during Burns's day still adhered to the orthodox doctrines of John Knox and the more extreme refinements of them made by some of his followers. Burns exposed these doctrines with amazing fullness and particularity in "Holy Willie's Prayer." According to these beliefs, Adam's sin caused all his progeny to be totally depraved. Christ's death did not open salvation to all men who chose Him and His example, but only to those whom God, for inscrutable reasons, elected. All are predestined to damnation or salvation. The antinomian belief (denounced by the General Assembly in 1720, but still prevalent) followed, that Christians need not obey the moral law to be saved. The elect were informed of their state by God's Effectual Calling, a moment of inner illumination calling them from their sinful ways. By emotional, evangelical preaching, the orthodox ministers castigated sin, portrayed the lurking devil and the torments he had prepared for those not chosen, and, paradoxically, attempted to create communally the occasion of the Effectual Calling. These beliefs and practices were those of the broadly-based Evangelical, the Popular, or the "Auld-Licht" (Old-Light) party within the Church of Scotland.

But these old-fashioned popular doctrines had been largely discredited and condemned by the Moderate or "New-Licht" party, which after the middle of the century dominated the General Assembly and by its support of patronage caused many parish ministers of Moderate persuasion to be ordained in defiance of the largely orthodox wishes of the kirk sessions and the parishioners. The Moderates, composed of the aristocratic, landed, cultured, more intellectual and educated men, and thus perhaps influenced by English latitudinarian and even deistic beliefs and by the moral philosophy of the Scottish universities, emphasized salvation by good moral practice determined by reason and Christ's teaching and example. The Evangelicals accused the Moderates of Socinianism (unitarianism) and Arminianism (salvation by works).

Like his more conservative father before him and like the civilized and learned minister Dalrymple of Ayr who baptised him, Burns belonged to the Moderate party. Burns's personal religious beliefs are complex and inconsistent; they vary from the humane and reasonable Calvinism of his father to the scepticism of the more advanced thought of the European Enlightenment of which he was well aware. But for the understanding of his satires, since satire by nature is negative, we need only know what he was against; and that, simply enough, was the Evangelical party and their beliefs. It is paradoxical that Burns, the great champion of the people and democracy, found himself, in matters of religion—because of genius, voluminous reading, and eager inquiry which removed him from his class—in league with the aristocrats in opposing the popular party.

LITERARY BACKGROUND

Burns's best poems are of a tradition entirely different from the English one, and thus cannot be classified by standards other than their own. His verse forms, language, and genres are those made popular by his predecessors in the eighteenth-century revival of Scottish literature: Robert Sempill of Beltrees, William Hamilton of Gilbertfield, Allan Ramsay, and, best of all, Robert Fergusson. These poets were writing in a tradition which had flowered most impressively in the late fifteenth and early sixteenth centuries with Robert Henryson, William Dunbar, and Gavin Douglas, when all Scots poets wrote in Scots. Since the early seventeenth century when James VI of Scotland took his court to London and John Knox wrote in English and the reformed church suppressed secular literature among the people, whatever poetry cultured Scotsmen wrote was, like the poetry of Drummond of Hawthornden, in English. Many older Scots poems had been printed in anthologies in the first quarter of Burns's century and, although the most modish and respectable Scottish poets wrote (poorly) in English, there had occurred a revival of original vernacular poetry, to which Burns was the last contributor until Hugh MacDiarmid touched it to life again in the twentieth century.

Burns, like these predecessors, composed in a literary language made up of a synthesis of dialect words from all over the Lowlands and of poetic words found in the vernacular literature. The very names of his stanzas show their origin ("Christis Kirk on the Green," "The Cherry and the Slae," "Habbie Simson"), and even his octosyllabic couplets in "The Twa Dogs" and "Tam o' Shanter" have more the rhythm of those in Ramsay's *Fables* or Fergusson's "Planestanes and Causey" than of those used by the English masters of the form in the previous age: Butler, Prior, Swift, and Gay. His epistles have almost nothing in common with those of Pope; but they are similar in many ways to Hamilton's and Ramsay's. His comic elegies are straight from the tradition that Sempill's "Piper of Kilbarchan" started when it was published at the beginning of the century. His satires have fewer direct Scots models than his other poems, but they are closer to some by Ramsay and Fergusson than to any by Pope. Two short poems by Ramsay gave Burns the idea for "The Jolly Beggers," and although the form is English, the stanzas of the recitatives and all but two of the tunes are Scots. The large majority of tunes for which Burns wrote lyrics are Scots and all of the best lyrics have at least a sprinkling of Scots words.

When it came to literary form and manner, Burns, the radical in politics, was ultraconservative and traditional. As a formal artist he invented almost nothing new, since he almost always had a model in his mind, and the models for all his best poems are Scots. Burns will not be properly appreciated unless we see him as a Scot writing in the old tradition of Scots vernacular literature, taking his place not with Pope or Gray or Wordsworth but with the other greatest Scottish poets of the Scots language, the late medieval William Dunbar and the twentieth-century Hugh MacDiarmid.

But two clarifications must be made. Although Burns is unquestionably in the mainstream of the Scots vernacular literary tradition, he undoubtedly brought a great deal of what he knew and admired from English literature even into his best poems. Although all his many sentimental and moralizing poems in the English mode, based on the style and in the mood of Pope, Thomson, Shenstone, Sterne, and Gray, are inferior because the tradition is alien to him, he often integrated English elements into his best Scots pieces. Setting aside the hundreds of verbal echoes from English poetry, which a reading of the footnotes in Thomas Crawford's recent book (see Bibliography) can demonstrate, we perceive examples of more internal or formal English influences. The bard's vigorous second song in "The Jolly Beggars" is English in tune and words. Although the main models for "To a Mouse" are three odes about animals by Fergusson (Bee, Butterfly, Gowdspink), it could not have been written without an appreciation of Gray's manner of a personal terminal twist in "Elegy Written in a Country Churchyard" or the moral extension from the animal world in "Ode to Spring." His view of Satan in a number of his poems derives almost as much from *Paradise Lost* as it does from the Scots folk devil. He turned the loose Scots tradition of the comic elegy into a true burlesque in "Poor Mailie's Elegy" because, we suspect, he learned about that kind of poetry from Dryden, Pope, and Gay.

The second clarification is related to the first. Although Burns worked conservatively with Scots models in his mind, he did so, as he wrote in his Preface to the Kilmarnock *Poems,* "rather with a view to kindle at their flame than for servile imitation" (see Appendix A). Not especially creative in form or matter, he nevertheless made many small innovations and left his distinctive imprint on the tradition he inherited. Mention has already been made of his innovation in the Scots comic elegy. He adapted Hamilton's and Ramsay's verse epistles to serious subjects. He made of the loose descriptions of a festival day in Fergusson's "Leith Races" a controlled satire of single purpose ("The Holy Fair"). He usually realized the potential of the form he inherited rather than invented one; he tightened the genres, brought them more under control. And line by line, with flashes of wit, breathtaking turns of phrase, a warm heart, a sharp eye for pretense, a peasant's refusal to be put upon, a fierce moral indignation, he made of traditional forms and matter, poetry distinctively individual.

The interests of Burns's poetry will be best served if there are no false expectations. Burns had very little visionary imagination of the kind that creates whole mythical or fictive worlds, like Hardy or Faulkner, Blake or Yeats, or even like the Pope of "The Rape of the Lock" and "The Dunciad." His poetic world is his real one, that of southwest Scotland. The closest he came to creating an imaginary world is in "The Jolly Beggars" and that, characteristically, is disconcertingly realistic, that is, based on the unattractive facts of Scots vagabondage.

Nor did Burns describe the outward forms of nature to any great extent. With some exceptions (e.g., "Elegy to Captain Matthew Henderson"), images of nature come in casually. It has often been noted that Burns lived his whole life within a few miles of the sea without including a description of it in his poetry. Burns is not a nature poet. Nor is he a poet of sensuous and lush imagery like Spenser and Keats, most of his imagery existing not for itself but for the metaphorical purposes of his wit. Nor does he present any grand scheme of things, a cosmic view, like Wordsworth or Whitman. He is not a philosophic poet.

Nor, finally, is he erudite and learned, like Donne and Eliot. His life of impoverished labor did not permit the leisure and energy required to learn languages and read widely and indulgently. Scottish music and song was the one body of formal subject matter which he knew more about than anybody else. The books he had read he seems almost to have memorized, but his allusions come from a rather narrow range of literature, although those to the Bible, particularly to the Old Testament, are impressive in their frequency and aptness.

What could a poet in the late eighteenth century do who was deprived of leisure to become learned and whose talents were not those of myth-making, of dramatic creation, of philosophical synthesis, or of descriptive image-making. He could, as Burns did, turn for his subject matter to the society around him and the folk culture which he knew. And he could use his natural talents of clear vision, humanity, and humor. And he could write, in the literary language of his country, epistles, satires, "manners-painting" poems (as he called them), and lyrics to his native music. When he ventured beyond these limitations, he almost invariably failed. But within them he created a body of poetry that ranks him with the more privileged poets who achieved greatness.

BIBLIOGRAPHY

Items preceded by an asterisk have helpful bibliographies.

BIBLIOGRAPHICAL

EGERER, J. W. *A Bibliography of Robert Burns:* Edinburgh and London: Oliver and Boyd, 1964. A primary bibliography, good for finding all editions and the first appearance of individual pieces, but poor for showing the relation of editions.

HEPBURN, A. G., *et al. Catalogue of Robert Burns Collection in the Mitchell Library.* Glasgow: Glasgow Corporation Public Libraries, 1959.

PRIMARY

BARKE, JAMES, SYDNEY GOODSIR SMITH, and J. DELANCEY FERGUSON, eds. *The Merry Muses of Caledonia.* London: W. H. Allen, 1965. Contains a number of bawdy songs composed and collected by Burns and not found in other editions.

* CHAMBERS, ROBERT, ed., revised by William Wallace. *The Life and Works of Robert Burns.* 4 vols. Edinburgh and London, 1896. Both prose and poetry arranged chronologically with biography and commentary interspersed. Good for Burns's non-epistolary prose and for a great mass of biographical and background information.

COOK, DAVIDSON, ed. "Annotations of Scottish Songs by Burns," *Annual Burns Chronicle and Club Directory*. XXXI (1922). Reprinted in *The Songs of Robert Burns* listed below. Prints an important discovery of Burns's manuscript that augments Dick's *Notes,* listed below.

DICK, JAMES C., ed. *Notes on Scottish Song by Robert Burns.* London, 1908. Reprinted in *The Songs of Robert Burns* listed below. These are critical notes that Burns wrote about his own songs along with Dick's voluminous and learned commentary.

*————, ed. *The Songs of Robert Burns.* London, 1903. Reprinted by Folklore Associates, Hatboro, Pa., 1962. One of the monuments of modern scholarship. The only reliable source for finding the music reproduced for which Burns wrote his lyrics. Over 150 pages of notes.

DOUGLAS, WILLIAM SCOTT, ed. *The Works of Robert Burns.* 6 vols. Edinburgh, 1777–1779. The first attempt to print all of Burns's poetry and prose. Only superceded by Chambers-Wallace (listed above), still valuable for annotation.

FERGUSON, J. DELANCEY, ed. *The Letters of Robert Burns.* 2 vols. Oxford: The Clarendon Press, 1931. Definitive. The beginning point of all biographical studies of Burns.

HENLEY, WILLIAM E., and THOMAS F. HENDERSON, eds. *The Poetry of Robert Burns.* "The Centenary Edition." 4 vols. Edinburgh, 1896. Reissued in 1901. The best edition for the text of and notes on the poems.

BIOGRAPHICAL

CARSWELL, CATHRINE. *The Life of Robert Burns.* London: Chatto and Windus, 1930. Many scholars scoff at this book because it is almost completely undocumented. But the author, a Scotswoman and a friend of D. H. Lawrence, knew all there was to be known about Burns and used the facts responsibly to produce the only readable and sympathetic, if often conjectural, narrative of Burns's life. Read this for Burns the man, then read Snyder for the documentation.

FERGUSON, DELANCEY. *Pride and Passion.* New York: Oxford University Press, 1939. A series of essays on the most important aspects of Burns's life. The best non-narrative biographical study.

* HECHT, HANS. *Robert Burns: The Man and His Work.* London, Edinburgh, Glasgow: William Hodge and Co., 1950. This and the longer book by Snyder are the best scholarly biographies.

* SNYDER, FRANKLIN B. *The Life of Robert Burns.* New York: Macmillan Company, 1932.

CRITICAL, LINGUISTIC, HISTORICAL

ANGELLIER, AUGUSTE. *Robert Burns: la vie, les oeuvres.* 2 vols. Paris, 1893.

ARNOLD, MATTHEW. "The Study of Poetry" (1880) in *Essays in Criticism. Second Series.* 1888. This essay, often anthologized, has an important section on Burns.

CARLYLE, THOMAS. "Burns," a review of J. G. Lockhart's *Life* (1828), collected in *Critical and Miscellaneous Essays,* often reprinted.

CRAWFORD, THOMAS. *Burns: A Study of the Poems and Songs.* Edinburgh and London: Oliver and Boyd, 1960. The best critical study to date.

DAICHES, DAVID. *Robert Burns.* New York: Rinehart and Company, Inc., 1950. Another good critical study. The first chapter explains clearly and accurately the development in the eighteenth century of Scottish vernacular literature before Burns.

REID, JAMES B. *A Complete Word and Phrase Concordance to the Poems and Songs of Robert Burns.* Glasgow, 1889.

WILSON, JAMES. *The Dialect of Robert Burns as Spoken in Central Ayrshire.* London: Oxford University Press, 1923.

WITTIG, KURT, *The Scottish Tradition in Literature.* Edinburgh: Oliver and Boyd, 1958. The best secondary source, along with Henderson's detailed notes (see above), to find the relation of Burns's poetry to Scots vernacular literature.

Note on the Text

It is the design of this edition to provide for the interest in Burns himself which the study of his poetry inevitably produces and to present all the kinds of his poetry with all their often disparate moods and views. Thus some of his underground bawdy poems and some of his pro-aristocratic poems, two kinds often ignored, are included. And thus a great deal of biographical information appears in the Introduction, the long first section, in the notes, and in the appendixes. The only kinds of poems systematically excluded are those inferior ones written in the alien English mode. There is collected here about thirty-five percent by page volume of Burns's non-lyric poems. Only about eight percent of Burns's three-hundred fifty songs are included because it was judged of overriding importance to have them appear with the musical scores.

The gloss provided in the margins should make Burns's poems easy to read. The student should avoid the natural tendency to substitute the English words in the margins for the Scots words in the text: they are merely as appropriate English synonyms as could be recalled and almost invariably are inadequate in tone and connotation to the meaning, which must be discovered by considerations of context. Gloss-words separated by a comma are alternatives. Most students will find the gloss too complete, but it can always be ignored.

Because this text does not provide accent marks to indicate Scots pronunciation, one should learn to pronounce, unless meter forbids, a written "-ed" inflection of verbs as an extra syllable, a common feature of Scots pronunciation. Burns almost always indicated an elision in Scots pronunciation with an apostrophe: thus, *marked*, but *hammer'd*. Before the reader proceeds very far in his reading, he will become aware of other problems of pronunciation, at which time he should turn to Appendix C. One brutalizes Burns's poems by reading them in English.

Under the title of each poem and song, there is placed in parentheses, first, the date of composition (if it is known) and, second, the date or dates of first publication.

For those poems published under Burns's supervision, the text is taken from their first printing in the editions of *Poems Chiefly in the Scottish Dialect,* that is, in those of 1786 (Kilmarnock), 1787, 1793 (both Edinburgh). The text of those poems first printed in the edition of 1787 is taken from the *true* first Edinburgh edition, for which Burns read proof (an edition determined by variants in each sheet which exists in two type settings).[1] The scores and texts of the songs are taken from Dick (see "Abbreviations") unless a footnote specifies otherwise. Certain changes have been made silently, i.e., without notice given in footnotes:

1. Italicized words and words composed of all upper-case letters, reduced to lower-case roman;

2. Some initial capitals, reduced to lower case;

3. Some *very few* marks of punctuation, including some apostrophes and hyphens within words, changed;

4. Old "s" changed to modern form;

5. Indecent, irreverant, and impolitic words, which Burns left completely or partially blank for prudential reasons, filled in (when not completely clear by context, from evidence of manuscripts or other editions).

6. Obvious typographical errors corrected.

Footnotes explain all textual sources for poems first printed during Burns's life in publications other than these editions (e.g., "Tam o' Shanter") and all changes incorporated into the text of the first printings not covered by the above principles and all changes resulting from Burns's later emendations.

---

[1] See Edwin Wolf, " 'Skinking' or 'Stinking'? A Bibliographical Study of the 1787 Edinburgh Edition of Burns' Poems," *The Library Chronicle of . . . the University of Pennsylvania,* XIV (April 1947), 3–14.

The text of posthumous poems or of those printed separately and never collected during Burns's life, unless recorded to the contrary in a footnote, is that of HH (see "Abbreviations"). A large exception is the text of "The Jolly Beggars," which is that of the best holograph manuscript, as explained in the first footnote to that poem: some of the notes for that poem are taken, with permission, from my edition published by The Gehenna Press, Northampton, Massachusetts, 1963.

ABBREVIATIONS

CW   Robert Burns. *The Life and Works,* ed. Robert Chambers, rev. William Wallace. 4 vol. Edinburgh and London, 1896.

Dick   Robert Burns. *The Songs of Robert Burns,* ed. James C. Dick. Hatboro, Pa.: Folklore Associates, 1962.

Egerer   J. W. Egerer. *A Bibliography of Robert Burns.* Edinburgh and London: Oliver and Boyd, 1964.

HH   Robert Burns. *The Poetry,* eds. William E. Henley and Thomas F. Henderson ("The Centenary Edition"). 4 vol. Edinburgh 1896. Reprint, 1901.

Letters   Robert Burns. *The Letters,* ed. J. DeLancey Ferguson. 2 vol. Oxford: Clarendon Press, 1931.

POEMS

Epistles and
Other Autobiographical Poems

Burns wrote these epistles and actually sent them to his correspondents, some of whom replied in kind, with little or no view to later publication. But he valued some enough (e.g., the two addressed to James Lapraik) to copy them into his Commonplace Book at a time when he had no plans to publish his poems. He was working from the Scottish models of Allan Ramsay and William Hamilton of Gilbertfield, who exchanged epistles (in 1719) employing the Standard Habbie stanza ($A_4A_4A_4B_2A_4B_2$; see, for instance, the stanza of "Epistle to J. Lapraik") to present epistolary platitudes about poetry, drinking and camaraderie, nationalism and the vernacular tradition, praise of the other's poetic gifts, and wishes for the other's good fortune.

Burns preserved these topics and the general tone of swaggering independence and jolly intimacy. But he extended the range of the genre by using it to express—unlike his predecessors—many subjects important to him and central to his life. Whereas Ramsay and Hamilton filled pages, ringing the changes wittily on almost nothing, Burns presents more matter: poverty, riches, sex, love, social feeling, injustice, happiness. And although generally employing the traditional Standard Habbie stanza, he occasionally experimented, as in "Epistle to Davie," by using the ancient and exacting Scottish stanza of Alexander Montgomerie's "Cherry and the Slae" (1597), which he had come across reprinted in Ramsay's anthology *The Ever Green* (1724).

Burns was as subject as most to the hyperbole and pose that letter-writing, even in prose, brings out. But although his attitudes in these epistles do not always express all of Burns, they do express real enough, if often contradictory, parts of him. For instance, when he shows his contempt for respectability, he is sincere, although we know that in

3

other moods he thought well of this quality. His favorite pose, often expressed in these epistles—the untaught, thoughtless, spontaneous, rustic bard—however pleasing to himself, is patently false.

Three pieces not epistles appear at the end of this section because they offer other insights into Burns the man and the poet. The first two we can consider as almost extemporaneous effusions, written for an occasion and then forgotten. "The Inventory" shows his manner of life on the farm at Mossgiel just before the publication of his book of poems. "Lines on Meeting with Lord Daer" shows Burns typically torn between a pride in recognition of his own merit and a sense of his own social inferiority. "The Vision" is obviously a more studied and finished piece, expressing complicated and long-pondered ideas. By impulse Burns most characteristically attacked the aristocracy with savage indignation. Here he presents the Scottish aristocrats and himself (and other peasants like himself) as parts of a single national revival.

EPISTLE TO DAVIE,[1] A BROTHER POET
January
(1785, 1786)

– 1 –

While winds frae off Ben-Lomond[2] blaw,   *blow*
And bar the doors wi' driving snaw,
   And hing us owre the ingle,   *hang; fireplace*
I set me down, to pass the time,
And spin a verse or twa o' rhyme,
   In hamely, westlin jingle,   *homely; west-country*
While frosty winds blaw in the drift,
   Ben to the chimla lug,   *In; chimney corner*
I grudge a wee the Great-folk's gift,
   That live sae bien an' snug: *prosperous*
      I tent less, and want less   *value*
        Their roomy fire-side:
      But hanker, and canker,
        To see their cursed pride.

– 2 –

It's hardly in a body's pow'r,
To keep, at times, frae being sour,
   To see how things are shar'd;
How best o' chiels are whyles in want,   *fellows; sometimes*
While Coofs on countless thousands rant,   *Fools; revel*
   And ken na how to wair't: *know not; spend it*

---

[1] David Sillar, teacher, grocer, fiddler, one year Burns's junior, since 1781 a member of Burns's drinking-debating society called the Bachelor's Club, for two years at that time a resident of Irvine about fifteen miles from Mossgiel where Burns lived.

[2] A distant mountain visible in the north from parts of Ayrshire.

bother   But Davie, lad, ne'er fash your head,
           Tho' we hae little gear;
        We're fit to win our daily bread,
sound   As lang's we're hale and fier:
More ask not   "Mair spier na, nor fear na,"[3]
             Auld age ne'er mind a feg;
           The last o't, the warst o't,
             Is only but to beg.

- 3 -

To lie in kilns and barns at e'en,
bones; blood   When banes are craz'd, and bluid is thin,
           Is, doubtless, great distress!
Yet then content could make us blest;
Ev'n then, sometimes we'd snatch a taste
           Of truest happiness.
The honest heart that's free frae a'
           Intended fraud or guile,
ball   However Fortune kick the ba',
always   Has ay some cause to smile:
           And mind still, you'll find still,
small   A comfort this nae sma';
           Nae mair then, we'll care then,
fall   Nae farther can we fa'.

- 4 -

What tho', like Commoners of air,
We wander out, we know not where,
without   But either house or hal'?
Yet Nature's charms, the hills and woods,
The sweeping vales, and foaming floods,
           Are free alike to all.

---

[3] In a footnote to this line in a manuscript, Burns claims it for Allan Ramsay, but the editors of "The Centenary Edition" could not find it (HH, I, 369–370).

In days when Daisies deck the ground,
  And Blackbirds whistle clear,
With honest joy, our hearts will bound,
  To see the coming year:
    On braes when we please then,   *hills, hillsides*
      We'll sit an' sowth a tune;   *hum*
    Syne rhyme till't, well time till't,   *Then*
      An' sing't when we hae done.

– 5 –

It's no in titles nor in rank;
It's no in wealth like Lon'on Bank,
  To purchase peace and rest.
It's no in makin muckle, mair: *a great deal; more*
It's no in books; it's no in Lear,   *Learning*
  To make us truly blest:
If Happiness hae not her seat
  An' centre in the breast,
We may be wise, or rich, or great,
  But never can be blest:
    Nae treasures, nor pleasures
      Could make us happy lang;
    The heart ay's the part ay,   *always is*
      That makes us right or wrang.

– 6 –

Think ye, that sic as you and I,
Wha drudge and drive thro' wet and dry,
  Wi' never-ceasing toil;
Think ye, are we less blest than they,
Wha scarcely tent us in their way,   *heed*
  As hardly worth their while?
Alas! how aft, in haughty mood,
  God's creatures they oppress!

good   Or else, neglecting a' that's guid,
        They riot in excess!
          Baith careless, and fearless,
            Of either Heaven or Hell;
          Esteeming, and deeming,
            It a' an idle tale!

– 7 –

Then let us chearfu' acquiesce;
Nor make our scanty Pleasures less
    By pining at our state:
And, even should Misfortunes come,
I, here wha sit, hae met wi' some,
And am   An's thankfu' for them yet,
give   They gie the wit of Age to Youth;
know   They let us ken oursel;
They make us see the naked truth,
    The real guid and ill;
       Tho' losses, and crosses,
         Be lessons right severe,
      There's wit there, ye'll get there,
       Ye'll find nae other where.

– 8 –

But tent me, Davie, Ace o' Hearts!
cards   (To say aught less wad wrang the cartes,
    And flatt'ry I detest)
This life has joys for you and I;
And joys that riches ne'er could buy,
    And joys the very best.
There's a' the Pleasures o' the Heart,
    The Lover an' the Frien':

Ye hae your Meg, your dearest part,
  And I my darling Jean![4]
    It warms me, it charms me,
      To mention but her name:
    It heats me, it beets me,   *fans*
      And sets me a' on flame!

- 9 -

O, all ye Pow'rs who rule above!
O Thou, whose very self art love!
  Thou know'st my words sincere!
The life-blood streaming thro' my heart,
Or my more dear Immortal part,
  Is not more fondly dear!
When heart-corroding care and grief
  Deprive my soul of rest,
Her dear idea brings relief
  And solace to my breast.
    Thou Being All-seeing,
      O, hear my fervent pray'r!
    Still take her, and make her,
      Thy most peculiar care!

- 10 -

All hail! ye tender feelings dear!
The smile of love, the friendly tear,
  The sympathetic glow!
Long since, this world's thorny ways
Had number'd out my weary days,
  Had it not been for you!

---

[4] Jean Armour (1765–1834), about three and a half years later to become Burns's wife.

Fate still has blest me with a friend
  In every care and ill;
And oft a more endearing band,
  A tie more tender still.
    It lightens, it brightens
      The tenebrific scene,
    To meet with, and greet with
      My Davie or my Jean!

– II –

O, how that Name inspires my style!
dashing   The words come skelpin' rank an' file,
Almost; know   Amaist before I ken!
runs   The ready measure rins as fine,
As Phoebus and the famous Nine
looking over   Were glowrin owre my pen.
spavin   My spaviet Pegasus will limp,
once; hot   Till ance he's fairly het;
hobble; limp; jump   And then he'll hilch, an' stilt, an' jimp,
run; rare   And rin an unco fit;
lest   But least then, the beast then
        Should rue this hasty ride,
alight; wipe   I'll light now, and dight now
        His sweaty, wizen'd hide.

EPISTLE TO J. LAPRAIK[1]

An Old Scottish Bard, April 1, 1785

(1785, 1786)

- 1 -

While briers an' woodbines budding green,
And Paitricks scraichan loud at e'en,   *Partridges screeching; evening*
An' morning Poussie whiddan seen,   *Rabbit scudding*
    Inspire my Muse,
This freedom, in an unknown frien',
    I pray excuse.

- 2 -

On Fasten-e'en[2] we had a rockin,   *meeting*
To ca' the crack and weave our stockin;   *have a chat*
And there was muckle fun and jokin,   *a great deal of*
    Ye need na doubt;
At length we had a hearty yokin,   *stint*
    At "sang about."   *song*

- 3 -

There was ae sang, amang the rest,   *one*
Aboon them a' it pleas'd me best,   *Above*
That some kind husband had addrest,
    To some sweet wife:

---

[1] James Lapraik, 32 years Burns's senior, was a member of an old landowning family near Muirkirk, Ayrshire, who published his poems in 1788 in hopes of repeating Burns's success.

[2] The evening of Shrove-Tuesday, the day before the fast of Lent, traditionally a time of merrymaking.

thrilled It thirl'd the heart-strings thro' the breast,
      A' to the life.

- 4 -

well I've scarce heard ought describ'd sae weel,
That gen'rous, manly bosoms feel;
Thought I, "Can this be Pope, or Steele,
work   Or Beattie's[3] wark?"
fellow They tald me 'twas an odd kind chiel
      About Muirkirk.

- 5 -

put; so eager as to fidget It pat me fidgean-fain to hear't,
enquired An' sae about him there I spier't;
Then a' that kent him round declar'd
genius   He had ingine;
That nane excell'd it, few cam near't
      It was sae fine.

- 6 -

That, set him to a pint of ale,
grave An' either douce or merry tale,
Or rhymes an' sangs he'd made himsel,
      Or witty catches,
'Tween Inverness an' Teviotdale;[4]
      He had few matches.

- 7 -

got; oath Then up I gat, an' swoor an aith,
plow; harness Tho' I should pawn my pleugh an' graith,

---

[3] James Beattie (1735-1803), a Scottish writer whose English poems Burns overrated.
[4] Inverness is in the northwest and Teviotdale in the southeast of Scotland; thus the phrase means "from one end of Scotland to the other."

Or die a cadger pownie's death,   *pedlar's pony's*
    At some dyke-back,   *Behind a wall*
A pint an' gill I'd gie them baith,   *glass; give; both*
    To hear your crack.

– 8 –

But, first an' foremost, I should tell,
Amaist as soon as I could spell,   *Almost*
I to the crambo-jingle fell;   *riming verse*
    Tho' rude an' rough,
Yet crooning to a body's sel,   *singing softly*
    Does weel eneugh.

– 9 –

I am nae poet, in a sense,
But just a Rhymer like by chance,
An' hae to Learning nae pretence;
    Yet, what the matter?
Whene'er my Muse does on me glance,
    I jingle at her.

– 10 –

Your critic-folk may cock their nose,
And say, "How can you e'er propose,
You wha ken hardly verse frae prose,   *know*
    To mak a sang?"   *song*
But, by your leaves, my learned foes,
    Ye're maybe wrang.   *wrong*

– 11 –

What's a' your jargon o' your Schools,
Your Latin names for horns an' stools?[5]

---

[5] Perhaps the horns of the cuckold and "cutty stools" (stools of repentence in the kirk).

If honest Nature made you fools,
  What sairs your Grammars?
Ye'd better taen up spades and shools,
  Or knappin-hammers.

serves
taken; shovels
sledge-hammers

– 12 –

Blockheads
go; Steers
then

A set o' dull, conceited Hashes
Confuse their brains in Colledge-classes!
They gang in Stirks, and come out Asses,
  Plain truth to speak;
An' syne they think to climb Parnassus
  By dint o' Greek!

– 13 –

Gie me ae spark o' Nature's fire,
That's a' the learning I desire;
Then, tho' I drudge thro' dub an' mire
  At pleugh or cart,
My Muse, tho' hamely in attire,
  May touch the heart.

– 14 –

spark; bright melody
bold; sly, clever
learning

O for a spunk o' Allan's glee,
Or Fergusson's,[6] the bauld an' slee,
Or bright Lapraik's, my friend to be,
  If I can hit it!
That would be lear eneugh for me,
  If I could get it.

---

[6] For more about Burns's attitude toward Allan Ramsay (1686–1758) and Robert Fergusson (1750–1774), his predecessors in the eighteenth-century revival of the Scots vernacular literary tradition, see his Preface to the Kilmarnock edition and his autobiographical letter to Dr. Moore (Appendixes A and B).

– 15 –

Now, Sir, if ye hae friends enow,   *enough*
Tho' real friends I b'lieve are few;
Yet, if your catalogue be fow,   *full*
    I'se no insist: *I'll not*
But, gif ye want ae friend that's true,
    I'm on your list.

– 16 –

I winna blaw about mysel,   *will not blow*
As ill I like my fauts to tell;   *faults*
But friends, an' folk that wish me well,
    They sometimes roose me;   *praise*
Tho', I maun own, as monie still   *must; many*
    As far abuse me.

– 17 –

There's ae wee faut they whyles lay to me, *one; sometimes*
I like the lasses—Gude forgie me!   *God forgive*
For monie a plack they wheedle frae me   *coin*
    At dance or fair:
Maybe some ither thing they gie me,
    They weel can spare.

– 18 –

But Mauchline[7] Race or Mauchline Fair,
I should be proud to meet you there;
We'se gie ae night's discharge to care,   *We'll give a*
    If we forgather;
And hae a swap o' rhymin-ware
    Wi' ane anither.

---

[7] The largest village near Burns's and his brother's farm at Mossgiel and the setting for both "The Jolly Beggars" and "The Holy Fair."

– 19 –

measure; we'll make The four-gill chap, we'se gar him clatter,
christen; steaming An' kirs'n him wi' reekin water;
Then; draught Syne we'll sit down an' tak our whitter,
    To cheer our heart;
An' faith, we'se be acquainted better
    Before we part.

– 20 –

Away; worldly Awa ye selfish, warly race,
good manners Wha think that havins, sense an' grace,
Ev'n love an' friendship should give place
coin   To catch-the-plack!
do not I dinna like to see your face,
talk   Nor hear your crack.

– 21 –

But ye whom social pleasure charms,
Whose hearts the tide of kindness warms,
Who hold your being on the terms,
    "Each aid the others,"
Come to my bowl, come to my arms,
    My friends, my brothers!

– 22 –

But, to conclude my lang epistle,
nub As my auld pen's worn to the grissle,
would make; tingle Two lines frae you wad gar me fissle,
    Who am most fervent,
While I can either sing or whistle,
    Your friend and servant.

SECOND EPISTLE TO J. LAPRAIK
April 21, 1785
(1785, 1786)

‒ 1 ‒

While new-ca'd kye rowte at the stake,   *newly-calved cows low*
An' pownies reek in pleugh or braik,   *ponies steam; harrow*
This hour on e'enin's edge I take,
      To own I'm debtor
To honest-hearted, auld Lapraik,   *old*
      For his kind letter.

‒ 2 ‒

Forjesket sair, with weary legs,   *Worn out sorely*
Rattlin the corn out-owre the rigs,   *across the ridges*
Or dealing thro' amang the naigs   *distributing; horses*
      Their ten-hours bite,[1]
My awkart Muse sair pleads and begs,   *awkward; sorely*
      I would na write.

‒ 3 ‒

The tapetless, ramfeezl'd hizzie,   *feckless; worn-out hussy*
She's saft at best an' something lazy,   *soft*
Quo' she, "Ye ken we've been sae busy   *know*
      This month an' mair,   *more*
That trowth, my head is grown right dizzie,   *truth*
      An' something sair."   *sore*

---

[1] A bit of fodder given to horses in harness at 10 a.m.

- 4 -

dull; put   Her dowff excuses pat me mad:
lazy, listless   "Conscience," says I, "ye thowless jad!
large piece   I'll write, an' that a hearty blaud,
very   This vera night;
So dinna ye affront your trade,
      But rhyme it right.

- 5 -

bold   "Shall bauld Lapraik, the king o' hearts,
Supposing that   Tho' mankind were a pack o' cartes,
Praise; well   Roose you sae weel for your deserts,
      In terms sae friendly,
show   Yet ye'll neglect to shaw your parts
      An' thank him kindly?"

- 6 -

Sae I gat paper in a blink,
went   An' down gaed stumpie in the ink:
Quoth I: "Before I sleep a wink,
      I vow I'll close it:
will not; rime   An' if ye winna mak it clink,
      By Jove I'll prose it!"

- 7 -

Sae I've begun to scrawl, but whether
together   In rhyme, or prose, or baith thegither,
Or some hotch-potch that's rightly neither,
      Let time mak proof;
nonsense   But I shall scribble down some blether
off-hand   Just clean aff-loof.

- 8 -

My worthy friend, ne'er grudge an' carp,
Tho' Fortune use you hard an' sharp;

Come, kittle up your moorlan harp   *tickle; moorland*
        Wi' gleesome touch!
Ne'er mind how Fortune waft an' warp;   *weaves*
        She's but a bitch.

- 9 -

She's gein me monie a jirt an' fleg,   *given; jerk; scare*
Sin' I could striddle owre a rig;   *straddle; ridge between furrows*
But by the Lord, tho' I should beg
        Wi' lyart pow,   *grey; head, poll*
I'll laugh, an' sing, an' shake my leg,
        As lang's I dow!   *can*

- 10 -

Now comes the sax an' twentieth simmer,   *six*
I've seen the bud upo' the timmer,   *timber*
Still persecuted by the limmer   *slut, whore, bitch*
        Frae year to year;
But yet, despite the kittle kimmer,   *fickle woman*
        I, Rob, am here.

- 11 -

Do ye envy the city gent,
Behint a kist to lie an' sklent;   *Behind; chest, counter; cheat*
Or purse-proud, big wi' cent per cent,
        An' muckle wame,   *huge belly*
In some bit Brugh to represent   *little Borough*
        A Baillie's name?   *Town magistrate's*

- 12 -

Or is't the paughty feudal Thane,   *haughty, proud*
Wi ruffl'd sark an' glancin cane,   *shirt; shining*
Wha thinks himsel nae sheep-shank bane,   *bone*
        But lordly stalks;

19

taken While caps an' bonnets aff are taen,
  As by he walks?

– 13 –

gives; good "O Thou wha gies us each guid gift!
load Gie me o' wit an' sense a lift,
  Then turn me, if Thou please, adrift,
   Thro' Scotland wide;
respectable citizens; country squires Wi' cits nor lairds[2] I wadna shift,
   In a' their pride!"

– 14 –

Were this the charter of our state,
"On pain o' hell be rich an' great,"
Damnation then would be our fate,
remedy   Beyond remead;
way But, thanks to Heaven, that's no the gate
  We learn our creed.

– 15 –

For thus the royal Mandate ran,
When first the human race began:
"The social, friendly, honest man,
  Whate'er he be,
'Tis he fulfils great Nature's plan,
  And none but he."

– 16 –

O Mandate, glorious and divine!
The followers o' the ragged Nine,[3]

---

[2] The "city gent," the "Baillie," and the "feudal Thane" of stanzas 11 and 12.

[3] The nine Muses are not ragged, of course; but since Burns believed all true devotees of the arts were likely to be (see line 3 of this stanza), he evidently conceived that which they followed to be so too.

Poor, thoughtless devils! yet may shine
    In glorious light,
While sordid sons o' Mammon's line
    Are dark as night!

– 17 –

Tho' here they scrape, an' squeeze, an' growl,
Their worthless neivefu' of a soul,   *fistful*
May in some future carcase howl,
    The forest's fright;
Or in some day-detesting owl
    May shun the light.

– 18 –

Then may Lapraik and Burns arise,
To· reach their native, kindred skies,
And sing their pleasures, hopes an' joys,
    In some mild sphere,
Still closer knit in friendship's ties
    Each passing year!

TO WILLIAM SIMPSON[1] OF OCHILTREE
May, 1785
(1785, 1786)

- 1 -

I gat your letter, winsome Willie;

handsomely   Wi' gratefu' heart I thank you brawlie;

must; would   Tho' I maun say't, I wad be silly,

very   An' unco vain,

Should I believe, my coaxin billie,

      Your flatterin strain.

- 2 -

I'll   But I'se believe ye kindly meant it:

should; loath   I sud be laith to think ye hinted

sideways squinted   Ironic satire, sidelins sklented,

      On my poor Musie;

flattering   Tho' in sic phraisin terms ye've penn'd it,

      I scarce excuse ye.

- 3 -

would; confused state   My senses wad be in a creel,

climb   Should I but dare a hope to speel,

Wi' Allan, or wi' Gilbertfield,[2]

hills   The braes o' fame;

---

[1] A landowning farmer, one year Burns's senior, educated at the University of Glasgow, and at the time of this epistle a schoolmaster in Ochiltree, a few miles south of Mauchline. He evidently wrote a verse epistle to Burns after reading one of the latter's poems in manuscript.

[2] William Hamilton of Gilbertfield (1665?-1751), important in the eighteenth-century vernacular revival as the author of the "Last Dying Words of Bonny Heck,"

Or Ferguson, the writer-chiel,[3]   *lawyer-fellow*
  A deathless name.

– 4 –

(O Ferguson! thy glorious parts,
Ill suited law's dry, musty arts!
My curse upon your whunstane hearts, *whinstone*
  Ye Enbrugh gentry!   *Edinburgh*
The tythe o' what ye waste at cartes *cards*
  Wad stow'd his pantry!)   *Would have supplied*

– 5 –

Yet when a tale comes i' my head,
Or lasses gie my heart a screed,   *give; rent*
As whyles they're like to be my dead, *sometimes; death*
  (O sad disease!)
I kittle up my rustic reed;   *tickle*
  It gies me ease.   *gives*

– 6 –

Auld Coila,[4] now, may fidge fu' fain, *be restless with eagerness*
She's gotten Bardies o' her ain,   *own*
Chiels wha their chanters winna hain, *Fellows; bagpipes will not spare*
  But tune their lays,

---

which reestablished a Scots tradition Burns brought to perfection in "The Death and Dying Words of Poor Mailie," and as Allan Ramsay's correspondent in the verse epistles mentioned in the headnote to this section.

[3] Robert Fergusson was not a lawyer but a clerk in a law firm; nor was he starved by the indifference of the Edinburgh gentry as is implied in the next stanza, where we can see Burns's tendency to identify with Fergusson and to view poets as victims of class injustice.

[4] Coila is the district of Kyle in Ayrshire, which lies between Cunningham north of the River Irvine and Carrick south of the River Doon. Later Burns gave this name to his local muse (see "The Vision").

Till echoes a' resound again

well-   Her weel-sung praise.

- 7 -

Nae Poet thought her worth his while,
To set her name in measur'd style;
She lay like some unkend-of isle
         Beside New Holland,
Or whare wild-meeting oceans boil

South of   Besouth Magellan.

- 8 -

Ramsay an' famous Ferguson

Gave; above   Gied Forth an' Tay a lift aboon;

many   Yarrow an' Tweed, to monie a tune,

Over   Owre Scotland rings;
While Irwin,[5] Lugar, Aire, an' Doon
         Naebody sings.

- 9 -

Th' Illissus, Tiber, Thames, an' Seine,
Glide sweet in monie a tunefu' line;

foot   But Willie set your fit to mine,
         An' cock your crest,

make; little brooks   We'll gar our streams an' burnies shine
         Up wi' the best.

- 10 -

old   We'll sing auld Coila's plains an' fells,
Her moors red-brown wi' heather bells,

---

[5] More commonly now called Irvine, a river in Ayrshire; Burns presents this and the other unsung local rivers (Aire = Ayr) in this line (see map) in counterdistinction to the four other rivers and streams elsewhere in Scotland he has just named.

Her banks an' braes, her dens an' dells,   *hills*
    Whare glorious Wallace[6]
Aft bure the gree, as story tells,   *bore off the prize*
    Frae Suthron billies.   *Southern men*

– II –

At Wallace' name, what Scottish blood
But boils up in a spring-tide flood!
Oft have our fearless fathers strode
    By Wallace' side,
Still pressing onward, red-wat-shod,   *-wet-*
    Or glorious dy'd!

– 12 –

O, sweet are Coila's haughs an' woods,   *hollows*
When lintwhites chant amang the buds,   *linnets*
And jinkin hares, in amorous whids,   *dodging; frisks*
    Their loves enjoy;
While thro' the braes the cushat croods   *pigeon coos*
    With wailfu' cry!

– 13 –

Ev'n winter bleak has charms to me,
When winds rave thro' the naked tree;
Or frosts on hills of Ochiltree
    Are hoary gray;
Or blinding drifts wild-furious flee,
    Dark'ning the day!

– 14 –

O Nature! a' thy shews an' forms   *shows*
To feeling, pensive hearts hae charms!

---

[6] William Wallace (1272?–1305), the greatest of Scots heroes, who fought for Scottish independence against Edward I of England.

Whether the Summer kindly warms,
    Wi' life an' light;
Or Winter howls, in gusty storms,
    The lang, dark night!

– 15 –

found   The Muse, nae Poet ever fand her,
    Till by himsel he learn'd to wander,
brook's   Adown some trottin burn's meander,
        An' no think lang:
    O, sweet to stray, an' pensive ponder
song   A heart-felt sang!

– 16 –

worldly   The warly race may drudge an' drive,
jostle; elbow their way   Hog-shouther, jundie, stretch,
        an' strive;
describe   Let me fair Nature's face descrive,
        And I, wi' pleasure,
    Shall let the busy, grumbling hive
Hum over   Bum owre their treasure.

– 17 –

    Fareweel, "my rhyme-composing" brither!
unacquainted with each other   We've been owre lang unkenn'd to ither:
    Now let us lay our heads thegither,
        In love fraternal:
dangle; rope   May Envy wallop in a tether,
        Black fiend, infernal!

– 18 –

    While Highlandmen hate tolls an' taxes;
herdsmen; good   While moorlan herds like guid, fat braxies;[7]

---

[7] Dead sheep given to a shepherd as a perquisite.

While Terra Firma, on her axis,
    Diurnal turns;
Count on a friend, in faith an' practice,
    In Robert Burns.[8]

---

[8] An independent 13-stanza "Postscript" added by Burns is here omitted (see HH, I, 172–175).

EPISTLE TO JAMES SMITH[1]

(1786, 1786)

- 1 -

slyest; shrewd Dear Smith, the sleest, pawkie thief,
theft That e'er attempted stealth or rief,
witch-spell Ye surely hae some warlock-breef
   Owre human hearts;
proof For ne'er a bosom yet was prief
   Against your arts.

- 2 -

For me, I swear by sun an' moon,
above And ev'ry star that blinks aboon,
shoes Ye've cost me twenty pair o' shoon,
going   Just gaun to see you;
And ev'ry ither pair that's done,
taken   Mair taen I'm wi' you.

- 3 -

gossip That auld, capricious carlin, Nature,
To mak amends for scrimpet stature,
She's turn'd you off, a human-creature
   On her first plan;
And in her freaks, on ev'ry feature
   She's wrote the Man.

- 4 -

taken Just now I've taen the fit o' rhyme,
yeasty My barmie noodle's working prime,

---

[1] James Smith, b. 1765, merchant of Mauchline and member of Burns's drinking-debating society, the Bachelor's Club.

My fancy yerket up sublime,   *fermented*
    Wi' hasty summon:
Hae ye a leisure-moment's time
    To hear what's comin?

– 5 –

Some rhyme a neebor's name to lash;
Some rhyme (vain thought!) for needfu' cash;
Some rhyme to court the countra clash,   *country talk*
    An' raise a din;
For me, an aim I never fash;   *trouble about*
    I rhyme for fun.

– 6 –

The star that rules my luckless lot,
Has fated me the russet coat,[2]
An' damn'd my fortune to the groat;   *fourpenny piece*
    But, in requit,
Has blest me with a random shot
    O' countra wit.   *country*

– 7 –

This while my notion's taen a sklent,   *time; slant*
To try my fate in guid, black prent;   *good; print*
But still the mair I'm that way bent,
    Something cries, "Hoolie!   *Softly!*
I red you, honest man, tak tent!   *counsel; heed*
    Ye'll shaw your folly.

– 8 –

"There's ither poets, much your betters,
Far seen in Greek, deep men o' letters,

---

[2] Made of coarse, homemade woollen cloth of reddish-brown or grey color, the traditional dress of country folk in Burns's day.

Hae thought they had ensur'd their debtors,
    A' future ages;
Now moths deform, in shapeless tatters,
    Their unknown pages."

– 9 –

Then farewell hopes o' Laurel-boughs
To garland my poetic brows!
Henceforth, I'll rove where busy ploughs
busy   Are whistling thrang,
hollows An' teach the lanely heights an' howes
song   My rustic sang.

– 10 –

careless I'll wander on, wi' tentless heed,
How never-halting moments speed,
Till Fate shall snap the brittle thread;
    Then, all unknown,
I'll lay me with th' inglorious dead,
    Forgot and gone!

– 11 –

But why, o' Death, begin a tale?
Just now we're living sound an' hale;
Then top and maintop crowd the sail,
    Heave Care o'er-side!
And large, before Enjoyment's gale,
    Let's tak the tide.

– 12 –

This life, sae far's I understand,
Is a' enchanted fairy-land,
Where Pleasure is the Magic-wand,
    That, wielded right,

Maks Hours like Minutes, hand in hand,
  Dance by fu' light.   *very*

- 13 -

The magic-wand then let us wield;
For, ance that five-an'-forty's speel'd,   *climbed*
See, crazy, weary, joyless Eild,   *Eld*
  Wi' wrinkl'd face,
Comes hostin, hirplan owre the field,   *coughing; limping*
  Wi' creepin pace.

- 14 -

When ance life's day draws near the gloamin,
Then fareweel vacant, careless roamin;
An fareweel chearfu' tankards foamin,
  An' social noise:
An' farewell dear, deluding woman,
  The joy of joys!

- 15 -

O Life! how pleasant in thy morning,
Young Fancy's rays the hills adorning!
Cold-pausing Cautions's lesson scorning,
  We frisk away,
Like school-boys, at th' expected warning,
  To joy an' play.

- 16 -

We wander there, we wander here,
We eye the rose upon the brier,
Unmindful that the thorn is near,
  Among the leaves;
And tho' the puny wound appear,
  Short while it grieves.

– 17 –

Some, lucky, find a flow'ry spot,
did sweat   For which they never toil'd nor swat;
They drink the sweet and eat the fat,
Without   But care or pain;
perhaps   And haply eye the barren hut
With high disdain.

– 18 –

With steady aim, Some Fortune chase;
Keen hope does ev'ry sinew brace;
Thro' fair, thro' foul, they urge the race,
And seize the prey:
quiet   Then canie, in some cozie place,
They close the day.

– 19 –

And others, like your humble servan',
people   Poor wights! nae rules nor roads observin,
To right or left eternal swervin,
They zig-zag on;
Till, curst with Age, obscure an' starvin,
They aften groan.

– 20 –

Alas! what bitter toil an' straining—
But truce with peevish, poor complaining!
Is Fortune's fickle Luna waning?
go   E'en let her gang!
Beneath what light she has remaining,
Song   Let's sing our Sang.

– 21 –

My pen I here fling to the door,
And kneel, "ye Pow'rs!" and warm implore,

"'Tho' I should wander Terra o'er,
  In all her climes,
Grant me but this, I ask no more,
  Ay rowth o' rhymes.   *Always plenty*

– 22 –

"Gie dreeping roasts to countra Lairds,   *Give dripping; country Squires*
Till icicles hing frae their beards;
Gie fine braw claes to fine Life-guards,   *handsome clothes*
  And Maids of Honor;
And yill an' whisky gie to cairds,[3]   *ale; tinkers*
  Until they sconner.   *sicken*

– 23 –

"A Title, Dempster[4] merits it;
A Garter gie to Willie Pitt;[5]
Gie wealth to some be-ledger'd cit,   *citizen*
  In cent per cent;
But give me real, sterling Wit,
  And I'm content.

– 24 –

"While ye are pleas'd to keep me hale,
I'll sit down o'er my scanty meal,
Be't water-brose, or muslin-kail,   *oatmeal porridge; meatless soup*
  Wi' chearfu' face,
As lang's the Muses dinna fail   *long; do not*
  To say the grace."

---

[3] Tinkers were noted for their affluence, relative to other vagrants, and for their fondness of drink; see the caird in "The Jolly Beggars."

[4] George Dempster (1732–1818), a Scottish M. P. at the time; he did not get the title.

[5] William Pitt, the Younger (1759–1806), Prime Minister; he refused the Order of the Garter offered him in 1790.

- 25 -

eye	An anxious e'e I never throws
ear	Behint my lug, or by my nose;
duck	I jouk beneath Misfortune's blows
well as	As weel's I may;
	Sworn foe to sorrow, care, and prose,
	I rhyme away.

- 26 -

sober, respectable	O ye douce folk that live by rule,
	Grave, tideless-blooded, calm and cool,
	Compar'd wi' you—O fool! fool! fool!
	How much unlike!
	Your hearts are just a standing pool,
wall	Your lives a dyke!

- 27 -

Nae hair-brained, sentimental[6] traces
In your unletter'd, nameless faces!
In arioso trills and graces
        Ye never stray,
But gravissimo, solemn basses
        Ye hum away.

- 28 -

	Ye are sae grave, nae doubt ye're wise;
wonder	Nae ferly tho' ye do despise
	The hairum-scairum, ram-stam boys,
	The rambling squad:
	I see ye upward cast your eyes—
know	—Ye ken the road—

---

[6] In the sense of compassionate, sympathetic, emotional—the sentiments of a Man of Feeling.

Whilst I—but I shall haud me there—   *hold*
Wi' you I'll scarce gang onie where—   *go any*
Then Jamie, I shall say nae mair,   *more*
      But quat my sang,   *quit*
Content wi' you to mak a pair,
      Whare'er I gang.

TO DAVIE
Second Epistle
(1786, 1789)[1]

– 1 –

Auld Neebor,
    I'm three times doubly o'er your debtor
old-fashioned   For your auld-farrant, frien'ly letter;
must; suspect   Tho' I maun say't, I doubt ye flatter,
        Ye speak sae fair:
chatter   For my puir, silly, rhymin clatter
serve   Some less maun sair.

– 2 –

    Hale be your heart, hale be your fiddle!
elbow; dance and jig   Lang may your elbuck jink an' diddle
struggle   To cheer you thro' the weary widdle
worldly   O' war'ly cares,
children's   Till bairns' bairns kindly cuddle
        Your auld grey hairs!

– 3 –

I suspect; foolish   But Davie, lad, I'm red ye're glaikit:
told   I'm tauld the Muse ye hae negleckit;
should; whipped   An' gif it's sae, ye sud be lickit
squirm   Until ye fyke;
hands; excused, stopped   Sic han's as you sud ne'er be faiket,
spared   Be hain't wha like.

---

[1] First published in *Poems by David Sillar,* Kilmarnock, 1789.

– 4 –

For me, I'm on Parnassus' brink,[2]
Rivin the words to gar them clink;   *tearing, tugging; make; rime*
Whyles daez't wi' love, whyles daez't wi' drink   *Sometimes dazed*
      Wi' jads or Masons,[3]   *girls*
An' whyles, but ay owre late I think,
      Braw sober lessons.   *Fine*

– 5 –

Of a' the thoughtless sons o' man
Commen' me to the Bardie clan: *Commend*
Except it be some idle plan
      O' rhymin clink—
The devil-haet that I sud ban!—   *-have it; should forbid*
      They never think.

– 6 –

Nae thought, nae view, nae scheme o' livin,
Nae cares to gie us joy or grievin,   *give*
But just the pouchie put the nieve in,   *pocket; fist*
      An' while ought's there,
Then, hiltie-skiltie, we gae scrievin,   *helter-skelter; sauntering*
      An' fash nae mair.   *care; more*

– 7 –

Leeze me on rhyme! It's ay a treasure,   *Blessings be on; always*
My chief, amaist my only pleasure;   *almost*
At hame, a-fiel', at wark or leisure,   *afield*
      The Muse, poor hizzie!

---

[2] The edition published at Kilmarnock, Burns's first appearance in print, came out in July, 1786 (Egerer, p. 4). This poem was probably written after his manuscript had been sent to the printer some month and a half before the book appeared.

[3] Burns had been an enthusiastic Freemason since at least mid-1784, when his name appeared as an officer in a Lodge at Tarbolton.

homespun   Tho' rough an' raploch be her measure,
                She's seldom lazy.

- 8 -

Hold   Haud to the Muse, my dainty Davie:
world; trick The warl' may play you monie a shavie,
               But for the Muse, she'll never leave ye,
poor   Tho' e'er sae puir;
spavin   Na, even tho' limpin wi' the spavie
                 Frae door to door!

TO MAJOR LOGAN[1]

(1786, 1834)

– 1 –

Hail, thairm-inspirin, rattlin Willie!   *gut-, string-*
Tho' Fortune's road be rough an' hilly
To every fiddling, rhyming billie,   *fellow, comrade*
     We never heed,
But take it like the unbrack'd filly   *unbroken*
     Proud o' her speed.

– 2 –

When, idly goavin, whyles we saunter,   *gazing; sometimes*
Yirr! Fancy barks, awa we canter,   *away*
Up hill, down brae, till some mishanter,   *mischance*
     Some black bog-hole,
Arrests us; then the scathe an' banter   *loss*
     We're forced to thole.   *endure*

– 3 –

Hale be your heart! hale be your fiddle!
Lang may your elbuck jink an' diddle,   *elbow dance and jig*
To cheer you through the weary widdle   *wriggle, struggle*
     O' this vile warl',   *world*
Until you on a cummock driddle,   *short cane totter*
     A grey-hair'd carl.   *old man*

---

[1] William Logan, a retired soldier, famous for his wit and violin music around Ayr, his home, where he lived with his mother and his sister ("honest Lucky" and "Susie" of stanza 13).

– 4 –

poverty	Come wealth, come poortith, late or soon,
always	Heaven send your heart-strings ay in tune,
fiddle-pegs above	And screw your temper-pins aboon
more	(A fifth or mair)
sorrowful	The melancholious, sairie croon
peevish	O' cankrie Care.

– 5 –

May still your life from day to day,
Nae *lente largo* in the play
But *allegretto forte* gay,
Harmonious flow,
bold A sweeping, kindling, bauld strathspey—
Encore! Bravo!

– 6 –

All	A' blessings on the cheery gang,
song	Wha dearly like a jig or sang,
wrong	An' never think o' right an' wrang
	By square an' rule,
gadflies; sting	But as the clegs o' feeling stang
	Are wise or fool.

– 7 –

-chosen	My hand-wal'd curse keep hard in chase
miserly	The harpy, hoodock, purse-proud race,
poverty	Wha count on poortith as disgrace!
	Their tuneless hearts,
	May fireside discords jar a bass
	To a' their parts!

– 8 –

But come, your hand, my careless brither!
world I' th' ither warl', if there's anither—

40

An' that there is, I've little swither   *doubt*
    About the matter—
We, cheek for chow, shall jog thegither—   *by jowl; together*
    I'se ne'er bid better!   *I'll; desire*

– 9 –

We've faults and failins—granted clearly!
We're frail, backsliding mortals merely;
Eve's bonie squad,[2] priests wyte them sheerly   *blame; wholly*
    For our grand fa';   *fall*
But still, but still—I like them dearly . . .
    God bless them a'!

– 10 –

Ochon for poor Castalian drinkers,[3]   *Alas*
When they fa' foul o' earthly jinkers!   *lively girls*
The witching, curs'd delicious blinkers
    Hae put me hyte,   *made; mad*
An' gart me weet my waukrife winkers   *made; wet; wakeful*
    Wi' girnin spite.   *raging*

– 11 –

But by yon moon—and that's high swearin!—
An' every star within my hearin,
An' by her een[4] wha was a dear ane   *eyes*
    I'll ne'er forget,
I hope to gie the jads a clearin   *give; clearing of accounts*
    In fair play yet!

---

[2] I.e., the pretty daughters of Eve, the antecedent of "them" in the last two lines of this stanza.

[3] Drinkers from the fountain of Castalia, on the slopes of Parnassus, sacred to the Muses.

[4] The eyes of Jean Armour, who had, in the poet's view, repudiated his love by bowing to the remonstrances of her father, giving the latter Burns's private paper declaring their irregular marriage.

– 12 –

My loss I mourn, but not repent it;
purse; lost I'll seek my pursie whare I tint it;
have arrived Ance to the Indies[5] I were wonted,
witching   Some cantraip hour
provided with an opportunity By some sweet elf I'll yet be dinted:
    Then *vive l'amour!*

– 13 –

Faites mes baissemains respectueusé[6]
To sentimental sister Susie
not to flatter And honest Lucky: no to roose you,
    Ye may be proud,
That sic a couple Fate allows ye
    To grace your blood.

– 14 –

more Nae mair at present can I measure,
in truth! An, trowth! my rhymin ware's nae treasure;
But when in Ayr, some half-hour's leisure,
    Be't light, be't dark,
Sir Bard will do himself the pleasure
    To call at Park.[7]

Robert Burns

Mossgiel, *30th October*, 1786

---

[5] Burns had, in fact, by the date appended to this epistle (if it is correct) given up his plan to emigrate to Jamaica (see *Letters*, I, 47), conceived in response to his loss of Jean Armour and the persecutions of her father.

[6] "Extend my respectful compliments"

[7] The name of Logan's house.

TO THE GUIDWIFE OF WAUCHOP HOUSE[1]
(1787, 1801)

– 1 –

Guid Wife,

  I mind it weel, in early date,   *remember; well*
  When I was beardless, young, and blate,   *bashful*
    An' first could thresh the barn,
  Or haud a yokin at the pleugh,   *hold; day's work*
  An', tho' forfoughten sair eneugh,   *tired sorely*
    Yet unco proud to learn;   *very*
  When first amang the yellow corn   *grain*
    A man I reckon'd was,
  An' wi' the lave ilk merry morn   *rest each*
    Could rank my rig and lass;[2]   *manage my strip of land*
      Still shearing, and clearing
        The tither stooked raw,   *successive rows of shocks*
      Wi' clavers an' havers   *gossip; nonsense*
        Wearing the day awa.   *away*

– 2 –

E'en then, a wish (I mind its pow'r),   *remember*
A wish that to my latest hour
  Shall strongly heave my breast,

---

[1] "Guidwife" means "mistress of the house." Burns sent this epistle to Elizabeth Scott, a literary lady of about 58 years of age, the wife of a gentleman farmer. He responded to an enthusiastic epistle in vernacular octosyllabic couplets, which Mrs. Scott sent him in reaction to reading the Kilmarnock edition.

[2] Each boy or man was given a strip ("rig") of barley to cut down and a girl to gather it after him. Burns recounts this incident more formally in his autobiographical letter to Dr. John Moore (see Appendix B, paragraph 3).

That I for poor auld Scotland's sake
Some usefu' plan or book could make,
   Or sing a sang at least.[3]
The rough burr-thistle spreading wide
barley   Amang the bearded bear,
wooden weeding pincers I turn'd the weeder-clips aside,
   An' spar'd the symbol dear.
    No nation, no station
      My envy e'er could raise;
without stain   A Scot still, but blot still,
      I knew nae higher praise.

– 3 –

But still the elements o' sang
In formless jumble, right an' wrang,
   Wild floated in my brain;
harvest   Till on that hairst I said before,
group   My partner in the merry core,
   She rous'd the forming strain.
buxom, cheerful, pretty girl I see her yet, the sonsie quean
   That lighted up my jingle,
artful eyes   Her witching smile, her pauky een
made   That gart my heart-strings tingle!
    I fired, inspired,
glance   At ev'ry kindling keek,
abashing; confusing But, bashing and dashing,
indeed   I feared ay to speak.

– 4 –

each good fellow Hale to the sex! (ilk guid chiel says):
Wi' merry dance on winter days,
   An' we to share in common!

---

[3] Burns's life-long ambition, here asserted, to contribute to Scottish culture is not often noted. It forms the main subject of "The Vision."

TO THE GUIDWIFE OF WAUCHOP HOUSE

The gust o' joy, the balm of woe,
The saul o' life, the heav'n below *soul*
  Is rapture-giving Woman.
Ye surly sumphs, who hate the name, *fools*
  Be mindfu' o' your mither:
She, honest woman, may think shame
  That ye're connected with her!
    Ye're wae men, ye're nae men *woefully deficient; no*
      That slight the lovely dears;
    To shame ye, disclaim ye,
      Ilk honest birkie swears. *each; fellow*

– 5 –

For you, no bred to barn and byre, *not; cowbarn*
Wha sweetly tune the Scottish lyre,
  Thanks to you for your line!
The marl'd plaid ye kindly spare,[4] *checked; are willing to do without*
By me should gratefully be ware; *worn*
  'Twad please me to the nine.
I'd be mair vauntie o' my hap, *more proud; wrap*
  Douce hingin owre my curple, *Decently hanging over my haunches*
Than onie ermine ever lap, *any; hung in folds*
  Or proud imperial purple.
    Farewell, then! lang hale, then,
      An' plenty be your fa'! *fortune*
    May losses and crosses
      Ne'er at your hallan ca'! *doorstep call*

R. Burns

March, 1787

---

[4] Mrs. Scott had offered this patriotic present:

    O, gif I kenn'd but whare ye baide *if; resided*
    I'd send to you a marled plaid
    'Twad haud your shoulders warm and braw, *keep; handsome*
    An' douce at kirk or market shaw. . . . *decent; show*

THE INVENTORY

In Answer to a Mandate by the Surveyor of Taxes[1]

(1786, 1799)

Sir, as your mandate did request,
I send you here a faithfu' list
goods; possessions; equipment O' guids an' gear an' a' my graith,
give; oath To which I'm clear to gie my aith.
Imprimis, then, for carriage cattle:—
I hae four brutes o' gallant mettle
wooden plow As ever drew before a pettle:
My lan'-afore's[2] a guid auld "has been,"
strong; willing An' wight an' wilfu' a' his days been.
well-going My lan'-ahin's a weel-gaun fillie,
often; Kilmarnock That aft has borne me hame frae Killie,
many An' your auld borough monie a time
In days when riding was nae crime.
once (But ance, when in my wooing pride
had to I, like a blockhead, boost to ride,
willing; I so urged on The wilfu' creature sae I pat to—
Lord, pardon a' my sins, an' that too!—
trick I play'd my fillie sic a shavie,
all; spavin She's a' bedevil'd wi' the spavie.)
worthy My fur-ahin's a wordy beast

---

[1] Note by Burns in a manuscript reported by HH, II, 336: "To Mr. Robt. Aiken in Ayr, in answer to his mandate requiring an account of servants, carriages, carriage horses, riding horses, wives, children." Aiken (1739–1807), a prosperous lawyer in Ayr and Burns's faithful mentor and friend since 1783, was also the tax-surveyor for the district.

[2] Burns explains in notes to this poem, the terminology of the traditional Scottish four-horse plow: the *lan'-afore* is "the fore-horse on the left"; the *lan'-ahin* is the "hindmost horse on the left hand"; the *fur-ahin* is the "hindmost horse on the right hand."

As e'er in tug or tow was traced. *plowtraces of rawhide or rope*
The fourth's a Highland Donald hastie, *Highland pony*
A damn'd red-wud Kilburnie blastie! *stark-mad Kilbirnie*
Foreby, a cowte, o' cowtes the wale, *Besides; colt; pick*
As ever ran afore a tail:
If he be spar'd to be a beast,
He'll draw me fifteen pund at least. *pounds sterling*

    Wheel-carriages I hae but few:
Three carts, an' twa are feckly new; *for the most part*
An auld wheelbarrow—mair for token, *more*
Ae leg an' baith the trams are broken: *One; both; shafts*
I made a poker o' the spin'le, *spindle, axle*
An' my auld mither brunt the trin'le. *burnt; wheel*

    For men, I've three mischievous boys,
Run-deils for fechtin an' for noise: *Regular devils; fighting*
A gaudsman ane, a thrasher t'other, *plowman one*
Wee Davoc hauds the nowte in fother. *keeps; cattle; fodder*
I rule them, as I ought, discreetly,
An' aften labour them completely;
An' ay on Sundays duly, nightly, *always*
I on the *Questions*[3] tairge them tightly: *cross-examine; rigorously*
Till, faith! wee Davoc's grown sae gleg, *keen, sharp*
Tho' scarcely langer than your leg, *taller*
He'll screed you aff "Effectual Calling"[4] *repeat, rattle; off*
As fast as onie in the dwalling. *any; dwelling*
    I've nane in female servan' station
(Lord keep me ay frae a' temptation!):
I hae nae wife—and that my bliss is—
An' ye hae laid nae tax on misses; *mistresses*
An' then, if kirk folks dinna clutch me, *do not*
I ken the deevils darena touch me. *know*

---

[3] The Shorter Catechism, in which the kirk required housemasters to examine their servants every Sunday.

[4] "What is Effectual Calling?"—one of the questions of the Shorter Catechism.

children; more	Wi' weans I'm mair than weel contented:
	Heav'n sent me ane mair than I wanted!
plump, friendly	My sonsie, smirking, dear-bought Bess,[5]
	She stares the daddie in her face,
	Enough of ought ye like but grace:[6]
	But her, my bonie, sweet wee lady,
	I've paid enough for her already;
if	An' gin ye tax her or her mither,
ye'll	By the Lord, ye'se get them a' thegither!

	But pray, remember, Mr. Aiken,
	Nae kind of licence out I'm takin:
	Frae this time forth, I do declare
I'll; hussy more	I'se ne'er ride horse nor hizzie mair;
puddle; tramp, wade	Thro' dirt and dub for life I'll paidle,
	Ere I sae dear pay for a saddle;
	I've sturdy stumps, the Lord be thankit,
ways; tramp	And a' my gates on foot I'll shank it.
	The Kirk and you may tak' you that,
pot	It puts but little in your pat:
book	Sae dinna put me in your beuk,
look	Nor for my ten white shillings leuk.

own	This list, wi' my ain hand I've wrote it,
	The day and date as under notit;[7]
	Then know all ye whom it concerns,
	Subscripsi huic, Robert Burns

---

[5] Elizabeth, born in May the previous year to Elizabeth Paton, a former servant at Burns's father's farm of Lochlie; Burns paid a fine of one guinea to the kirk for his transgression and supported the younger Elizabeth in the household of Mossgiel until his death.

[6] Perhaps, "grace is the only quality of her face which her daddy's face does *not* have."

[7] Some editions insert as the last line: "Mossgiel, February 22d, 1786" (e.g., CW, I, 310).

LINES ON MEETING WITH LORD DAER[1]
(1786, 1799)

- 1 -

This wot ye all whom it concerns:
I, Rhymer Rab, *alias* Burns,
    October twenty-third,
A ne'er-to-be-forgotten day,
Sae far I sprachl'd up the brae   *clambered*
    I dinner'd wi' a Lord.

- 2 -

I've been at drucken Writers' feasts,   *drunken Lawyers'*
Nay, been bitch-fou 'mang godly Priests—   *-drunk*
    Wi' rev'rence be it spoken!—
I've even join'd the honor'd jorum,   *convivial gathering*
When mighty Squireships o' the Quorum[2]   *Court*
    Their hydra drouth did sloken.   *thirst, drought; slake*

- 3 -

But wi' a Lord!—stand out my shin!   *chin (?), shoes (?)*
A Lord, a Peer, an Earl's son!—
    Up higher yet, my bonnet!
An' sic a Lord!—lang Scotch ell[3] twa   *two*

---

[1] Basil William Douglas-Hamilton, Lord Daer (1763-1794), the second son of the fourth Earl of Selkirk and a student of Professor Dugald Steward (1753-1828), who had invited Burns to Catrine House, near Mauchline, where Lord Daer happened to be present. The stanza Burns uses in this poem is an English one employed by Allan Ramsay (HH, II, 341-342).

[2] Court composed of Justices of the Peace.

[3] A Scots ell is more than three feet.

Our Peerage he looks o'er them a',
As I look o'er my sonnet.

– 4 –

But O, for Hogarth's magic pow'r

bewildered gaze To show Sir Bardie's willyart glow'r,
An' how he star'd an' stammer'd,

looking vacantly as if; a bridle When, goavin's he'd been led wi' branks,
An' stumpin on his ploughman shanks,

stumbled He in the parlour hammer'd!

– 5 –

To meet good Stewart little pain is,
Or Scotia's sacred Demosthenes:[4]
Thinks I: "They are but men"!

blundered But "Burns"!—"My Lord"!—Good God! I doited,

knocked My knees on ane anither knoited

went in As faultering I gaed ben.

– 6 –

corner I sidling shelter'd in a neuk,

stole; look An' at his Lordship staw a leuk,
Like some portentous omen:
Except good sense and social glee
An' (what surpris'd me) modesty,
I marked nought uncommon.

– 7 –

I watch'd the symptoms o' the Great—

gentleman's The gentle pride, the lordly state,
The arrogant assuming:

Not a trace of The fient a pride, nae pride had he,

---

[4] Probably Dr. Hugh Blair (1718–1800), holder of the Chair of Rhetoric at Edinburgh University (HH, II, 342).

Nor sauce, nor state, that I could see,
    Mair than an honest ploughman!

– 8 –

Then from his Lordship I shall learn
Henceforth to meet with unconcern
    One rank as well's another;
Nae honest, worthy man need care
To meet with noble youthfu' Daer,
    For he but meets a brother.

THE VISION

(1786, 1786)

Duan[1] First

– I –

	The sun had clos'd the winter-day,
quit	The Curlers[2] quat their roaring play,
Rabbit taken	And hunger'd Maukin taen her way,
kitchen-	To kail-yards green,
snows each	While faithless snaws ilk step betray
	Whare she has been.

– 2 –

flail	The Thresher's weary flingin-tree,
live-	The lee-lang day had tired me;
eye	And when the Day had clos'd his e'e,
	Far i' the West,
Back; Parlor	Ben i' the Spence, right pensivelie,
went	I gaed to rest.

– 3 –

lonely; fireside	There, lanely, by the ingle-cheek,
smoke	I sat and ey'd the spewing reek,
cough-; fumes	That fill'd, wi' hoast-provoking smeek,
dwelling	The auld, clay biggin;
rats	An' heard the restless rattons squeak
rafters	About the riggin.

---

[1] Burns's note: "Duan, a term of Ossian's for the different divisions of a digressive poem. See his *Cath-Loda,* vol. ii. of M'Pherson's Translation." Ossian, of course, is the supposed author of a Gaelic epic forged by James Macpherson.

[2] Curling is a game similar to shuffle board played on the ice in Scotland.

– 4 –

All in this mottie, misty clime,   *dusty*
I backward mus'd on wasted time,
How I had spent my youthfu' prime,
      An' done naething,
But stringing blethers up in rhyme,   *nonsense*
      For fools to sing.

– 5 –

Had I to guid advice but harkit,
I might, by this, hae led a market,
Or strutted in a Bank and clarkit   *clerked*
      My Cash-Account;
While here, half-mad, half-fed, half-sarkit,   *-shirted*
      Is a' th' amount.

– 6 –

I started, mutt'ring "blockhead! coof!"   *fool*
An' heav'd on high my wauket loof,   *calloused palm*
To swear by a' yon starry roof,
      Or some rash aith,   *oath*
That I henceforth would be rhyme-proof
      Till my last breath—

– 7 –

When click! the string the snick did draw;   *latch*
And jee! the door gaed to the wa';   *went; wall*
And by my ingle-lowe I saw,   *fireplace-flame*
      Now bleezan bright,   *blazing*
A tight, outlandish Hizzie, braw,   *well-shaped; handsome*
      Come full in sight.

– 8 –

Ye need na doubt, I held my whisht;   *noise, peace*
The infant aith, half-form'd, was crusht;   *oath*

stared; as if; thrust   I glowr'd as eerie's I'd been dusht,
In some wild glen;
When sweet, like modest Worth, she blusht,
inside   And stepped ben.

– 9 –

Green, slender, leaf-clad Holly-boughs
Were twisted, gracefu', round her brows,
I took her for some Scottish Muse,
By that same token;
And come to stop those reckless vows,
Would soon been broken.

– 10 –

A "hair-brain'd, sentimental trace" [3]
Was strongly marked in her face;
A wildly-witty, rustic grace
Shone full upon her;
Her eye, ev'n turn'd on empty space,
Beam'd keen with Honor.

– 11 –

bright   Down flow'd her robe, a tartan sheen,
barely   Till half a leg was scrimply seen;
And such a leg! my bonie Jean[4]
Could only peer it;
straight; sound and trim   Sae straught, sae taper, tight an' clean
Nane else came near it.

---

[3] Quoted from his own "Epistle to James Smith," see p. 34.

[4] Jean Armour, of course. In anger with what he considered her betrayal, Burns changed the line in the Kilmarnock edition to refer to Elizabeth Paton (see p. 48, note 5):

"And such a leg! my Bess, I ween."

—but changed it back for the next edition.

54

– 12 –

Her Mantle large, of greenish hue,
My gazing wonder chiefly drew;
Deep lights and shades, bold-mingling, threw
    A lustre grand;
And seem'd, to my astonish'd view,
    A well-known Land.

– 13 –

Here, rivers in the sea were lost;
There, mountains to the skies were tost;
Here, tumbling billows mark'd the coast
    With surging foam;
There, distant shone Art's lofty boast,
    The lordly dome.

– 14 –

Here, Doon pour'd down his far-fetch'd floods;
There, well-fed Irwine stately thuds:
Auld hermit Aire staw thro' his woods,[5]   *stole*
    On to the shore;
And many a lesser torrent scuds
    With seeming roar.

– 15 –

Low, in a sandy valley spread,
An ancient borough[6] rear'd her head;
Still, as in Scottish Story read,   *History*
    She boasts a Race
To ev'ry nobler virtue bred,
    And polish'd grace.[7]

---

[5] The three main rivers of Ayrshire (see map). Aire = Ayr.

[6] The borough of Ayr.

[7] In the Edinburgh edition of 1787 Burns here added seven stanzas giving details of what he saw on his Muse's mantle, particularly the accomplishments of local families. He also added a stanza, here omitted, after the 5th stanza of Duan Second.

Duan Second

– I –

With musing-deep, astonish'd stare,
I view'd the heavenly-seeming Fair;
A whisp'ring throb did witness bear
 Of kindred sweet,
When with an elder Sister's air
 She did me greet.

– 2 –

"All hail! my own inspired Bard!
In me thy native Muse regard!
Nor longer mourn thy fate is hard,
 Thus poorly low!
I come to give thee such reward,
 As we bestow.

– 3 –

"Know, the great Genius of this Land,
Has many a light aerial band,
Who, all beneath his high command,
 Harmoniously,
As Arts or Arms they understand,
 Their labors ply.[8]

– 4 –

"They Scotia's race among them share:
Some fire the Sodger on to dare;
Some rouse the Patriot up to bare
 Corruption's heart;

---

[8] The supernatural machinery clearly derives from Alexander Pope's "Rape of the Lock," but there are also clear parallels with Allan Ramsay's "Vision" (see Thomas Crawford, *Robert Burns,* Edinburgh and London, 1960, p. 187 and note).

Some teach the Bard, a darling care,
        The tuneful Art.

– 5 –

" 'Mong swelling floods of reeking gore,
They ardent, kindling spirits pour;
Or, mid the venal Senate's roar,
        They, sightless, stand,
To mend the honest Patriot-lore,
        And grace the hand.

– 6 –

"Hence, Fullarton, the brave and young;
Hence, Dempster's truth-prevailing tongue;
Hence, sweet, harmonious Beattie sung
        His 'Mistrel lays,'
Or tore, with noble ardour stung,
        The sceptic's bays.[9]

– 7 –

"To lower Orders are assign'd
The humbler ranks of Human-kind,
The rustic Bard, the lab'ring Hind,
        The Artisan;
All chuse, as various they're inclin'd,
        The various man.

– 8 –

"When yellow waves the heavy grain,
The threat'ning storm, some, strongly rein,

---

[9] These represent the three classes: (1) Colonel William Fullarton (b. 1754) a *soldier* from Ayrshire; (2) George Dempster, M. P. (see p. 33, note 4), a *politician;* (3) James Beattie (see p. 12, note 3), a *poet.* The last two lines refer to Beattie's attempt to answer David Hume's scepticism about miracles.

Some teach to meliorate the plain,
　　With tillage-skill;
And some instruct the Shepherd-train,
　　Blythe o'er the hill.

– 9 –

"Some hint the Lover's harmless wile;
Some grace the Maiden's artless smile;
Some soothe the Lab'rer's weary toil
　　For humble gains,
And make his cottage-scenes beguile
　　His cares and pains.

– 10 –

"Some, bounded to a district-space,
Explore at large Man's infant race,
To mark the embryotic trace
　　Of rustic Bard;
And careful note each opening grace,
　　A guide and guard.

– 11 –

"Of these am I—Coila[10] my name:
And this distict as mine I claim,
Where once the Campbells,[11] chiefs of fame,
　　Held ruling pow'r:
I mark'd thy embryo-tuneful flame,
　　Thy natal hour.

– 12 –

"With future hope I oft would gaze,

---

[10] The Muse of the district of Kyle, see p. 23, note 4.
[11] The Loudoun branch of the Campbells, who still owned land in Ayr, including Burns's farm of Mossgiel.

Fond, on thy little, early ways:
Thy rudely caroll'd, chiming phrase,
    In uncouth rhymes;
Fir'd at the simple, artless lays
    Of other times.

– 13 –

"I saw thee seek the sounding shore,
Delighted with the dashing roar;
Or when the North his fleecy store
    Drove thro' the sky,
I saw grim Nature's visage hoar,
    Struck thy young eye.

– 14 –

"Or when the deep green-mantled earth
Warm cherish'd ev'ry floweret's birth,
And joy and music pouring forth,
    In ev'ry grove,
I saw thee eye the gen'ral mirth
    With boundless love.

– 15 –

"When ripen'd fields and azure skies,
Call'd forth the Reapers' rustling noise,
I saw thee leave their ev'ning joys,
    And lonely stalk,
To vent thy bosom's swelling rise,
    In pensive walk.

– 16 –

"When youthful Love, warm-blushing, strong,
Keen-shivering, shot thy nerves along,
Those accents, grateful to thy tongue,
    Th' adored Name,

I taught thee how to pour in song
　　To soothe thy flame.[12]

– 17 –

"I saw thy pulse's maddening play,
Wild-send thee Pleasure's devious way,
Misled by Fancy's meteor-ray,
　　By Passion driven;
But yet the light that led astray
　　Was light from Heaven.

– 18 –

"I taught thy manners-painting strains
The loves, the ways of simple swains,
Till now, o'er all my wide domains
　　Thy fame extends;
And some, the pride of Coila's plains,
　　Become thy friends.

– 19 –

"Thou canst not learn, nor can I show,
To paint with Thomson's landscape glow;
Or wake the bosom-melting throe
　　With Shenstone's art;
Or pour, with Gray,[13] the moving flow
　　Warm on the heart.

– 20 –

"Yet, all beneath th' unrivall'd Rose,
The lowly Daisy sweetly blows;

---

[12] Burns often recounted this episode which linked first love with first poetic composition—see paragraph 3 of his autobiographical letter, Appendix B, and "To the
Guidwife of Wauchop House."

[13] James Thomson, William Shenstone, Thomas Gray, eighteenth-century poets of
the English tradition.

Tho' large the forest's Monarch throws
    His army-shade,
Yet green the juicy Hawthorn grows
    Adown the glade.

– 21 –

"Then never murmur nor repine;
Strive in thy humble sphere to shine;
And trust me, not Potosi's mine,
    Nor King's regard,
Can give a bliss o'ermatching thine,
    A rustic Bard.

– 22 –

"To give my counsels all in one:
Thy tuneful flame still careful fan;
Preserve the dignity of Man,
    With Soul erect;
And trust the Universal Plan
    Will all protect.

– 23 –

"And wear thou this"—She solemn said,
And bound the Holly round my head:
The polish'd leaves and berries red
    Did rustling play;
And, like a passing thought, she fled
    In light away.

Comic and Sentimental Poems

In the two poems about sheep with which this section opens, we can see how Burns worked with the Scots vernacular tradition, using what was helpful but adapting freely to suit his purposes. In "The Death and Dying Words of Poor Mailie," Burns followed the last-dying-words genre (see p. 22, note 2) which recounts comic autobiographical detail in the dying words of its subject. Burns added a dramatic frame, interesting and serious themes (notions of freedom, new methods of agriculture, and insights into social climbing), and a kind of shape and unity not found in the simple enumeration of his models. In "Poor Mailie's Elegy" Burns's model was the Scots comic elegy, a non-serious lament for the passing of a local worthy whose life is retold in a loose collection of anecdotes and descriptions. The form was not burlesque, because it lacked the characteristic discrepancy between the lowness of the matter and the elevation of the expression which marks all mock writing. Burns turned this loose comic tradition of nostalgic biography into a true mock elegy by informing the entire poems with his extravagant sorrow over the loss of what, in spite of the humanizing, is just a sheep. To appreciate the changes he has made in the Scots elegiac genre, one should compare this poem with Burns's close imitation of the tradition of the comic elegy, "Tam Samson's Elegy."

"To a Mouse" approaches the brink of sentimentality without falling in, because the tenderness of feeling toward the mouse is presented in the concrete language and detail of the peasants' world and because the moral extension of the last two stanzas is accomplished with precision and concentration.

In "Death and Doctor Hornbook" Burns shows his mastery of verse narrative, a form he rarely employed. He wrote only two other long narrative poems, "Tam o' Shanter" and "The Twa Dogs." But "Hornbook," like "Twa Dogs," soon becomes dialogue. In other obvious ways, "Hornbook" is very similar to and a forerunner of "Tam o' Shanter": both present a local character's tipsy roadside encounter at midnight with the supernatural. "Hornbook" is not a personal satire because the emphasis is clearly on the comedy of character and the dramatic reactions and relations between the characters, not on causing injury to the butt of the tale. Burns succeeds in adapting the idiom of country speech to the requirements of his form. There appears here a distinctive Scottish quality of literature, the grotesque and off-beat humor of realistic fantasy that results from combining concrete, earthy, and commonplace detail with the eerie supernatural.

"Scotch Drink" and "To a Haggis" are not celebrations of Scottish whisky and a traditional Scottish dish but lusty and vigorous expressions of Scottish nationalism in which the humorous effect is created by our recognition of the intended extravagance of the praise. "Grim Grizzle" is a burlesque of the traditional ballad.

THE DEATH AND DYING WORDS OF
POOR MAILIE,

Mollie

Ewe; Very

The Author's Only Pet Yowe: An Unco Mournfu' Tale

(1782 or 1783, 1786)

together	As Mailie, an' her lambs thegither,
one	Was ae day nibbling on the tether,
hoof; cast; loop	Upon her cloot she coost a hitch,
floundered	An' owre she warsl'd in the ditch:
	There, groanin, dying, she did ly,
doddering	When Hughoc[1] cam doytan by.

staring eyes	Wi' glowrin een, an' lifted han's
	Poor Hughoc like a statue stan's;
	He saw her days were near-hand-ended,
woe is	But, wae's my heart! he could na mend it!
	He gaped wide, but naething spak.
	At length poor Mailie silence brak:—

"O thou, whase lamentable face
Appears to mourn my woefu' case!
My dying words attentive hear,
An' bear them to my Master dear.

	"Tell him, if e'er again he keep
much money as will	As muckle gear as buy a sheep,
more	O, bid him never tye them mair,
	Wi' wicked strings o' hemp or hair!

---

[1] Burns's note in a manuscript: "Hughoc was an odd, glowran [staring], gapin callan [lad] about three-fourths as wise as other folk" (CW, I, 89).

But ca them out to park or hill,   *drive*
An' let them wander at their will;
So, may his flock increase an' grow
To scores o' lambs, an' packs o' woo'!²   *wool*

  "Tell him, he was a Master kin',   *kind*
An' ay was guid to me an' mine;
An' now my dying charge I gie him,   *give*
My helpless lambs, I trust them wi' him.

  "O, bid him save their harmless lives,
Frae dogs an' tods, an' butchers' knives! *foxes*
But gie them guid cow-milk their fill,   *give*
Till they be fit to fend themsel;   *for themselves*
An' tent them duly, e'en an' morn,   *tend*
Wi' teats o' hay an' ripps o' corn.   *handfuls*

  "An' may they never learn the gaets, *ways*
Of ither vile, wanrestfu' pets!   *restless*
To slink thro' slaps, an' reave an' steal, *holes in the fence*
At stacks o' pease, or stocks o' kail!   *cabbage*
So may they, like their great forbears,
For monie a year come thro' the sheers:
So wives will gie them bits o' bread,   *give*
An' bairns greet for them when they're dead. *children weep*

  "My poor toop-lamb, my son an' heir, *tup-lamb (i.e., ram)*
O, bid him breed him up wi' care!
An' if he live to be a beast,
To pit some havins in his breast!   *put; manners*
An' warn him—what I winna name—³

---

² Mailie here counsels the poet to abandon the traditional practice of tethering a few sheep to provide wool for the household and to go into sheep raising in a modern, big way in enclosed fields.
³ "An' warn him ay at ridin time," (1786).

ewes   To stay content wi' yowes at hame;
run; wear out his hooves   An' no to rin an' wear his cloots,
unmannerly   Like other menseless, graceless brutes.

next; little ewe   "An' niest, my yowie, silly thing;
Gude keep thee frae a tether string!
O, may thou ne'er forgather up,
ram   Wi' onie blastet, moorlan toop;[4]
remember; nibble; mix   But ay keep mind to moop an' mell,
Wi' sheep o' credit like thysel!

"And now, my bairns, wi' my last breath,
both   I lea'e my blessin wi' you baith:
An' when you think upo' your Mither,
Mind to be kind to ane anither.

"Now, honest Hughoc, dinna fail,
To tell my Master a' my tale;
An' bid him burn this cursed tether,
shall; bladder   An' for thy pains thou'se get my blather."

This said, poor Mailie turn'd her head,
eyes   An' clos'd her een amang the dead!

---

[4] I.e., a Scottish black-faced sheep; Mailie snobbishly counsels her ewe, of English (i.e., upper-class) descent, to avoid the company of Scottish (i.e., lower-class) rams.

POOR MAILIE'S ELEGY

(1786?, 1786)

- 1 -

Lament in rhyme, lament in prose,
Wi' saut tears trickling down your nose;   *salt*
Our Bardie's fate is at a close,
     Past a' remead!   *remedy*
The last, sad cape-stane of his woes;
     Poor Mailie's dead!

- 2 -

It's no the loss of warl's gear,   *worldly possessions*
That could sae bitter draw the tear,
Or mak our Bardie, dowie, wear   *drooping*
     The mourning weed: *dress*
He's lost a friend an' neebor dear   *neighbor*
     In Mailie dead.

- 3 -

Thro' a' the toun she trotted by him;   *farm*
A lang half-mile she could descry him;
Wi' kindly bleat, when she did spy him,
     She ran wi' speed:
A friend mair faithfu' ne'er cam nigh him,   *more*
     Than Mailie dead.

- 4 -

I wat she was a sheep o' sense,   *know*
An' could behave hersel wi' mense: *good manners*

67

I'll say't she never brak a fence,
Thro' thievish greed.
parlor Our Bardie, lanely, keeps the spence
Sin' Mailie's dead.

– 5 –

valley Or, if he wanders up the howe,
ewe Her livin image in her yowe,
to; knoll Comes bleating till him, owre the knowe,
For bits o' bread;
roll An' down the briny pearls rowe
For Mailie dead.

– 6 –

no offspring; rams She was nae get o' moorlan tips,
matted fleece; rumps Wi' tauted ket, an' hairy hips;
For her forbears were brought in ships,
Frae 'yont the Tweed:[1]
came under the clipping shears A bonier fleesh ne'er cross'd the clips
Than Mailie's dead.

– 7 –

Woe befall Wae worth the man wha first did shape
unlucky; rope That vile, wanchancie thing—a rape!
grimace It maks guid fellows grin an' gape,
Wi' chokin dread;
An' Robin's bonnet wave wi' crape
For Mailie dead.

– 8 –

O a' ye Bards on bonie Doon!
bagpipes An' wha on Aire your chanters tune!

---

1 To the south of the River Tweed, i.e., from England (see p. 66, note 4)

Come, join the melancholious croon   *lament*
    O' Robin's reed!
His heart will never get aboon!   *rejoice*
    His Mailie's dead!

TO A MOUSE

On Turning Her Up in Her Nest With The Plough, November 1785
(1785, 1786)

– 1 –

sleek; cowering

Wee, sleeket, cowran, tim'rous beastie,
O, what a panic's in thy breastie!
Thou need na start awa sae hasty,

rushing scamper   Wi' bickering brattle!
would; loath to run   I wad be laith to rin an' chase thee,
staff to remove clay from plow   Wi' murd'ring pattle!

– 2 –

I'm truly sorry Man's dominion
Has broken Nature's social union,
An' justifies that ill opinion,
     Which makes thee startle,
At me, thy poor, earth-born companion,
     An' fellow mortal!

– 3 –

sometimes   I doubt na, whyles, but thou may thieve;
What then? poor beastie, thou maun live!
odd ear; quantity of 24 sheaves   A daimen icker in a thrave
Is   'S a sma' request;
rest   I'll get a blessin wi' the lave,
     An' never miss't!

– 4 –

tiny house   Thy wee-bit housie, too, in ruin!
feeble walls; winds   Its silly wa's the win's are strewin!
build   An' naething, now, to big a new ane,

70

O' foggage green!   *rank grass*
An' bleak December's winds ensuin,
    Baith snell an' keen!   *biting*

– 5 –

Thou saw the fields laid bare an' wast,
An' weary winter comin fast,
An' cozie here, beneath the blast,
    Thou thought to dwell,
Till crash! the cruel coulter past
    Out thro' thy cell.   *Right*

– 6 –

That wee bit heap o' leaves an' stibble,   *stubble*
Has cost thee monie a weary nibble!   *many*
Now thou's turned out, for a' thy trouble,
    But house or hald,   *Without; holding*
To thole the winter's sleety dribble,   *endure*
    An' cranreuch cauld!   *hoar-frost cold*

– 7 –

But Mousie, thou art no thy-lane,   *not alone*
In proving foresight may be vain: *experiencing that*
The best laid schemes o' Mice an' Men
    Gang aft agley,   *Go often askew*
An' lea'e us nought but grief an' pain,
    For promis'd joy!

– 8 –

Still, thou art blest, compared wi' me!
The present only toucheth thee:
But Och! I backward cast my e'e,   *eye*
    On prospects drear!
An' forward, tho' I canna see,
    I guess an' fear!

DEATH AND DOCTOR HORNBOOK[1]
A True Story
(1785, 1787)

- 1 -

Some books are lies frae end to end,
And some great lies were never penn'd:
know   Ev'n ministers, they hae been keen'd
      In holy rapture,
fib   A rousing whid at times to vend,[2]
      And nail't wi' Scripture.

- 2 -

going   But this that I am gaun to tell,
      Which lately on a night befel,
      Is just as true's the Deil's in hell
        Or Dublin city:
approaches us   That e'er he nearer comes oursel
Is a great   'S a muckle pity.

---

[1] Doctor Hornbook is Burns's name for John Wilson (d. 1839), a schoolmaster in Tarbolton, who as a sideline kept a small grocery shop where he also, according to Gilbert Burns, "added the sale of a few medicines to his stock in trade," and advertized on a shop-bill that "advice would be given in common disorders at the shop gratis" (CW, I, 150). Burns's note to "Hornbook's," stanza 13; "This gentleman, Dr. Hornbook, is professionally a brother of the sovereign order of the ferula; but, by intuition and inspiration, is at once an apothecary, surgeon, and physician." He was secretary of Burns's Masonic lodge at Tarbolton from 1782 to 1787. Burns later was on good terms with him (see *Letters,* II, 42–43, 376).

[2] An improved line by Burns inserted in the third Edinburgh edition (1794) for

"Great lies and nonsense baith to vend."

- 3 -

The clachan yill had made me canty,   *village ale; merry*
I was na fou, but just had plenty: *drunk*
I stacher'd whyles, but yet took tent ay   *staggered sometimes; care*
    To free the ditches;
An' hillocks, stanes, an' bushes, kenn'd ay   *stones; knew*
    Frae ghaists an' witches.

- 4 -

The rising moon began to glowr   *gaze*
The distant Cumnock Hills out-owre: *over*
To count her horns, wi' a' my pow'r,
    I set mysel,
But whether she had three or four,
    I cou'd na tell.

- 5 -

I was come round about the hill,
And todlin down on Willie's mill,
Setting my staff wi' a' my skill
    To keep me sicker;   *steady*
Tho' leeward whyles, against my will,   *sometimes*
    I took a bicker.   *short run*

- 6 -

I there wi' Something does forgather,   *did encounter*
That pat me in an eerie swither;   *put; dread*
An awfu' scythe, out-owre ae shouther,   *across one shoulder*
    Clear-dangling, hang;   *hung*
A three-tae'd leister on the ither   *-pronged spear*
    Lay, large an' lang.

– 7 –

two	Its stature seem'd lang Scotch ells[3] twa;
	The queerest shape that e'er I saw,
not any belly; at all	For fient a wame it had ava;
	And then its shanks,
small	They were as thin, as sharp an' sma'
wooden sides to ox bridles	As cheeks o' branks.

– 8 –

Good evening	"Guid-een," quo' I; "Friend! hae ye been
mowing	mawin,
sowing	When ither folk are busy sawin?"
stand	It seem'd to mak a kind o' stan',
	But naething spak;
going	At length, says I: "Friend, whare ye gaun,
	Will ye go back?"

– 9 –

hollow	It spak right howe: "My name is Death,
scared	But be na' fley'd." Quoth I: "Guid faith,
Ye may have; stop	Ye're may be come to stap my breath;
heed; comrade	But tent me, billie;
advise; well; harm	I red ye weel, take care o' skaith,
large knife	See, there's a gully!"

– 10 –

	"Gudeman," quo' he, "put up your whittle,
	I'm no design'd to try its mettle;
would be difficult	But if I did, I wad be kittle
outwitted	To be mislear'd,
would not	I wad na mind it, no that spittle
Over	Out-owre my beard."

---

[3] A Scottish "ell" is somewhat more than three feet.

- 11 -

"Weel, weel!" says I, "a bargain be't;
Come, gie's[4] your hand, an' say we're gree't; *give us; agreed*
We'll ease our shanks, an' tak a seat:
 Come, gie's your news!
This while ye hae been monie a gate, *many a road*
 At monie a house."[5]

- 12 -

"Ay, ay!" quo' he, an' shook his head,
"It's e'en a lang, lang time indeed *really*
Sin' I began to nick the thread *Since*
 An' choke the breath:
Folk maun do something for their bread, *must*
 An' sae maun Death.

- 13 -

"Sax thousand years are near-hand fled *Six; nearly*
Sin' I was to the butching bred, *Since; butchering*
An' monie a scheme in vain's been laid *many*
 To stap or scar me; *stop*
Till ane Hornbook's ta'en up the trade, *taken*
 And faith! he'll waur me. *worst*

- 14 -

"Ye ken Jock Hornbook i' the Clachan? *Village*
Deil mak his king's-hood in a spleuchan!— *scrotum into a tobacco pouch*
He's grown sae weel acquaint wi' *Buchan*[6]
 And ither chaps,

---

[4] "gies" in all editions, here and two lines from here.
[5] Burns's note (1787): "An epidemical fever was then raging in that country."
[6] Burns's note (1787): "Buchan's Domestic Medicine." William Buchan's book (1769) was popular in country households.

children hold The weans haud out their fingers laughin,
poke   An' pouk my hips.

– 15 –

"See, here's a scythe, an' there's a dart,
They hae pierc'd monie a gallant heart;
But Doctor Hornbook wi' his art
    An' cursed skill,
both Has made them baith no worth a fart,
The devil a one   Damn'd haet they'll kill!

– 16 –

yesterday evening "Twas but yestreen, nae farther gane,
one I threw a noble throw at ane;
Wi' less, I'm sure, I've hundreds slain;
    But deil-ma-care!
went tinkle; bone It just play' dirl on the bane,
more   But did nae mair.

– 17 –

"Hornbook was by, wi' ready art,
An' had sae fortify'd the part,
That when I looked to my dart,
    It was sae blunt,
Not a bit of it would Fient haet o't wad hae pierc'd the heart
cabbage stalk   Of a kail-runt.

– 18 –

"I drew my scythe in sic a fury,
almost tumbled I near-hand cowpit wi' my hurry,
But yet the bauld Apothecary
    Withstood the shock:
I might as well have try'd a quarry
    O' hard whin-rock.

– 19 –

"Ev'n them he canna get attended,
Altho' their face he ne'er had kend it,   *known*
Just shit in a kail-blade an' send it,   *cabbage-leaf*
      As soon's he smells 't,
Baith their disease, and what will mend it,
      At once he tells't.

– 20 –

"And then a' doctor's saws and whittles   *knives*
Of a' dimensions, shapes, an' mettles,
A' kinds o' boxes, mugs, and bottles,
      He's sure to hae;
Their Latin names as fast he rattles
      As A B C.

– 21 –

"Calces o' fossils, earth, and trees;
True Sal-marinum o' the seas;
The Farina of beans an' pease,
      He has't in plenty;
Aqua-fontis, what you please,
      He can content ye.

– 22 –

"Forbye some new, uncommon weapons,   *Besides*
Urinus Spiritus of capons;
Or Mite-horn shavings, filings, scrapings,
      Distill'd per se;
Sal-alkali o' Midge-tail clippings,
      And mony mae."   *many more.*

− 23 −

Woe is	"Waes me for Johnie God's-Hole[7] now,"
this	Quoth I, "if that thae news be true!
-enclosure; daisies	His braw calf-ward whare gowans grew
	Sae white and bonie,
tear it up; plow	Nae doubt they'll rive it wi' the plew:
	They'll ruin Johnie!"

− 24 −

groaned; unearthly	The creature grain'd an eldritch laugh,
need not; plow	And says: "Ye nedna yoke the pleugh,
enough	Kirk-yards will soon be till'd eneugh,
	Tak ye nae fear:
many a ditch	They'll a' be trench'd wi monie a sheugh
two-	In twa-three year.

− 25 −

straw (i.e., bed)	"Whare I kill'd ane, a fair strae death
	By loss o' blood or want o' breath,
oath	This night I'm free to tak my aith,
	That Hornbook's skill
cloth	Has clad a score i' their last claith
drop	By drap an' pill.

− 26 −

Weaver	"An honest Wabster to his trade,
two fists	Whase Wife's twa nieves were scarce weel- bred,

---

[7] The parish gravedigger, who evidently as an extra means of support keeps calves in the churchyard. The speaker mistakenly thinks that Hornbook has been preventing the death of villagers and here reacts by expressing his sympathy for the coming financial ruin of the gravedigger.

Gat tippence-worth to mend her head
    When it was sair;   *sore*
The wife slade cannie to her bed,   *slid quietly*
    But ne'er spak mair.   *spoke more*

– 27 –

"A countra Laird had taen the batts,   *country Squire; taken; colic*
Or some curmurring in his guts,   *commotion*
His only son for Hornbook sets,   *sets his eye, intention*
    An' pays him well,
The lad, for twa guid gimmer-pets,   *two good pet ewes*
    Was Laird himsel.

– 28 –

"A bonie lass, ye kend her name,
Some ill-brewn drink had hov'd her wame;   *swollen; belly*
She trusts hersel, to hide the shame,
    In Hornbook's care;
Horn sent her aff to her lang hame   *long home*
    To hide it there.

– 29 –

"That's just a swatch o' Hornbook's way;   *sample*
Thus goes he on from day to day,
Thus does he poison, kill, an' slay,
    An's weel paid for't;
Yet stops me o' my lawfu' prey,   *keeps me from*
    Wi' his damn'd dirt!

– 30 –

"But, hark! I'll tell you of a plot,
Tho' dinna ye be speakin o't: *don't*
I'll nail the self-conceited Sot,
    As dead's a herrin;

Next; bet   Niest time we meet, I'll wad a groat,
reward   He gets his fairin!"

- 31 -

But just as he began to tell,
old; struck   The auld kirk-hammer strak the bell
beyond twelve Some wee short hour ayont the twal,
       Which raised us baith:
I took the way that pleas'd mysel,
       And sae did Death.

SCOTCH DRINK

(1785 or 1786; 1786)

> *Gie him strong Drink until he wink,* Give
> *That's sinking in despair;*   Who's
> *An' liquor guid to fire his bluid,* good; blood
> *That's prest wi' grief an' care:*
> *There let him bowse, an' deep carouse,*
> *Wi' bumpers flowing o'er,*
> *Till he forgets his loves or debts,*
> *An' minds his griefs no more.*
> SOLOMON'S PROVERBS, XXXI. 6, 7.

– 1 –

Let other Poets raise a fracas
'Bout vines, an' wines, an' druken Bacchus,[1] drunken
An' crabbed names an' stories wrack us, torment
  An' grate our lug: ear
I sing the juice Scotch bear can mak us, barley
  In glass or jug.

– 2 –

O thou, my Muse! guid auld Scotch drink!
Whether thro' wimplin worms thou jink, winding; frisk
Or, richly brown, ream owre the brink, cream
  In glorious faem,   foam

---

[1] Compare lines in Robert Fergusson's "Caller Water," a poem in the same stanza which ostensibly praises fresh water (but really pretty lasses) and which Burns's "Scotch Drink" lovingly burlesques:

> "The fuddlin Bardies now-a-days drinking
> Rin maukin-mad in Bacchus praise." mad as a hare

Inspire me, till I lisp an' wink,
    To sing thy name!

– 3 –

valleys   Let husky Wheat the haughs adorn,
Oats; bearded   An' Aits set up their awnie horn,
An' Pease an' Beans, at een or morn,
    Perfume the plain:
Blessings on   Leeze me on thee, John Barleycorn,
    Thou king o' grain!

– 4 –

chews; cud   On thee aft Scotland chows her cood,
pliable barley cakes; pick   In souple scones, the wale o' food!
Or tumbling in the boiling flood
cabbage   Wi' kail an' beef;
But when thou pours thy strong heart's blood,
    There thou shines chief.

– 5 –

belly   Food fills the wame, an' keeps us livin;
Tho' life's a gift no worth receivin,
When heavy-dragg'd wi' pine an' grievin;
    But oil'd by thee,
careering   The wheels o' life gae down-hill, scrievin,
    Wi' rattlin glee.

– 6 –

confused Learning   Thou clears the head o' doited Lear,
Thou chears the heart o' drooping Care;
sore   Thou strings the nerves o' Labor sair,
    At's weary toil;
Thou ev'n brightens dark Despair
    Wi' gloomy smile.

– 7 –

Aft, clad in massy siller weed,   *Often; silver dress*
Wi' Gentles thou erects thy head;   *Gentlefolk*
Yet, humbly kind in time o' need,
     The poor man's wine:
His wee drap parritch, or his bread,   *little bit of porridge*
     Thou kitchens fine.   *givest fine relish to*

– 8 –

Thou art the life o' public haunts:
But thee, what were our fairs and rants?   *Without; frolics*
Ev'n godly meetings o' the saunts,[2]   *saints*
     By thee inspir'd,
When, gaping, they besiege the tents,
     Are doubly fir'd.

– 9 –

That merry night we get the corn in,   *grain*
O sweetly, then, thou reams the horn in! *overflowest*
Or reekin on a New-Year mornin   *steaming*
     In cog or bicker,   *large wooden bowl or a small one*
An' just a wee drap sp'ritual burn[3] in,   *whisky*
     An' gusty sucker!   *sugar*

– 10 –

When Vulcan gies his bellows breath,   *gives*
An' Ploughmen gather wi' their graith, *gear*
O rare! to see thee fizz an' freath   *froth*
     I' th' lugget caup!   *two-handed cup*
Then Burnewin comes on like death   *(the blacksmith)*
     At ev'ry chaup.   *stroke*

---

[2] A reference to the open-air communion service, the setting of "The Holy Fair."
[3] I.e., spiritual water (whiskey) put into ale to make a posset.

- 11 -

iron   Nae mercy, then, for airn or steel:
bony; fellow   The brawnie, bainie, ploughman chiel,
            Brings hard owrehip, wi' sturdy wheel,
                The strong forehammer,
stithy; anvil   Till block an' studdie ring an' reel,
                Wi' dinsome clamour.

- 12 -

squalling babies   When skirlin weanies see the light,
chatter brightly   Thou maks the gossips clatter bright,
impotent fellows   How fumbling coofs their dearies slight;
Woe betide   Wae worth the name!
midwife   Nae howdie gets a social night,
coin from   Or plack frae them.[4]

- 13 -

            When neebors anger at a plea,
mad   An' just as wud as wud can be,
-brew   How easy can the barley-brie
                Cement the quarrel!
            It's aye the cheapest Lawyer's fee,
                To taste the barrel.

- 14 -

            Alake! that e'er my Muse has reason,
charge   To wyte her countrymen wi' treason!

---

[4] Burns cleaned up this stanza for the second edition (1787) by substituting the last three lines as printed here; in the first edition (1786), the midwives at the party in celebration of the birth reflect on the capacity of men to give sexual pleasure, not, as here, to conceive:

                "Wae worth them for't!
whole, hale   While healths gae round to him, wha, tight
Gives   Gies famous sport."

But monie daily weet their weason   *wet; throat*
    Wi' liquors nice,
An' hardly, in a winter season,
    E'er spier her price.   *ask*

– 15 –

Wae worth that Brandy, burnan trash!
Fell source o' monie a pain an' brash!   *sickness*
Twins monie a poor, doylt,   *Deprives many; stupid;*
        druken hash,   *drunken fellow*
    O' half his days;
An' sends, beside, auld Scotland's cash
    To her warst faes.   *worst foes*

– 16 –

Ye Scots, wha wish auld Scotland well!
Ye chief, to you my tale I tell,
Poor, plackless devils like mysel!   *penniless*
    It sets you ill,   *becomes*
Wi' bitter, dearthfu' wines to mell,   *expensive; meddle*
    Or foreign gill.   *drink*

– 17 –

May Gravels round his blather wrench,   *bladder*
An' Gouts torment him, inch by inch,
Wha twists his gruntle wi' a glunch   *mouth, sneer*
    O' sour disdain,
Out owre a glass o' Whiskey-punch   *At a*
    Wi' honest men!

– 18 –

O Whisky! soul o' plays an' pranks!
Accept a Bardie's gratefu' thanks!
When wanting thee, what tuneless cranks   *lacking*

Are my poor Verses!
Thou comes—they rattle i' their ranks

Close to each other's asses   At ither's arses!

- 19 -

Thee, Ferintosh! O sadly lost!
Scotland lament frae coast to coast!

cough   No colic grips, an' barkin hoast,
     May kill us a';
For loyal Forbes' Chartered boast

taken away   Is taen awa![5]

- 20 -

Those; -doctors   Thae curst horse-leeches o' th' Excise,
stills   Wha mak the Whiskey stells their prize!
Hold   Haud up thy han', Deil! ance, twice, thrice!
spies   There, seize the blinkers!
brimstone   An' bake them up in brunstane pies
     For poor damn'd Drinkers.

- 21 -

give   Fortune! if thou'll but gie me still
Whole trousers   Hale breeks, a scone, an' whiskey gill,
abundance   An' rowth o' rhyme to rave at will,
     Tak a' the rest,
An' deal't about as thy blind skill
     Directs thee best.

---

[5] The family of Forbes of Culloden had since 1690 the privilege to make whisky free of duty at Ferintosh (a synonym for whisky, as in the first line of this stanza). When this privilege was abolished in 1785, the price of whisky went up.

ADDRESS TO A HAGGIS[1]
(1786, 1786)[2]

- 1 -

Fair fa' your honest, sonsie face, *Good luck to; jolly*
Great Chieftain o' the Puddin-race!
Aboon them a' ye tak your place, *Above*
     Painch, tripe, or thairm: *Paunch; small intestine*
Weel are ye wordy of a grace *worthy*
     As lang's my arm. *long as*

- 2 -

The groaning trencher there ye fill,
Your hurdies like a distant hill, *buttocks*
Your pin[3] wad help to mend a mill
     In time o' need,
While thro' your pores the dews distil
     Like amber bead.

- 3 -

His knife see Rustic-Labor dight, *wipe*
An' cut ye up wi' ready slight, *skill*
Trenching your gushing entrails bright,
     Like onie ditch;

---

[1] A kind of large, round, sausage-like pudding made of a sheep's stomach stuffed with ground sheep's heart, lungs, liver and with oatmeal, suet, and flavoring, boiled and served steaming hot.

[2] First published in the *Caledonian Mercury,* 20 December 1786, then collected in the second edition (1787). The text here is from the latter.

[3] The wooden skewer used to close the opening of the casing.

And then, O what a glorious sight,
-steaming   Warm-reekin, rich!

– 4 –

horn-spoon   Then, horn for horn they stretch an' strive,
Devil   Deil tak the hindmost, on they drive,
-swollen bellies soon   Till a' their weel-swall'd kytes belyve
          Are bent like drums;
most; burst   Then auld Guidman, maist like to rive,
"God be thanked!" murmers   "Bethankit!" hums.

– 5 –

over   Is there that owre his French ragout,
would sicken   Or olio that wad staw a sow,
    Or fricassee wad mak her spew
disgust   Wi' perfect sconner,
    Looks down wi' sneering, scornfu' view
          On sic a dinner?

– 6 –

    Poor devil! see him owre his trash,
feeble; rush   As feckless as a wither'd rash,
thin leg; mere   His spindle shank a guid whip-lash,
fist; nut   His nieve a nit;
bloody   Thro' bluidy flood or field to dash,
          O how unfit!

– 7 –

    But mark the Rustic, haggis-fed,
    The trembling earth resounds his tread,
large fist   Clap in his walie nieve a blade,
    He'll make it whissle;
lop off   An' legs, an' arms, an' heads will sned
tops of thistle   Like taps o' thrissle.

– 8 –

Ye Pow'rs, wha mak mankind your care,
And dish them out their bill o' fare,
Auld Scotland wants nae skinking ware,   *thin, watery*
    That jaups in luggies;   *splashes in bowls*
But, if ye wish her gratefu' prayer,
    Gie her a Haggis!   *Give*

"GRIM GRIZZEL[1] WAS A MIGHTY DAME..."
(post 1788?, 1896)

Grim Grizzel was a mighty Dame
Weel kend on Cluden-side:[2]
Grim Grizzel was a mighty Dame
a great deal of   O' meikle fame and pride.

When gentles met in gentle bowers
hall   And nobles in the ha',
Grim Grizzel was a mighty Dame,
all   The loudest o' them a'.

Where lawless Riot rag'd the night
not go   And Beauty durst na gang,
Grim Grizzel was a mighty Dame
Whom no; would wrong   Wham nae man e'er wad wrang.

Nor had Grim Grizzel skill alane
hall   What bower and ha' require;
But she had skill, and meikle skill,
cowbarn   In barn and eke in byre.

One   Ae day Grim Grizzel walked forth,
As she was wont to do,

---

[1] Burns discovered the name "Grizzle Grimme" and the lady's dwelling of "Lincluden" in a comic epitaph which he took down, as he wrote, from "an old tombstone" (HH, II, 275, 458–459). For this hilarious tale of the heroic exploits of a lady from long ago, Burns adopted the manner of the ballad.

[2] A small river which falls into the Nith at Lincluden (mentioned in the last line of the poem), one and one-half miles northwest of Dumfries.

Alang the banks o' Cluden fair,
  Her cattle for to view.

The cattle sh[at] o'er hill and dale
  As cattle will incline,
And sair it grieved Grim Grizzel's heart   *sorely*
  Sae muckle muck to tine.   *So much manure to lose*

And she has ca'd on John o' Clods,   *called*
  Of her herdsmen the chief,
And she has ca'd on John o' Clods,
  And tell'd him a' her grief:—   *all*

"Now wae betide thee, John o' Clods!   *woe*
  I gie thee meal and fee,   *give*
And yet sae meikle muck ye tine
  Might a' be gear to me!   *all be property for*

"Ye claut my byre, ye sweep my byre,   *rake; cowbarn*
  The like was never seen;
The very chamber I lie in
  Was never half sae clean.

"Ye ca' my kye adown the loan   *drive; cows; down; lane*
  And there they a' discharge: *all*
My Tammie's hat, wig, head and a'
  Was never half sae large!

"But mind my words now, John o' Clods,
  And tent me what I say: *heed what*
My kye shall shit ere they gae out,   *cows; before; go*
  That shall they ilka day.   *every*

"And mind my words now, John o' Clods,
  And tent now wha ye serve;
ye'll; go   Or back ye'se to the Colonel gang,
  Either to steal or starve."

Then John o' Clods he looked up
then   And syne he looked down;
  He looked east, he looked west,
round   He looked roun' and roun'.

mountain-ash   His bonnet and his rowantree club
From; fall   Frae either hand did fa';
eyes   Wi' lifted een and open mouth
all   He naething said at a'.

At length he found his trembling tongue,
folded   Within his mouth was fauld:—
One   "Ae silly word frae me, madam,
If; dare; bold   Gin I daur be sae bauld.

"Your kye will at nae bidding shit,
  Let me do what I can;
  Your kye will at nae bidding shit
any   Of onie earthly man.

Mire-   "Tho' ye are great Lady Glaur-hole,
  For a' your power and art
  Tho' ye are great Lady Glaur-hole,
will not   They winna let a fart."

woe   "Now wae betide thee, John o' Clods!
  An ill death may ye die!
  My kye shall at my bidding shit,
  And that ye soon shall see."

Then she's ta'en Hawkie by the tail,   *she has taken*
  And wrung wi' might and main,
Till Hawkie rowted through the woods   *bellowed*
  Wi' agonising pain.

"Shit, shit, ye bitch," Grim Grizzel roar'd,
  Till hill and valley rang;
"And shit, ye bitch," the echoes roar'd
  Lincluden wa's amang.   *walls among*

Manners-Painting Poems

In "The Vision" Burns has Coila, his Muse, explain how from his early years she has taught him "manners-painting strains/The Loves, the ways of simple swains" (p. 60). He is always good at such painting when he is not thus Anglo-genteel and sentimentally pastoral. He shared with Prior, Pope, Gay, and Goldsmith the eighteenth-century preoccupation with the behavior of social man, with the comedy of manners. His descriptions are never pure, that is, they serve other purposes of humor or sentiment; and his "manners-painting strains" are best seen in his satires. But there are a group of poems which seem more than the rest mainly descriptive, three of which appear in this section.

"The Auld Farmer's . . . Salutation," written in broader Scots than is found in any other of his poems in this collection, evokes the remembrance of things past. It is a poem more of moving nostalgia than, as it is usually taken, of companionable tenderness to animals. The old mare could just as well be the farmer's wife, as we can see if we compare this poem with "John Anderson, My Jo," a lyric of strikingly similar purpose. Because of his unusually close association with her, the mare is a living memorial of all the days of his life since his marriage; her beauty, strength, grace, faithfulness, endurance, and patience were his, and her present stately tranquility he now enjoys too. The poem evokes a universal feeling, the sad sense of days gone by.

"Tam Samson's Elegy" conservatively uses the Scots form of the comic elegy, which he modified for "Poor Mailie's Elegy," to accomplish its traditional purpose of presenting a humorous portrait.

Burns seems to have written "The Cotter's Saturday Night" as a show piece to put in the Kilmarnock edition, and an idyll (much like Goldsmith's old Auburn in "The Deserted Village"), presenting what he wanted his readers to believe about the Scots peasantry from which he sprang. It should be compared with its model by Fergusson, "The Farmer's Ingle," which opens:

Whan gloaming gray out o'er the welkin keeks,	*peeps*
Whan Bawtie ca' his owsen to the byre,	*drives*
Whan Thrasher John, sair dung, his barn-	*worn-out;*
door steeks,	*closes*
Whan lusty lasses at the dighting tire:	*winnowing*
What bangs fu' leal the e'enings caming cauld,	*beats truly*
And gars snaw-tapit winter freeze in vain;	*makes*
Gars dowie mortals look baith blythe and bauld,	*doleful*
Nor fley'd wi a' the poortith o' the plain;	*frightened; poverty*
Begin, my Muse, and chant in hamely strain.	

THE AULD FARMER'S NEW YEAR MORNING SALUTATION TO HIS AULD MARE MAGGIE, ON GIVING HER THE ACCUSTOMED RIPP OF CORN *ha* TO HANSEL IN THE NEW-YEAR *as a ceremonia*

(1786, 1786)

– 1 –

A Guid New-year I wish thee, Maggie!
old belly Hae, there's a ripp to thy auld baggie:
sway-backed; knobby Tho' thou's howe-backet now, an' knaggie,
      I've seen the day
have gone; colt Thou could hae gaen like onie staggie,
Over the lea   Out-owre the lay.

– 2 –

art drooping Tho' now thou's dowie, stiff, an' crazy,
An' thy auld hide as white's a daisie,
glossy I've seen thee dappl't, sleek an' glaizie,
      A bonie gray:
prepared; dared; excite He should been tight that daur't to raize thee,
Once   Ance in a day.

– 3 –

Thou ance was i' the foremost rank,
goodly; sturdy, supple A filly buirdly, steeve, an' swank;
well An' set weel down a shapely shank,
ever trod earth   As e'er tread yird;
have; ditch An' could hae flown out-owre a stank
any   Like onie bird.

96

– 4 –

It's now some nine-an'-twenty year
Sin' thou was my Guidfather's Meere;   *Since; Father-in-law's Mare*
He gied me thee, o' tocher clear,   *gave; dowry*
    An' fifty mark;
Tho' it was sma', 'twas weel-won gear,   *small; property*
    An' thou was stark.

– 5 –

When first I gaed to woo my Jenny,   *went*
Ye then was trottan wi' your Minnie: *Mother*
Tho' ye was trickie, slee, an' funnie: *sly; frisky*
    Ye ne'er was donsie;   *mischievous*
But hamely, tawie, quiet, an' cannie,   *friendly; tractable; gentle*
    An' unco sonsie.   *good tempered*

– 6 –

That day, ye pranc'd wi' muckle pride,   *a great deal of*
When ye bure hame my bonie Bride: *bore home*
An' sweet an' gracefu' she did ride,
    Wi' maiden air!
Kyle-Stewart[1] I could bragged wide,   *could have challenged, boasted*
    For sic a pair.

– 7 –

Tho' now ye dow but hoyte and hoble,   *can; limp*
An' wintle like a saumont-coble,   *wobble; salmon-boat*
That day, ye was a jinker noble,   *pacer*
    For heels an' win'!   *wind*
An' ran them till they a' did wauble,   *wobble*
    Far, far behin'!

---

[1] Kyle, the middle district of Ayrshire, between the rivers Irvine and Doon, is itself divided by the river Ayr into Kyle-Stewart on the north and King's Kyle on the south.

– 8 –

skittish   When thou an' I were young and skiegh,

tedious   An' Stable-meals at Fairs were driegh,

would; whinny   How thou wad prance, an' snore, an' skriegh,
          An' tak the road!

out of the way   Town's-bodies ran, an' stood abiegh,
          An' ca't thee mad.

– 9 –

When thou was corn't, an' I was mellow,

just   We took the road ay like a Swallow:

Horse races at weddings   At Brooses thou had ne'er a fellow,
          For pith an' speed;

But ev'ry tail thou pay't them hollow,

Wherever; went   Whare'er thou gaed.

– 10 –

small; droop-rumped; beasts   The sma', droop-rumpl't hunter cattle,

perhaps have worsted thee in a spurt   Might aiblins waur't thee for a brattle;

six   But sax Scotch mile, thou try't their mettle,

made; wheeze   An' gar't them whaizle:

switch   Nae whip nor spur, but just a wattle

willow   O' saugh or hazle.

– 11 –

Thou was a noble Fittie-lan',[2]

rawhide or rope plow-traces   As e'er in tug or tow was drawn!

eight; work   Aft thee an' I, in aught hours' gaun,
          On guid March-weather,

six roods to our own measurement   Hae turn'd sax rood beside our han'

together   For days thegither.

---

2 The inside horse of the rear pair in a four-horse plow.

- 12 -

Thou never braing't, an' fetch't,   *lunged violently; pulled unevenly;*
     an' flisket;   *moved impatiently*
But thy auld tail thou wad hae whisket, *would have switched*
An' spread abreed thy weel-fill'd brisket, *abroad; breast*
   Wi' pith an' pow'r,
Till sprittie knowes wad rair't, an' risket,
   An' slypet owre.[3]

- 13 -

When frosts lay lang, an' snaws were deep, *long; snows*
An' threaten'd labor back to keep,
I gied thy cog a wee bit heap   *gave; dish*
   Aboon the timmer: *Above; edge*
I ken'd my Maggie wad na sleep *knew; would not*
   For that, or Simmer.   *before Summer*

- 14 -

In cart or car thou never reestet; *stood still*
The steyest brae thou wad hae fac't it; *steepest hill*
Thou never lap, an' sten't, an' breastet, *leaped; stretched; sprang forward*
   Then stood to blaw;   *blow*
But just thy step a wee thing hastet, *little quickened*
   Thou snoov't awa.   *pushed on ahead*

- 15 -

My Pleugh is now thy bairntime a', *Team; all thy issue*
Four gallant brutes as e'er did draw;
Forbye sax mae, I've sell't awa, *Besides six more; away*
   That thou hast nurst:
They drew me thretteen pund an' twa, *thirteen pounds and two*
   The vera warst.   *At the very least*

---

[3] "Until little hills full of roots would have given forth a crackling, grating, tearing sound and the clods fallen smoothly over."

– 16 –

hard day's work; two; done Monie a sair daurg we twa hae wrought,
world An' wi' the weary warl' fought!
An' monie an anxious day I thought
We wad be beat!
Yet here to crazy Age we're brought,
Wi' something yet.

– 17 –

An' think na, my auld trusty Servan',
thou art That now perhaps thou's less deservin,
An' thy auld days may end in starvin;
bushel For my last fow,
Quarter-peck; one A heapet Stimpart, I'll reserve ane
Laid by for you.

– 18 –

We've worn to crazy years thegither;
totter We'll toyte about wi' ane anither;
watchful; change Wi' tentie care I'll flit thy tether,
reserved portion of land To some hain'd rig,
stretch Whare ye may nobly rax your leather
small Wi' sma' fatigue.

TAM SAMSON'S ELEGY[1]

(1786, 1787)

An honest man's the noblest work of God.

POPE[2]

- I -

Has auld Kilmarnock seen the Deil?	*Devil*
Or great Mackinlay[3] thrawn his heel?	*sprained his ankle*
Or Robertson[4] again grown well	
To preach an' read?	
'Na, waur than a'!' cries ilka chiel,	*worse; all; everybody*
'Tam Samson's dead!'	

- 2 -

Kilmarnock lang may grunt an' grane,	*groan*
An' sigh, an' sob, an' greet her lane,	*weep alone*
An' cleed her bairns, man, wife an' wean,	*clothe; offspring; child*
In mourning weed;	*clothes*
To Death she's dearly pay'd the kane,	*rent in kind*
Tam Samson's dead!	

---

[1] Thomas Samson (1722-1795), a nurseryman, seedsman, and sportsman of Kilmarnock. Burns's note to this poem in its first printing: "When this worthy old Sportsman went out last muir-fowl season, he supposed it was to be, in Ossian's phrase, 'the last of his fields,' and expressed an ardent wish to die and be buried in the muirs. On this hint the author composed his Elegy and Epitaph."

[2] "Essay on Man," IV, 248.

[3] James Mackinlay (1756-1841), strictly orthodox minister of the second charge of Laigh Kirk, Kilmarnock, described by Burns in a note as "a great favourite with the million." He appears prominently in "The Ordination."

[4] John Robertson (1732-1799), moderate minister of the first charge of the same kirk as Mackinlay's described by Burns in a note as "an equal favourite with the *few*, . . . at that time ailing."

- 3 -

The Brethren o' the mystic level[5]

angle May hing their head in wofu' bevel,

While by their nose the tears will revel,

any Like ony bead;

has given; heavy blow Death's gien the Lodge an unco devel:

Tam Samson's dead!

- 4 -

When Winter muffles up his cloak,

And binds the mire like a rock;

lakes When to the loughs the Curlers[6] flock,

Wi' gleesome spied,

Who; mark Wha will they station at the cock,

Tam Samson's dead?

- 5 -

Corps He was the king of a' the Core,

To guard, or draw, or wick a bore,

Or up the rink like Jehu[7] roar

In time o' need;

But now he lags on Death's hog-score,

Tam Samson's dead!

- 6 -

Salmon Now safe the stately Sawmont sail,

And Trouts bedropp'd wi' crimson hail,

---

[5] Freemasons

[6] A Scots game, something like shuffleboard, played on ice. The next stanza uses curling terms: "to guard" is to defend a well-placed stone with another; "to draw" is to send a stone into a good position by hitting it with another; "to wick a bore" is to send a stone through an opening by an oblique hit. The "hog-score" is the line the curling stone must cross if it is not to be considered out of play.

[7] A wild driver, see 2 *Kings* 9:20.

And Eels, weel-kend for souple tail, *well-known*
  And Geds for greed,   *Pikes*
Since, dark in Death's fish-creel, we wail
  Tam Samson dead!

– 7 –

Rejoice, ye birring Paitricks a'; *whirring Partridges*
Ye cootie Moorcocks, crousely craw; *feather-legged, boldly crow*
Ye Maukins, cock your fud fu' braw *Rabbits; tail; finely*
  Withoutten dread;
Your mortal Fae is now awa, *Foe; away*
  Tam Samson's dead!

– 8 –

That woefu' morn be ever mourn'd,
Saw him in shootin graith adorn'd, *attire*
While pointers round impatient burn'd,
  Frae couples free'd; *leashes*
But Och! he gaed and ne'er return'd! *went*
  Tam Samson's dead!

– 9 –

In vain Auld-age his body batters,
In vain the Gout his ancles fetters,
In vain the burns cam down like waters, *streams come*
  An acre braid! *broad*
Now ev'ry auld wife, greetin, clatters: *weeping*
  "Tam Samson's dead!"

– 10 –

Owre monie a weary hag he limpit, *Over many; piece of broken ground*
An' ay the tither shot he thumpit, *still; other*
Till coward Death behint him jumpit,
  Wi! deadly feide; *hate*

Now he proclaims wi' tout o' trumpet,
    Tam Samson's dead!

— 11 —

When at his heart he felt the dagger,
He reel'd his wonted bottle-swagger,
But yet he drew the mortal trigger
well-   Wi' weel-aim'd heed;
"Lord, five!" he cry'd, an' owre did stagger;
    Tam Samson's dead!

— 12 —

Each; brother Ilk hoary Hunter mourn'd a brither;
Ilk Sportsman-youth bemoan'd a father;
stone Yon auld gray stane, amang the heather,
    Marks out his head;
nonsense Whare Burns has wrote, in rhyming blether:
    "Tam Samson's dead!"

— 13 —

When August winds the heather wave,
And Sportsmen wander by yon grave,
Three volleys let his mem'ry crave
powder   O' pouther an' lead,
Till Echo answers frae her cave,
    Tam Samson's dead!

— 14 —

Heav'n rest his saul whare'er he be!
many more Is th' wish o' monie mae than me:
two faults He had twa fauts, or maybe three,
remedy   Yet what remead?
One; lack Ae social, honest man want we:
    Tam Samson's dead!

THE EPITAPH

Tam Samson's weel-worn clay here lies: *well-*
   Ye canting Zealots, spare him!
If honest worth in Heaven rise,
   Ye'll mend or ye win near him.   *ere ye get*

PER CONTRA

Go, Fame, an' canter like a filly
Thro' a' the streets an neuks o' Killie;   *nooks; Kilmarnock*
Tell ev'ry social honest billie   *fellow*
   To cease his grievin;
For yet, unskaith'd by Death's gleg gullie,   *unharmed; quick, sharp knife*
   Tam Samson's livin!   *living*

THE COTTER'S SATURDAY NIGHT

Inscribed to R. Aiken, Esq.[1]

(1786?, 1786)

Let not ambition mock their useful toil,
Their homely joys, and destiny obscure;
Nor Grandeur hear, with a disdainful smile,
The short and simple annals of the poor.

GRAY.[2]

– 1 –

My lov'd, my honor'd, much respected friend,
  No mercenary Bard his homage pays;
With honest pride, I scorn each selfish end,
  My dearest meed, a friend's esteem and praise:
  To you I sing, in simple Scottish lays,[3]
The lowly train in life's sequester'd scene;
  The native feelings strong, the guileless ways,
What Aiken in a Cottage would have been;
Ah! tho' his worth unknown, far happier there
    I ween!

– 2 –

blows; moan   November chill blaws loud wi' angry sugh;
  The short'ning winter-day is near a close;

---

[1] For Robert Aiken, Burns's lawyer friend and patron, see p. 46, note 1.

[2] Thomas Gray's "Elegy Written in a Country Churchyard."

[3] Hardly an accurate description of the largely English diction of the Spenserian stanzas to follow, with their echoes of Gray, Pope, Edward Young, James Thomson, William Collins, Goldsmith, and Milton. Burns had not read Spenser at this time and probably derived his stanza from William Shenstone's "The Schoolmistress."

The miry beasts retreating frae the pleugh;
   The black'ning trains o' craws to their repose: *crows*
   The toil-worn Cotter frae his labor goes,
This night his weekly moil is at an end,
   Collects his spades, his mattocks, and his hoes,
Hoping the morn in ease and rest to spend,
And weary, o'er the moor, his course does
     hameward bend.

- 3 -

At length his lonely Cot appears in view,
   Beneath the shelter of an aged tree;
The' expectant wee-things, toddlan, stacher   *stagger*
     through
    To meet their Dad, wi' flichterin noise and   *fluttering*
     glee.
    His wee bit ingle, blinkan bonilie,   *fireplace*
His clean hearth-stane, his thrifty Wifie's smile,   *-stone*
   The lisping infant, prattling on his knee,
Does a' his weary kiaugh and care beguile,   *anxiety*
And makes him quite forget his labor and his
     toil.

- 4 -

Belyve, the elder bairns come drapping in,   *After awhile; children*
   At Service out, amang the Farmers roun';   *round about*
Some ca' the pleugh, some herd, some tentie rin   *drive; carefully*
   A cannie errand to a neebor town: *private*
   Their eldest hope, their Jenny, woman grown,
In youthfu' bloom, love sparkling in her e'e,   *eyes*
   Comes hame; perhaps, to shew a braw new   *handsome*
     gown,
Or deposite her sair-won penny-fee,   *hard-; -wages*
To help her Parents dear, if they in hardship be.

- 5 -

With joy unfeign'd, brothers and sisters meet,
enquiries   And each for other's weelfare kindly spiers:
The social hours, swift-wing'd, unnotic'd fleet;
wonders   Each tells the uncos that he sees or hears.
The Parents partial eye their hopeful years;
Anticipation forward points the view;
The Mother, wi' her needle and her sheers,
makes old clothes; almost Gars auld claes look amaist as weel's the new;
The Father mixes a' wi admonition due.

- 6 -

Their Master's and their Mistress's command,
youngsters all   The younkers a' are warned to obey;
diligent And mind their labors wi' an eydent hand,
trifle   And ne'er, tho' out o' sight, to jauk or play:
"And O! be sure to fear the Lord alway!
And mind your duty, duely, morn and night!
go   Lest in temptation's path ye gang astray,
Implore His counsel and assisting might:
They never sought in vain that sought the Lord
    aright."

- 7 -

But hark! a rap comes gently to the door;
    Jenny, wha kens the meaning o' the same,
Tells how a neebor lad came o'er the moor,
    To do some errands, and convey her hame.
The wily Mother sees the conscious flame
Sparkle in Jenny's e'e, and flush her cheek;
    With heart-struck anxious care, enquires his name,
almost While Jenny hafflins is afraid to speak;
Weel-pleas'd the Mother hears, it's nae wild,
    worthless Rake.

- 8 -

With kindly welcome, Jenny brings him ben;   *inside*
   A strappan youth, he takes the Mother's eye;
Blythe Jenny sees the visit's no ill taen;   *taken*
    The Father cracks of horses, pleughs, and kye.   *talks; cows*
    The Youngster's artless heart o'erflows wi' joy,
But blate and laithfu', scarce can weel behave;   *bashful; sheepish*
    The Mother, wi' a woman's wiles, can spy
What makes the youth sae bashfu' and sae grave;
Weel-pleas'd to think her bairn's respected like
    the lave.

- 9 -

O happy love! where love like this is found!
   O heart-felt raptures! bliss beyond compare!
I've paced much this weary, mortal round,
    And sage experience bids me this declare—
    "If Heaven a draught of heavenly pleasure
      spare,
One cordial in this melacholy Vale,
   'Tis when a youthful, loving, modest Pair,
In other's arms, breathe out the tender tale
Beneath the milk-white thorn that scents the
    ev'ning gale."

- 10 -

Is there, in human form, that bears a heart—
   A Wretch! a Villain! lost to love and truth!
That can, with studied, sly, ensnaring art,
    Betray sweet Jenny's unsuspecting youth?
    Curse on his perjur'd arts! dissembling, smooth!
Are Honor, Virtue, Conscience, all exil'd?
   Is there no Pity, no relenting Ruth,

Points to the Parents fondling o'er their Child?
Then paints the ruin'd Maid, and their
   distraction wild!

– 11 –

But now the Supper crowns their simple board,
   The healsome Porritch, chief o' Scotia's food;
The soupe their only Hawkie does afford,
   That, 'yont the hallan snugly chows her cood;
The Dame brings forth, in complimental
      mood,
To grace the lad, her weel-hain'd kebbuck, fell;
   And aft he's prest, and aft he ca's it guid;
The frugal Wifie, garrulous, will tell,
How 'twas a towmond auld, sin' Lint was i' the
      bell.

wholesome Porridge
milk; Cow
beyond; wall; cud

-saved cheese; pungent
oft; calls

twelvemonth old; since Flax;
flower

– 12 –

The chearfu' Supper done, wi' serious face,
   They, round the ingle, form a circle wide;
The Sire turns o'er, wi' patriarchal grace,
   The big ha'-Bible, ance his Father's pride!
His bonnet rev'rently is laid aside,
His lyart haffets wearing thin and bare;
   Those strains that once did sweet in Zion
      glide,
He wales a portion with judicious care,
And "Let us worship God!" he says, with
   solemn air.

hall-; once

grey side-locks

chooses

– 13 –

They chant their artless notes in simple guise;
   They tune their hearts, by far the noblest aim:

Perhaps *Dundee's*[4] wild-warbling measures rise,
   Or plaintive *Martyrs,* worthy of the name;
   Or noble *Elgin* beets the heaven-ward flame,   *fans*
The sweetest far of Scotia's holy lays:
   Compar'd with these, Italian trills are tame;
The tickl'd ears no heart-felt raptures raise;
Nae unison hae they, with our Creator's praise.

– 14 –

The priest-like Father reads the sacred page,
   How Abram was the friend of God on high;
Or, Moses bade eternal warfare wage,
   With Amalek's ungracious progeny;
   Or, how the royal Bard did groaning lye
Beneath the stroke of Heaven's avenging ire;[5]
   Or Job's pathetic plaint, and wailing cry;
Or rapt Isaiah's wild, seraphic fire;
Or other Holy Seers that tune the sacred lyre.

– 15 –

Perhaps the Christian volume is the theme,
   How guiltless blood for guilty man was shed;
How He who bore in Heaven the second name,
   Had not on Earth whereon to lay His Head;
   How His first followers and servants sped;
The Precepts sage they wrote to many a land:
   How he,[6] who lone in Patmos banished,
Saw in the sun a might angel stand,
And heard great Bab'lon's doom pronounc'd by
    Heaven's command.

---

[4] This and the names in the next two lines are titles to common hymns.

[5] For God's aid to Moses against the Amalekites and for His punishment of David for adultery with Bathsheba and the murder of Uriah, see Exodus 17:8–16 and 2 Samuel 12:7–18.

[6] St. John the Divine (see Revelations 1:9).

– 16 –

Then kneeling down to Heaven's Eternal King,
   The Saint, the Father, and the Husband prays:
Hope "springs exulting on triumphant wing," [7]
   That thus they all shall meet in future days:
   There, ever bask in uncreated rays,
No more to sigh, or shed the bitter tear,
   Together hymning their Creator's praise,
In such society, yet still more dear;
While circling Time moves round in an eternal
    sphere.

– 17 –

Compar'd with this, how poor Religion's pride,
   In all the pomp of method, and of art;
When men display to congregations wide,
   Devotion's ev'ry grace, except the heart!
   The Power, incens'd, the Pageant will desert,
The pompous strain, the sacerdotal stole:
   But haply, in some Cottage far apart,
May hear, well-pleas'd, the language of the Soul,
And in His Book of Life the Inmates poor
    enroll.

– 18 –

Then homeward all take off their sev'ral way;
   The youngling Cottagers retire to rest!
The Parent-pair their secret homage pay,
   And proffer up to Heaven the warm request,
   That He who stills the raven's clam'rous nest,
And decks the lily fair in flow'ry pride,
   Would, in the way His Wisdom sees the best,

---

[7] Quoted somewhat inaccurately from Pope's "Windsor Forest"; Burns identified
the work in a footnote to this line.

For them and for their little ones provide;
But chiefly, in their hearts with Grace Divine
    preside.

– 19 –

From scenes like these, old Scotia's grandeur
    springs,
  That makes her lov'd at home, rever'd abroad:
Princes and lords are but the breath of kings,
  "An honest man's the noblest work of God";[8]
  And certes, in fair Virtue's heavenly road,
The cottage leaves the palace far behind;
  What is a lordling's pomp? a cumbrous load,
Disguising oft the wretch of human kind,
Studied in arts of Hell, in wickedness refin'd!

– 20 –

O Scotia! my dear, my native soil!
  For whom my warmest wish to Heaven is sent!
Long may thy hardy sons of rustic toil,
  Be blest with health, and peace, and sweet
    content!
  And O! may Heaven their simple lives prevent
From Luxury's contagion, weak and vile!
  Then, howe'er crowns and coronets be rent,
A virtuous Populace may rise the while,
And stand a wall of fire around their much-loved
    Isle.

– 21 –

O Thou! who pour'd the patriotic tide,
  That stream'd thro' Wallace's undaunted heart,[9]

---

[8] Corrected from "noble" in the edition of 1793 (Pope's "Essay on Man," IV, 248).
[9] "That streamed through great unhappy Wallace' heart," in editions to that of 1793.
For Wallace, see p. 25, note 6.

Who dar'd to, nobly, stem tyrannic pride,
  Or nobly die, the second glorious part:
  (The patriot's God, peculiarly Thou art,
  His friend, inspirer, guardian, and reward!)
  O never, never Scotia's realm desert;
But still the Patriot, and the Patriot-Bard
In bright succession raise, her ornament and
  Guard!

Political, Social, Economic, Personal Satire

Satire may be defined as an indirect or disguised attack on a historic particular. All the pieces in this section have attack as their subsidiary purpose at least, have objects of attack in some degree related to particulars in Burns's world, and use as their means, disguises and indirections such as fable, ironic voice, surprising antithesis or balance, and metaphor. Thus they all can be considered as satires or as satiric in part.

"The Twa Dogs" is a defense of the simple life, a very ancient theme. It is a contribution to the primitivist literary tradition of anti-luxury in eighteenth-century England from Swift's view of the Houyhnhnms to Goldsmith's villagers of old Auburn. But its realism sets it apart: the language, the situation of the dogs in the Scottish beast-fable tradition, and the images—all are alive, earthy, real; the life of the simple cotters is happy but not idyllic or completely removed from the miseries of crushing poverty. The poem defends a way of life, but as part of this defense, attacks an alternative, the life of the aristocracy. The argument turns on two misunderstandings of the native Luath, the dramatic turning points in the dialogue.

"To a Louse" is a Horatian satire on social pretense. In satire Burns characteristically assumes another, often ironic, voice; here he at first identifies with Jenny and her class and appears as socially outraged by the behavior of the louse. The poet shifts his address from the louse to Jenny, and finally to Providence or the reader in the direct statement of the ostensible moral. The louse in its ubiquity links all classes in a kind of egalitarianism. The humor derives from the physical setting (the poet observing the back of the pretty girl in the pew in front of him), from the behavior of the heroic louse with the poet's shifting attitudes to it (contempt, pity, anger, admiration), and from Jenny's dawning recognition of the louse's presence. The last line suggests that ostentatious piety in church is made irrational by the absurdity of the human condition.

"Address to the Unco Guid" employs a modification of the ancient Scots stanza of "Christ's Kirk on the Green" to defend behavior based on social impulse and to attack the critics of such behavior, those who live their lives in cold and withdrawn reason and piety. The poem turns upon the old conflict between passion and reason. The attack and defense each have four or five distinct points.

"Address of Beelzebub" is Burns's most fierce and angry satire, more so than "Holy Willie's Prayer," because it is unrelieved by any comic exposure of hypocrisy. He attacks the Highland landowners not only for cruel indifference to their tenants but for their anti-democratic political attitudes. The best way to keep the tenants under control, Burns ironically suggests, is to prevent them from adopting any of the new political ideals arising in America. Since the poem was written in 1786, it shows that Burns's Jacobin moods after the fall of the Bastille had seeds in earlier attitudes.

The remaining three pieces are little more than squibs. It is enlightening to compare "Adam Armour's Prayer" with "Holy Willie's Prayer," for in spite of their obvious similarity the former fails to achieve stature because it has very little point. The treatment is almost purely comic. Adam's moral selfrighteousness and hypocrisy are not emphasized by vigorous ironic attack. In the fragment "On William Creech" Burns attempted the heroic couplet in the manner of Alexander Pope, as he did very often after his stay in Edinburgh. We see Burns in a ballad vein in "The Dean of the Faculty," thoroughly involved in the politics of his times.

THE TWA DOGS

A Tale

(1785–1786, 1786)

'Twas in that place o' Scotland's isle
That bears the name of auld King Coil,[1]
Upon a bonie day in June,
When wearing thro' the afternoon,
5 Twa dogs, that were na thrang at hame,   *Two; not busy at home*
Forgathered ance upon a time.   *Meet once*

The first I'll name, they ca'd him Caesar,   *called*
Was keepit for His Honor's pleasure: *kept*
His hair, his size, his mouth, his lugs,   *ears*
10 Shew'd he was nane o' Scotland's dogs;   *none*
But whalpit some place far abroad,   *whelped*
Whare sailors gang to fish for cod.   *go*

His locked, letter'd braw brass-collar   *handsome*
Shew'd him the gentleman an' scholar;
15 But tho' he was o' high degree,
The fient a pride, na pride had he;   *Not a trace of*
But wad hae spent an hour caressan,   *would*
Ev'n wi' a tinkler-gipsy's messan;   *tinker-; mongrel*
At kirk or market, mill or smiddie,   *smithy*
20 Nae tawted tyke, tho' e'er sae duddie, *matted-haired dog; ragged*
But he wad stan't, as glad to see him,   *would have stood*
An' stroan't on stanes an' hillocks wi' him. *pissed; stones*

---

[1] Erroneous folk etymology for Kyle, the central district of Ayrshire.

other		The tither was a ploughman's collie,
fellow		A rhyming, ranting, raving billie,
	25	Wha for his friend an' comrade had him,
called		And in his freaks had Luath ca'd him,
		After some dog in Highland sang,[2]
a long time ago		Was made lang syne, Lord knows how lang.

wise		He was a gash an' faithfu' tyke,
leaped; ditch or wall	30	As ever lap a sheugh or dyke.
pleasant; white-striped		His honest, sonsie, baws'nt face,
Always got; every		Ay gat him friends in ilka place;
shaggy		His breast was white, his towzie back,
		Weel clad wi' coat o' glossy black;
friendly	35	His gawsie tail, wi' upward curl,
buttocks		Hung owre his hurdies wi' a swirl.

fond of each other		Nae doubt but they were fain o' ither,
very intimate; together		And unco pack an' thick thegither;
now; scented		Wi' social nose whyles snuff'd an' snowket;
Now; moles; dug up	40	Whyles mice and moudewurks they howket;
Now		Whyles scour'd awa' in lang excursion,
each other		An' worry'd ither in diversion;
		Till tir'd at last wi' mony a farce,
		They sat them down upon their arse,[3]
	45	An' there began a lang digression
		About the lords o' the creation.

---

[2] Burns's note: "Cuchullin's dog in Ossian's Fingal." Burns, who himself owned a dog by this name, here alludes of course to James Macpherson's supposed translations of ancient Gaelic epic, the counterfeit character of which Burns never seems to have suspected.

[3] Burns or his editor Creech made these two lines more polite (but less effective) by substituting in 1794:

Until wi' daffin weary grown
Upon a knowe they sat them down.

CAESAR

I've aften wonder'd, honest Luath,
What sort o' life poor dogs like you have;
An' when the gentry's life I saw,
50 What way poor bodies liv'd ava.   *at all*

  Our Laird gets in his racked rents, *Squire*
His coals, his Kane, an' a' his stents: *Rent in kind; dues*
He rises when he likes himsel;
His flunkies answer at the bell;
55 He ca's his coach; he ca's his horse; *calls*
He draws a bonie, silken purse
As lang's my tail, whare thro' the steeks, *long as; stitches*
The yellow letter'd Geordie keeks. *Guinea peeps*

  Frae morn to een it's nought but toiling,
60 At baking, roasting, frying, boiling;
An' tho' the gentry first are steghan, *cramming*
Yet ev'n the ha' folk fill their peghan *servants of the hall; stomach*
Wi' sauce, ragouts, an sic like trashtrie, *trash*
That's little short o' downright wastrie, *waste*
65 Our whipper-in,[4] wee, blastet wooner, *shrivelled-up wonder*
Poor, worthless elf, it eats a dinner,
Better than ony tenant-man
His Honor has in a' the lan':
An' what poor cot-folk[5] pit their painch in, *cottagers put in their paunch*
70 I own it's past my comprehension.

LUATH

Trowth, Caesar, whyles they're[6] *In truth; sometimes;*
  fash't enough: *troubled*

---

[4] A minor official of the hunt in charge of the hounds.
[5] As distinct from a tenant, a cotter, like Burns's father, rented or leased his land.
[6] their (1786).

digging; ditch		A cotter howkan in a sheugh,
stones building a wall		Wi' dirty stanes biggan a dyke,
Clearing soil from		Bairan a quarry, an' sic like;
	75	Himsel, a wife, he thus sustains,
litter; ragged children		A smytrie o' wee duddie weans,
hands' labor		An' nought but his han'-darg to keep
thatch and rope (to bind it)		Them right an' tight in thack an' raep.
sore		An' when they meet wi' sair disasters,
	80	Like loss o' health or want o' masters,
almost would		Ye maist wad think, a wee touch langer,
must		An' they maun starve o' cauld and hunger:
have known		But how it comes, I never kent yet,
		They're maistly wonderfu' contented;
stalwart men; women	85	An' buirdly chiels, an' clever hizzies,
		Are bred in sic a way as this is.

CAESAR

		But then, to see how ye're neglecket,
		How huff'd, an' cuff'd, an' disrespecket!
		Lord man, our gentry care as little
	90	For delvers, ditchers, an' sic cattle;
go		They gang as saucy by poor folk,
would; badger		As I wad by a stinkan brock.
rent-day		I've notic'd, on our Laird's court-day,
woeful		(An' mony a time my heart's been wae),
	95	Poor tenant bodies, scant o' cash,
must endure; steward's abuse		How they maun thole a factor's snash:
		He'll stamp an' threaten, curse an' swear,
seize		He'll apprehend them, poind their gear;
must stand		While they maun staun', wi' aspect humble,
	100	An' hear it a', an' fear an' tremble![7]

---

[7] Burns said that he drew the portrait of this factor from one who thus mistreated his father (see Appendix B).

I see how folk live that hae riches;
But surely poor-folk maun be wretches!   *must*

LUATH

    They're no sae wretched's ane wad think;   *as one would*
Tho' constantly on poortith's brink,   *poverty's*
105 They're sae accustom'd wi' the sight,
The view o't gies them little fright.   *of it gives*

    Then chance an' fortune are sae guided,
They're ay in less or mair provided;   *always*
An' tho' fatigu'd wi' close employment,
110 A blink o' rest's a sweet enjoyment.   *moment*
    The dearest comfort o' their lives,
Their grushie weans an' faithfu' wives;   *thriving children*
The prattling things are just their pride,
That sweetens a' their fire-side.

115 An' whyles twalpennie-worth o' nappy[8]   *at times; twelvepence; ale*
Can mak the bodies unco happy: *very*
They lay aside their private cares,
To mind the Kirk and State affairs;
They'll talk o' patronage[9] an' priests,
120 Wi' kindling fury i' their breasts,
Or tell what new taxation's comin,
An' ferlie at the folk in Lon'on.   *marvel; London*

    As bleak-fac'd Hallowmass returns,
They get the jovial, rantan kirns,   *harvest festivities*
125 When rural life, of ev'ry station,
Unite in common recreation;

[8] A quart of ale would cost twelve-pence Scots or a penny sterling.
[9] The practice of presenting a minister to a charge of a kirk by a nobleman who had the gift as a right or possession; (see Introduction; p. xxii).

glances   Love blinks, Wit slaps, an' social Mirth
Forgets there's Care upo' the earth.

     That merry day the year begins,
winds   130 They bar the door on frosty win's;
ale smokes; froth The nappy reeks wi' mantling ream,
An' sheds a heart-inspiring steam;
smoking; snuff-box The luntan pipe, an' sneeshin mill,
Are handed round wi' right guid will;
genial; talking cheerfully 135 The cantie, auld folks crackan crouse,
The young anes ranting thro' the house—
pleased My heart has been sae fain to see them,
That I for joy hae barket wi' them.

     Still it's owre true that ye hae said,
too 140 Sic game is now owre aften play'd;
There's monie a creditable stock
orderly O' decent, honest, fawsont folk,
Are riven out baith root an' branch,
Some rascal's pridefu' greed to quench,
145 Wha thinks to knit himsel the faster
In favor wi' some gentle master,
perhaps busy Wha, aiblins thrang a parliamentin,
good; soul For Britain's guid his saul indentin—

CAESAR

Faith; know Haith lad ye little ken about it;
150 For Britain's guid! guid faith! I doubt it.
going Say rather, gaun as Premiers lead him,
no as An' saying *aye* or *no*'s they bid him:
At operas an' plays parading,
Mortgaging, gambling, masquerading:
155 Or maybe, in a frolic daft,
To Hague or Calais takes a waft,

To make a tour an' tak a whirl,
To learn *bon ton*, an' see the worl'.

There, at Vienna or Versailles,
160 He rives his father's auld entails;[10]   *tears*
Or by Madrid he takes the rout,
To thrum guittars an' fecht wi' nowt;   *fight with cattle*
Or down Italian Vista startles,   *stampedes*
Whore-hunting amang groves o' myrtles:
165 Then bowses drumlie German-water,   *guzzles muddy*
To mak himsel look fair an' fatter,
An' purge the bitter ga's an' cankers   *galls*
O' curst Venetian bores an' chancres.[11]

For Britain's guid! for her destruction!
170 Wi' dissipation, feud an' faction!

LUATH

Hech man! dear sirs! is that the gate   *way*
They waste sae mony a braw estate!   *fine*
Are we sae foughten and harass'd   *troubled*
For gear ta gang that gate at last!   *money to go; way*

175   O would they stay aback frae courts,
An' please themsels wi' countra sports,

---

[10] By legal action the heir causes to be declared invalid the father's "entails," that is restrictions placed on the inheritance, so that he can have the freer use of it.

[11] Less concrete and specific lines substituted in 1787:

> An' clear the consequential sorrows,
> Love-gifts of Carnival signoras.

The last words of this couplet first appeared as "b—res and ch—ncres." The second is clear (venereal ulcers), and the first is probably "bores," figurative for female pudenda.

would   It wad for ev'ry ane be better,
            The laird, the tenant, an' the cotter!
those; wild; fellows   For thae frank, rantan, ramblan billies,
Not one   180   Fient haet o' them's ill-hearted fellows:
timber   Except for breakin o' their timmer,
mistress   Or speakin lightly o' their limmer,
            Or shootin of a hare or moor-cock,
            The ne'er-a-bit they're ill to poor folk.

     185   But will ye tell me, master Caesar:
            Sure great folk's life's a life o' pleasure?
bother   Nae cauld nor hunger e'er can steer them,
very; frighten   The vera thought o't need na fear them.

CAESAR

once   Lord man, were ye but whyles whare I am,
     190   The gentles, ye wad ne'er envy them!

            It's true, they need na starve or sweat,
            Thro' winter's cauld, or summer's heat;
grinding labor   They've nae sair-wark to craze their banes,
groans   An' fill auld-age wi' grips an' granes;
     195   But human-bodies are sic fools,
            For a' their colledges an' schools,
            That when nae real ills perplex them,
enough   They mak enow themsels to vex them;
always; fret   An' ay the less they hae to sturt them,
     200   In like proportion, less will hurt them.

            A country fellow at the pleugh,
            His acre's till'd, he's right eneugh;
            A country girl at her wheel,
dozen; very well   Her dizzen's done, she's unco weel;
worst   205   But Gentlemen, an' Ladies warst,
lack   Wi' ev'n down want o' wark are curst,
            They loiter, lounging, lank an' lazy;

Tho' deil-haet ails them, yet uneasy;   *nothing at all*
Their days insipid, dull an' tasteless;
210 Their nights unquiet, lang an' restless.

  An' ev'n their sports, their balls an' races,
Their galloping through public places,
There's sic parade, sic pomp an' art,
The joy can scarcely reach the heart.

215 The men cast out in party-matches,   *fall out*
Then sowther a' in deep debauches.   *solder*
Ae night, they're mad wi' drink an' whoring, *One*
Niest day their life is past enduring.   *Next*

  The ladies arm-in-arm in clusters,
220 As great an' gracious a' as sisters;   *all*
But hear their absent thoughts o' ither, *each other*
They're a' run deils an' jads thegither. *downright devils, evil women*
Whyles, owre the wee bit cup an' platie, *Sometimes, over; tiny cup and saucer*
They sip the scandal-potion pretty;
225 Or lee-lang nights, wi' crabbit leuks *live-long; looks*
Pore owre the devil's picture'd beuks; *playing cards (books)*
Stake on a chance a farmer's stackyard,
An' cheat like onie unhang'd blackguard.

  There's some exceptions, man an' woman;
230 But this is Gentry's life in common.

  By this, the sun was out o' sight,
An' darker gloamin brought the night:
The bum-clock humm'd wi' lazy drone, *beetle*
The kye stood rowtan i' the loan;   *cows; lowing; path*
235 When up they gat, an' shook their lugs, *ears*
Rejoic'd they were na men, but dogs;
An each took off his several way,   *different*
Resolv'd to meet some ither day.

TO A LOUSE

On Seeing One On a Lady's Bonnet at Church

(1786?, 1786)

- 1 -

going; crawling wonder	Ha! whare ye gaun, ye crowlan ferlie?
marvellously	Your impudence protects you sairly:
can't deny that; swagger	I canna say but ye strunt rarely,
	Owre gawze and lace,
	Tho' faith! I fear ye dine but sparely
	On sic a place.

- 2 -

wonder	Ye ugly, creepan, blastet wooner,
saint	Detested, shunn'd by saunt an' sinner,
dare; foot	How daur ye set your fit upon her,
	Sae fine a lady!
	Gae somewhere else and seek your dinner,
	On some poor body.

- 3 -

Get off!; sideburns squat	Swith! in some beggar's hauffet squattle;
scramble	There ye may creep, and sprawl, and sprattle,
	Wi' ither kindred, jumping cattle,
	In shoals and nations;
bone (comb); dare	Whare horn nor bane ne'er daur unsettle
	Your thick plantations.

- 4 -

hold	Now haud you there, ye're out o' sight,

Below the fatt'rils, snug an' tight,   *gewgaws, falderals*
Na, faith ye yet! ye'll no be right,   *confound you!*
          Till ye've got on it—
The vera tapmost, towrin' height   *very*
          O' Miss's bonnet.

– 5 –

My sooth! right bauld ye set your nose out,
As plump an' grey as onie grozet: *any gooseberry*
O for some rank, mercurial rozet,   *rosin*
          Or fell, red-smeddum,   *deadly; -powder*
I'd gie ye sic a hearty dose o't,   *give; of it*
          Wad dress your droddum!   *Would lash; backside*

– 6 –

I wad na been surpriz'd to spy
You on an auld wife's flainen toy;   *flannel cap*
Or aiblins some bit duddie boy,   *perhaps; little ragged*
          On's wyliecoat;   *undershirt*
But Miss's fine Lunardi![1] fye!
          How daur ye do't?   *dare*

– 7 –

O Jenny, dinna toss your head,   *do not*
An' set your beauties a' abroad!   *abroad*
Ye little ken what cursed speed
          The blastie's makin!   *shrivelled-up dwarf is*
Thae winks an' finger-ends, I dread,   *Those*
          Are notice takin!

---

[1] A fashionable balloon-shaped bonnet named after the Italian balloonist who had made demonstration ascents in England and Scotland in 1784 and 1785; the point is that Jenny is very much in the height of style.

would; give   O wad some Pow'r the giftie gie us
To see oursels as others see us!
many   It wad frae monie a blunder free us,
An' foolish notion:
leave   What airs in dress an' gait wad lea'e us,
An' ev'n devotion!

ADDRESS TO THE UNCO GUID, *unusually good*
Or the Rigidly Righteous
(1785 or 1786, 1787)

> *My son, these maxims make a rule,*
>   *An' lump them ay thegither:*
> *The rigid Righteous is a fool,*
>   *The Rigid Wise anither;*
> *The cleanest corn that e'er was dight*   grain; sifted
>   *May hae some pyles o' caff in;*   bits of chaff
> *So ne'er a fellow-creature slight*
>   *For random fits o' daffin.*   fun-making, folly
>   SOLOMON *Eccles, 7:16*[1]

– I –

O ye wha are sae guid yoursel,
    Sae pious and sae holy,
Ye've nought to do but mark and tell
    Your Neebours' fauts and folly!   faults
Whase life is like a weel-gaun mill,   well-going
    Supplied wi' store o' water,

---

[1] Burns took his clues for this loose paraphrase from several verses of the Authorized Version of Ecclesiastes:

All things have I seen in the days of my vanity: there is a just man that perisheth in his righteousness, and there is a wicked man that prolongeth his life in his wickedness. (7:15)

Be not righteous over much; neither make thyself over wise: why shouldest thou destroy thyself? (7:16)

For there is not a just man upon earth, that doeth good, and sinneth not. (7:20)

129

heaped-up hopper is   The heaped happer's ebbing still,

clapper   An still the clap plays clatter![2]

- 2 -

Corps, Company   Hear me, ye venerable Core,
As counsel for poor mortals,

sober   That frequent pass douce Wisdom's door

giddy   For glaikit Folly's portals;
I, for their thoughtless, careless sakes

propose   Would here propone defences,

stupid   Their donsie tricks, their black mistakes,
Their failings and mischances.

- 3 -

Ye see your state wi' theirs compared,

comparison   And shudder at the niffer,
But cast a moment's fair regard
What makes the mighty differ;
Discount what scant occasion gave,
That purity ye pride in,

often more; rest   And (what's aft mair than a' the lave)
Your better art o' hiding.

- 4 -

Think, when your castigated pulse

Gives   Gies now and then a wallop,
What ragings must his veins convulse,
That still eternal gallop:
Wi' wind and tide fair i' your tail,
Right on ye scud your sea-way;

---

2 The image is of a prosperous, efficient flour mill, with a full mill-pond, a hopper constantly supplied and overflowing with grain, a clapper continually in noisy, bustling operation. The flour produced in this mill does not give the appearance at least of having any of the chaff in it mentioned by "Solomon" in the epigraph.

But, in the teeth o' baith to sail,
  It maks an unco leeway.   *unusual*

- 5 -

See Social-life and Glee sit down
  All joyous and unthinking,
Till, quite transmugrify'd, they're grown
  Debauchery and Drinking:
O' would they stay to calculate
  Th' eternal consequences;
Or your more dreaded hell to state,
  Damnation of expenses!

- 6 -

Ye high, exalted, virtuous dames,
  Tied up in godly laces,
Before ye gie poor Frailty names,   *give*
  Suppose a change o' cases;
A dear-lov'd lad, convenience snug,
  A treach'rous inclination—
But, let me whisper i' your lug,   *ear*
  Ye're aiblins nae temptation.   *You are perhaps no*

- 7 -

Then gently scan your brother Man,
  Still gentler sister Woman;
Tho' they may gang a kennin wrang,   *go; trace, suspicion wrong*
  To step aside is human:
One point must still be greatly dark,
  The moving Why they do it;
And just as lamely can ye mark
  How far perhaps they rue it.

– 8 –

Who made the heart, 'tis He alone
   Decidedly can try us,
He knows each chord its various tone,
   Each spring, its various bias:
Then at the balance let's be mute,
   We never can adjust it;
What's done we partly may compute,
   But know not what's resisted.

ADDRESS OF BEELZEBUB

(1786, 1818)

To the Right Honorable the Earl of Breadalbane, President of the Right Honorable the Highland Society, which met on the 23rd of May last, at the Shakespeare, Covent Garden, *to concert ways and means to frustrate the designs of five hundred Highlanders who, as the Society were informed by Mr. M'Kenzie of Applecross, were so audacious as to attempt an escape from their lawful lords and masters whose property they were, by emigrating from the lands of Mr. Macdonald of Glengary to the wilds of Canada, in search of that fantastic thing—Liberty.*[1]

Long life, my lord, an' health be yours,
Unskaith'd by hunger'd Highland boors!   *Unscathed*
Lord grant nae duddie, desperate beggar,   *ragged*
Wi' dirk, claymore, or rusty trigger,   *Highland sword*

---

[1] Beëlzebub is one of Burns's many names for the Devil. With his usual (but not invariable) hostility to the aristocracy, Burns seems to have misinterpreted the motives of the Society, at least on this occasion. According to an account in the *Edinburgh Advertiser* of May 30, 1786, it had "agreed to cooperate with government to frustrate their design [of the crofters' planning to emigrate]; and to recommend to the principal noblemen and gentlemen in the Highlands to endeavour to prevent emigration, by improving the fisheries, agriculture, and manufactures, and particularly to enter into a subscription for that purpose" (CW, I, 347). But if Burns did this particular group an injustice in his fierce attack, large-scale emigration after the middle of the century was generally caused not only by population increases but by cruel and rapacious land-owners in the western Highlands and the Islands. Further, if Burns saw the newspaper story above, he would have reacted to the notion of cooperating "with government to frustrate their design" with an instant rage that would have inhibited thought.

rob   May twin auld Scotland o' a life
She likes—as butchers[2] like a knife!

Faith! you and Applecross were right
To keep the Highland hounds in sight!
would offer   I doubt na! they wad bid nae better
If allowed; across   Than let them ance out owre the water!
those   Then up amang thae lakes and seas,
They'll mak what rules and laws they please:
Some daring Hancock, or a Franklin,
blood   May set their Highland bluid a-ranklin;
Some Washington again may head them;
Or some Montgomerie,[3] fearless, lead them;
Till (God knows what may be effected
When by such heads and hearts directed)
Poor dunghill sons of dirt an' mire
May to Patrician rights aspire!
Nae sage North now, nor sager Sackville,[4]
To watch and premier owre the pack vile!
An' whare will ye get Howes and Clintons[5]
To bring them to a right repentance?
scare   To cowe the rebel generation,
An' save the honor o' the nation?

---

[2] HH gives "lambkins" (II, 154), but the single surviving manuscript, which is in Burns's hand (National Library of Scotland), and the first printing (*The Scots Magazine*, Feb. 1818) both have "butchers," a better reading in any case because Beëlzebub is *not* being ironic (although Burns, of course, is).

[3] John Hancock, Benjamin Franklin, George Washington are well known. Richard Montgomery (1736–1775) was an American major general who died in battle at Quebec.

[4] Lord North was Prime Minister of Britain from 1770 to 1782. George Viscount Sackville ("sage" ironically, perhaps because he ran from the enemy at the battle of Minden during the Seven Years' War) was the British Secretary of State for the Colonies during the Revolutionary War.

[5] William Howe (1729–1814) and Henry Clinton (1738–1795) were in turn commanders-in-chief of the British forces in America from Bunker Hill to Yorktown.

They, an' be damn'd! what right hae they
To meat or sleep or light o' day,
Far less to riches, pow'r, or freedom,
But what your lordship likes to gie them?   *give*

But hear, my lord! Glengary, hear!
Your hand's owre light on them, I fear:
Your factors, grieves, trustees, and bailies,   *stewards; farm-overseers*
I canna say but they do gaylies: *can't deny that; pretty*
They lay aside a' tender mercies,
An' tirl the hullions to the birses.   *strip; scum; hairy hides*
Yet while they're only poind and herriet,   *distrained; robbed*
They'll keep their stubborn Highland spirit.
But smash them! crush them a' to spails,   *chips*
An' rot the dyvors i' the jails!   *bankrupts*
The young dogs, swinge them to the labour: *beat*
Let wark an' hunger mak them sober!
The hizzies, if they're aughtlins fawsont,   *girls; at all good-looking*
Let them in Drury Lane[6] be lesson'd!
An' if the wives an' dirty brats
Come thiggin at your doors an' yetts,   *begging; gates*
Flaffin wi' duds an' grey wi' beas',   *Flapping with rags; vermin*
Frightin awa your deuks an' geese,   *ducks*
Get out a horsewhip or a jowler,   *bulldog*
The langest thong, the fiercest growler,
An' gar the tatter'd gypsies pack   *make*
Wi' a' their bastards on their back!

Go on, my Lord! I lang to meet you,
An' in my "house at hame" to greet you.
Wi common lords ye shanna mingle: *shall not*
The benmost neuk beside the ingle,   *inmost corner; fireside*

---

[6] The whore-house district in London.

135

At my right han' assigned your seat
'Tween Herod's hip an' Polycrate,
complain   Or (if you on your station tarrow)
Between Almagro and Pizarro,[7]
A seat, I'm sure ye're weel deservin't;
An' till ye come—your humble servant,

BEELZEBUB

HELL,
1st June, Anno Mundi 5790

---

[7] Beëlzebub gives Breadalbane the choice of sitting between either pair of favorites: two near-eastern pagan tyrants or two Spanish conquerors of South America.

ADAM ARMOUR'S[1] PRAYER

(1786, 1803)

– 1 –

Gude pity me, because I'm little!   *God*
For though I am an elf o' mettle,
And can like onie wabster's shuttle   *any weaver's*
      Jink there or here,   *Dodge*
Yet, scarce as lang's a guid kail-whittle,   *good cabbage-knife*
      I'm unco queer.   *unusually funny*

– 2 –

An' now Thou kens our woefu' case:
For Geordie's jurr we're in disgrace,[2]   *maid*
Because we stang'd her through the place,   *rode her on a rail*
      An' hurt her spleuchan;   *vagina (literally: purse)*
For whilk we daurna show our face   *which we dare not*
      Within the clachan.   *village*

– 3 –

An' now we're dern'd in dens and hollows,   *hid*
And hunted, as was William Wallace,[3]
Wi' constables—thae blackguard fallows—   *those*
      An' sodgers baith;   *soldiers both*

---

[1] Burns's brother-in-law to be, then only 15 years of age.

[2] Adam with some other village hoodlums in a fit of moral righteousness had ridden Agnes Wilson out of town on a rail as a vigilante-type punishment for what the Mauchline kirk represented as "lewd and immoral practices" (CW, I, 247). Agnes was "jurr" (journeywoman maid) of "Geordie" (George Gibson), a tavern keeper in Mauchline. Adam is represented in the poem as in hiding from the Gibsons, who have threatened legal action against those who had committed this outrage against their maid.

[3] The great Scots patriot, see p. 25, note 6.

But Gude preserve us frae the gallows,
    That shamefu' death!

– 4 –

self   Auld, grim, black-bearded Geordie's sel'—
over   O, shake him owre the mouth o' Hell!
hang   There let him hing, an' roar, an' yell
        Wi' hideous din,
    And if he offers to rebel,
        Then heave him in!

– 5 –

glance   When Death comes in wi' glimmerin blink,
drunken   An' tips auld drucken Nanse[4] the wink,
Satan give her backside a whack   May Sautan gie her doup a clink
gate   Within his yett,
    An' fill her up wi' brimstone drink
hot   Red-reekin het.

– 6 –

half-witted   Though Jock an' hav'rel Jean[5] are merry,
    Some devil seize them in a hurry,
    An' waft them in th' infernal wherry
        Straught through the lake,
give   An' gie their hides a noble curry
oak (i.e., an oak stick)   Wi' oil of aik!

– 7 –

As for the jurr—puir worthless body!—
She's got mischief enough already;

---

4 The wife of George Gibson, Agnes or Poosie Nansie or Nanse, who gives her nam
to the tavern where Burns sets the events of "The Jolly Beggars."

5 The son and daughter of George and Agnes Gibson. Jean as "Racer Jess" appea
with a group of whores in "The Holy Fair."

Wi' stanget hips and buttocks bluidy   *hips that have been ridden on a rail*
    She's suffer'd sair;   *sorely*
But may she wintle in a woody   *wriggle on a gallows rope*
    If she whore mair!

ON WILLIAM CREECH[1]

(1788, 1808)

A little upright, pert, tart, tripping wight,
And still his precious self his dear delight;
Who loves his own smart shadow in the streets
Better than e'er the fairest She he meets.
Much specious lore, but little understood
(Veneering oft outshines the solid wood),
His solid sense by inches you must tell,
But mete his subtle cunning by the ell![2]
A man of fashion, too, he made his tour,[3]
Learn'd "Vive la bagatelle et vive l'amour":
So travell'd monkies their grimace improve,
Polish their grin—nay, sigh for ladies' love!
His meddling vanity, a busy fiend,
Still making work his selfish craft must mend.

---

[1] This is a fragment of a longer autobiographical poem which Burns never completed. William Creech (1745-1815) was the most prominent Edinburgh publisher of his day, who brought out the editions of Burns's *Poems* of 1787, 1793, and 1794. He was honest (barely), but very unwilling to part with money. He struck a hard bargain with Burns for the edition of 1787, made excuses for delaying payment on sums received for subscription copies of that edition, maddeningly delayed paying Burns the sum of one hundred guineas for the absolute copyright for the poems in the same edition, and for the additional poems printed in the edition of 1793 (including "Tam o' Shanter"!) paid nothing. After repeated dunning he gave twenty presentation copies.

[2] The Scots ell is a measure of over three feet.

[3] Creech had been tutor during the grand tour of Lord Kilmaurs, the brother of the fourteenth Earl of Glencairn, Burns's patron.

THE DEAN OF THE FACULTY[1]
A New Ballad
Tune: The Dragon of Wantley[2]
(1796; 1808, 1840)

– I –

Dire was the hate at Old Harlaw[3]
　That Scot to Scot did carry;
And dire the discord Langside[4] saw
　For beauteous, hapless Mary.
But Scot to Scot ne'er met so hot,
　Or were more in fury seen, Sir,
Then 'twixt Hal and Bob for the famous job,
　Who should be the Faculty's Dean, Sir.

---

[1] As a result of Henry Erskine's public opposition to the repressive Sedition Bill then before Parliament, the Tory majority of the Faculty of Advocates, the Scottish bar association, expelled him as their Dean at the annual election early in 1796. Erskine (1746–1817) had held this office since 1786, was generally popular, and tended, like Burns, toward libertarian Foxite Whiggism; Burns had met him in 1786. Robert Dundas (1758–1819), the new Dean, besides being politically repugnant to Burns had also incurred Burns's anger by an earlier personal affront (see *Letters,* II, 64–65). This ballad was written as an attack on Dundas and his conservative supporters in the Faculty of Advocates. "Hal" and "Bob" or "Bobby" in the poem are Henry Erskine and Robert Dundas respectively.

[2] An old broadside ballad, humorous, gross, and still popular in Burns's time. The rough metrics of the poem are in keeping with the manner of a popular ballad; Burns wrote these words to be sung; for the tune see Dick, p. 258.

[3] A bloody battle, often called "Red Harlow" (1411), in northeast Scotland near Aberdeen where Donald, Lord of the Isles, with his Highland army was stopped in his attempt to claim the earldom of Ross by local lairds and burgesses under the leadership of the Earl of Mar.

[4] The place in Scotland where in 1568 the Protestant army loyal to the infant King James VI defeated the forces loyal to his mother, Mary Queen of Scots. This was the last conflict between Mary's and the Protestants' forces before her flight to England.

- 2 -

This Hal for genius, wit, and lore
    Among the first was number'd;
But pious Bob, 'mid learning's store
    Commandment the Tenth[5] remember'd.
Yet simple Bob the victory got,
    And won his heart's desire:
Which shows that Heaven can boil the pot,
Devil   Tho' the Deil piss in the fire.

- 3 -

Squire Hal, besides, had in this case
    Pretensions rather brassy;
For talents, to deserve a place,
    Are qualifications saucy.
So their worships of the Faculty,
    Quite sick of Merit's rudeness,
Chose one who should owe it all, d'ye see,
    To their gratis grace and goodness.

- 4 -

As one on Pisgah purg'd was the sight
    Of a son of Circumcision,
So, may be, on this Pisgah height
    Bob's purblind mental vision.
Nay, Bobby's mouth may be open'd yet,
    Till for eloquence you hail him,
And swear that he has the Angel met
    That met the Ass of Balaam.[6]

---

[5] "Thou shalt not covet thy neighbor's house. . . ."

[6] From the top of Pisgah, God showed Moses the Promised Land just before his death (Deuteronomy 34:1-4). Balaam cursed and beat his ass when it would not continue because of the invisible angel which stood in its path (Numbers 22).

THE DEAN OF THE FACULTY

– 5 –

In your heretic sins may ye live and die,
  Ye heretic Eight-and-Thirty![7]
But accept, ye sublime majority,
  My congratulations hearty!
With your honors, as with a certain King,[8]
  In your servants this is striking,
The more incapacity they bring
  The more they're to your liking.

---

[7] I.e., the thirty-eight advocates who had voted for Henry Erskine (against one
hundred twenty-three for Dundas).

[8] George III.

Kirk Satires

The poems in this section have been called anti-Calvinist or ecclesiastical satires, but kirk satires seems a better name for them because, like all genuine satire, their attack is almost always *ad hominem*. They all assail a certain faction of ministers in the kirk of the time, but they continue to be relevant because the religious zealots and tyrants whom Burns flays are still with us, if in modified forms. But because satire attacks historical particulars, in order to understand these poems fully, we must have some knowledge of the organization of the Church of Scotland and the two main parties within it during the last quarter of the eighteenth century, a subject already treated in the Introduction.

"The Holy Fair," in both its situations and its language, ironically juxtaposes the spirit and the flesh, the religious and the secular. The purpose is to expose (1) the inadequacy of orthodox Calvinism to adapt itself to the full and warm humanity of its practitioners and (2) the hypocrisy that this religion of unreality leads to. This ironic contrast is totally informing and is seen in the title, in the allegorical device of Fun attending a communion service, and in the structure, which alternates between secular scenes in the tavern and on the road and pseudo-religious scenes in the churchyard.

"Holy Willie's Prayer" attacks extreme Calvinist doctrine and the resulting mental state of its believers, by allowing us to overhear a typical zealot's prayer and thus to understand the operation of his mind. Holy Willie's language is naturally the Scots-English used by the kirk, sprinkled with Biblical quotations and vernacular barnyard expressions in moments of excitement. As an early example of the dramatic monologue, the poem can be fruitfully compared with those by Tennyson and Browning.

"Address to the Deil" is more comic than satiric, because it is more general than particular. But it does have its particular thrusts: (1) against the orthodox and folk superstition of an intimate and ubiquitous devil, (2) against the motivation of a religion based on fear of him, and (3) against the inhumanity of a religion which could damn for eternity even the worst of sinners.

The three remaining poems are known only to students of Burns. Invariably in these satires Burns adopts, for ironic effect, the voice of the opposing party. In "The Ordination" he jubilates over the arrival of an Evangelical minister but degrades the Evangelical party by using diction and figures which equate their affairs and beliefs to barnyard matters. In "The Twa Herds" we again hear the voice of the Evangelical, this time exhorting the two quarrelling Old-Licht ministers to patch up their differences so as to get back to the pressing business of protecting the faithful against Moderate inroads. The whole is informed by the metaphor of the shepherd protecting his flock against its natural enemies. "The Kirk's Alarm" is a cruder but more robust piece. Like Pope's *Dunciad,* it is Burns's final fling against his enemies, the Evangelicals; he caricatures the ecclesiastical rogues stanza by stanza and impales each with his sharp verbal stakes. His hatred carries him along with such force that he disdains the fastidious attention to a single ironic point of view, sometimes praising his enemies tongue-in-cheek, at others directly lashing them.

THE HOLY FAIR[1]

(1785, 1786)

A robe of seeming truth and trust
Hid crafty observation;
And secret hung, with poison'd crust,
The dirk of Defamation;
A mask that like the gorget show'd,
Dye-varying, on the pigeon;
And for a mantle large and broad,
He wrapt him in Religion.

HYPOCRISY A-LA-MODE[2]

– I –

summer   Upon a simmer Sunday morn,
       When Nature's face is fair,
I walked forth to view the corn,
fresh   An' snuff the callor air.
The rising sun, owre Galston Muirs,
      Wi' glorious light was glintan;
hopping; furrows   The hares were hirplan down the furs,

---

[1] Burns's note (1787): "'Holy Fair' is a common phrase in the West of Scotland for a sacramental occasion." By "sacramental occasion" Burns meant all the events connected with the annual communion service, which took place in the summer. The sacrament was administered at tables within the church, where Burns did not take us in this poem. Meanwhile ministers from neighboring parishes preached from a movable, covered pulpit outside. A shelter was provided for dignitaries. In Mauchline the communion service took place on the second Sunday of August, and the preaching was done in the churchyard, close to the village taverns. The "holy fair" was attended from far and wide: about 1240 communicants attended in 1785, of whom only 400 belonged to the Mauchline congregation.

[2] This epigraph or motto is of Burns's composition.

The lav'rocks they were chantan — *larks*
    Fu' sweet that day. — *Very (Full)*

– 2 –

As lightsomely I glowr'd abroad, — *gazed*
    To see a scene sae gay,
Three hizzies, early at the road, — *young women*
    Cam skelpan up the way. — *hurrying*
Twa had manteeles o' dolefu' black, — *two; mantles*
    But ane wi' lyart lining; — *one with grey*
The third, that gaed a wee a-back, — *walked a bit behind*
    Was in the fashion shining
        Fu' gay that day.

– 3 –

The twa appear'd like sisters twin,
    In feature, form, an' claes; — *clothes*
Their visage wither'd, lang an' thin,
    An' sour as ony slaes: — *wild plums (sloes)*
The third cam up, hap-step-an'-lowp, — *hop-; -jump*
    As light as ony lambie,
An' wi' a curchie low did stoop, — *curtsey*
    As soon as e'er she saw me,
        Fu' kind that day.

– 4 –

Wi' bonnet aff, quoth I, "Sweet lass,
    I think ye seem to ken me;
I'm sure I've seen that bonie face,
    But yet I canna name ye,"
Quo' she, an' laughan as she spak,
    An' taks me by the han's,
"Ye, for my sake, hae gi'en the feck — *most part*
    Of a' the Ten Comman's
        A screed some day. — *rip*

– 5 –

"My name is Fun[3]—your cronie dear,
The nearest friend ye hae;
An' this is Superstition here,
An' that's Hypocrisy.

going I'm gaun to Mauchline Holy Fair,
fun-making To spend an hour in daffin:
wrinkled Gin ye'll go there, yon runkl'd pair,
We will get famous laughin
At them this day."

– 6 –

Quoth I, "Wi' a' my heart, I'll do't;
shirt I'll get my sunday's sark on,
An' meet you on the holy spot;
we'll have Faith, we'se hae fine remarkin!"
went; breakfast- (porridge-) Then I gaed hame at crowdie-time,
An' soon I made me ready;
filled For roads were clad, frae side to side,
Wi' monie a wearie body,
In droves that day.

– 7 –

complacent; clothes Here, farmers gash, in ridin graith,
jogging Gaed hoddan by their cotters;
strapping; fine broadcloth There, swankies young, in braw braid-claith,
Are springan owre the gutters.
striding barefoot; crowded The lasses, skelpan barefit, thrang,
In silks an' scarlets glitter;

---

[3] Burns's formal model for this poem is Robert Fergusson's "Leith Races," where the
speaker meets only one allegorical companion, Mirth, who unlike Burns's Fun, stay
with the speaker throughout the day of festivities. Burns also imitates Fergusson'
stanza, a modification of the more exacting one used in the famous medieval Scots poem
about a community festival day, "Christ's Kirk on the Green."

Wi' sweet-milk cheese, in monie a whang,   *chunk*
    An' farls, bak'd wi' butter,   *cakes*
        Fu' crump that day.   *crisp*

– 8 –

When by the plate we set our nose,
    Weel heaped up wi' ha'pence,
A greedy glowr black-bonnet[4] throws,   *stare*
    An' we maun draw our tippence.   *must*
Then in we go to see the show:
    On ev'ry side they're gath'ran;
Some carryan dails, some chairs an' stools,   *planks*
    An' some are busy bleth'ran   *chattering*
        Right loud that day.

– 9 –

Here stands a shed to fend the show'rs,
    An' screen our countra gentry;
There, Racer Jess,[5] an' twa-three whores,
    Are blinkan at the entry.   *leering*
Here sits a raw o' tittlan jads,   *girls*
    Wi' heaving breasts an' bare neck;
An' there a batch o' wabster lads,   *weaver*
    Blackguarding frae Kilmarnock,
        For fun this day.

– 10 –

Here, some are thinkan on their sins,
    An' some upo' their claes;   *clothes*
Ane curses feet that fyl'd his shins,
    Anither sighs an' prays:

---

[4] The kirk elder holding the collection plate at the entrance to the churchyard.
[5] See p. 138, note 5.

On this hand sits a chosen[6] swatch,
   Wi' screw'd-up, grace-proud faces;
On that, a set o' chaps, at watch,
busy beckoning (by winks) to   Thrang winkan on the lasses
     To chairs that day.

– 11 –

O happy is that man, an' blest![7]
   Nae wonder that it pride him!
own   Whase ain dear lass, that he likes best,
   Comes clinkan down beside him!
Wi' arm repos'd on the chair back,
   He sweetly does compose him;
Which, by degrees, slips round her neck,
palm   An's loof upon her bosom
     Unkend that day.

– 12 –

Now a' the congregation o'er
   Is silent expectation;
climbs   For Moodie[8] speels the holy door,
   Wi' tidings o' damnation:[9]
the Devil   Should Hornie, as in ancient days,
   'Mang sons o' God present him,
very   The vera sight o' Moodie's face
own hot   To's ain het hame had sent him
     Wi' fright that day.

---

[6] Changed in 1787 from "Elect" (1786).

[7] HH notes (I, 331) that this line echoes Psalm 146, stanza 2, verse 1 of the Scottish Metrical Version. Burns's Scottish audience would all hear the echo. This carnal application of a phrase with holy overtones contributes to the ironic yoking of the spirit and the flesh throughout this poem.

[8] Alexander Moodie, minister in Riccarton since 1761, an Auld Licht or member of the Orthodox or Evangelical or Popular party.

[9] Improved in second edition (1787) from "salvation" (1786).

- 13 -

Hear how he clears the points o' Faith
   Wi' rattlin and thumpin!
Now meekly calm, now wild in wrath,
   He's stampan, an' he's jumpan!
His lengthen'd chin, his turn'd-up snout,
   His eldritch squeel an' gestures,   *unearthly*
O how they fire the heart devout—
   Like cantharidian plaisters   *plasters*
      On sic a day!

- 14 -

But hark! the tent has chang'd its voice;
   There's peace an' rest nae langer;
For a' the real judges rise,
   They canna sit for anger.
Smith[10] opens out his cauld harangues,
   On practice and on morals;
An' aff the godly pour in thrangs,   *off; crowds*
   To gie the jars an' barrels   *give*
      A lift that day.

- 15 -

What signifies his barren shine,
   Of moral pow'rs an' reason?
His English style, an' gesture fine
   Are a' clean out o' season.
Like Socrates or Antonine,
   Or some auld pagan heathen,
The moral man he does define,
   But ne'er a word o' faith in
      That's right that day.

---

[10] George Smith, minister of Galston since 1778, presented in this poem as a New Licht or member of the Moderate party, while in reality he was somewhat vacillating.

– 16 –

In guid time comes an antidote

poisoned   Against sic posion'd nostrum;

river's mouth   For Peebles, frae the water-fit,[11]

Ascends the holy rostrum:

See, up he's got the word o' God,

prim   An' meek an' mim has view'd it,

taken   While Common-sense has taen the road,

An' aff, an' up the Cowgate[12]

Fast, fast that day.

– 17 –

next   Wee Miller[13] niest, the Guard relieves,

rattles off by rote   An' Orthodoxy raibles,

Tho' in his heart he weel believes,

An' thinks it auld wives' fables:

fellow   But faith! the birkie wants a manse,

gives them what they want So, cannilie he hums them;

Altho' his carnal wit an' sense

Almost half-way   Like hafflins-wise o'ercomes him

At times that day.

– 18 –

all the rooms; Tavern Now, butt an' ben, the Change-house fills,

ale-cup   Wi' yill-caup Commentators;

crackers and glasses of whiskey Here's crying out for bakes an' gills,

-measure   An' there the pint-stowp clatters;

crowded   While thick an' thrang, an' loud an' lang,

Wi' Logic an' wi' Scripture,

---

11 William Peebles, minister since 1778 at Newton (at the mouth of the River A⸱ thus "water-foot"), an Evangelical.

12 Burns's note (1787): "A street so called which faces the tent in Mauchline."

13 Alexander Millar, "assistant minister at St. Michael's" (Burns's handwritten not⸱ here presented as a Moderate masquerading for prudential reasons as an Evangelic⸱

They raise a din, that in the end
  Is like to breed a rupture
    O' wrath that day.

– 19 –

Leeze me Drink! it gies us mair   *Blessings on*
  Than either School or Colledge;
It kindles Wit, it waukens Lear,   *Learning*
  It pangs us fou o' Knowledge: *crams; full*
Be't whisky-gill or penny wheep,   *weak beer*
  Or ony stronger potion,
It never fails, on drinkin deep,
  To kittle up our notion,   *tickle*
    By night or day.

– 20 –

The lads an' lasses, blythely bent
  To mind baith saul an' body,
Sit round the table, weel content,
  An' steer about the toddy: *stir*
On this ane's dress, an' that ane's leuk,
  They're makin observations;
While some are cozie i' the neuk,   *corner*
  An' forming assignations
    To meet some day.

– 21 –

But now the Lord's ain trumpet touts,
  Till a' the hills are raran,   *roaring*
And echoes back return the shouts;
  Black Russell[14] is na spairan:
His piercin words, like Highlan swords,
  Divide the joints an' marrow;

---

[14] John Russell, minister in Kilmarnock since 1774, an Evangelical.

153

His talk o' Hell, whare devils dwell,
Our vera "Sauls does harrow"[15]
Wi' fright that day!

– 22 –

A vast, unbottom'd, boundless pit,

full of flaming brimstone   Fill'd fou o' lowan brunstane,

Whase raging flame, an' scorching heat,

Would; whinstone   Wad melt the hardest whun-stane!

The half-asleep start up wi' fear,
An' think they hear it roaran,
When presently it does appear,

neighbor   'Twas but some neebor snoran
Asleep that day.

– 23 –

too long   'Twad be owre lang a tale to tell,
How monie stories past;

ale   An' how they crouded to the yill,
When they were a' dismist:

went; wooden bowls; mugs   How drink gaed round, in cogs an' caups,

forms; benches   Amang the furms an' benches;

An' cheese an' bread, frae women's laps,

large pieces   Was dealt about in lunches,

chunks   An' dawds that day.

– 24 –

jolly; wise   In comes a gawsie, gash Guidwife,
An' sits down by the fire,

---

[15] Burns's note (1786): "Shakespeare's Hamlet." The quotation is inexact:

I could a tale unfold whose lightest word
Would harrow up thy soul (I, v).

154

Syne draws her kebbuck an' her knife; *Then; cheese*
  The lasses they are shyer:
The auld guidmen, about the grace, *farmers*
  Frae side to side they bother;
Till some ane by his bonnet lays,
  An' gies them't, like a tether, *gives; rope*
    Fu' lang that day. *Very (Full)*

– 25 –

Waesucks! for him that gets nae lass, *Alas!*
  Or lasses that hae naething!
Sma' need has he to say a grace,
  Or melvie his braw claithing! *soil with meal; fine clothing*
O Wives, be mindfu', ance yoursel,
  How bonie lads ye wanted;
An' dinna for a kebbuck-heel *do not; end of a cheese*
  Let lasses be affronted
    On sic a day!

– 26 –

Now Clinkumbell, wi' rattlan tow, *(the bell-ringer); rope*
  Begins to jow an' croon; *swing; toll*
Some swagger hame, the best they dow, *can*
  Some wait the afternoon.
At slaps the billies halt a blink, *gaps in hedge or fence*
  Till lasses strip their shoon: *shoes*
Wi' faith an' hope, an' love an' drink,
  They're a' in famous tune
    For crack that day. *talk*

– 27 –

How monie hearts this day converts
  O' sinners and o' lasses!

by   Their hearts o' stane, gin night, are gane
        As saft as ony flesh is.
full, drunk   There's some are fou o' love divine;
        There's some are fou o' brandy;
        An' monie jobs that day begin,
Fornication   May end in Houghmagandie
        Some ither day.

HOLY WILLIE'S PRAYER[1]

(1785, 1789)[2]

And send the godly in a pet to pray.

POPE[3]

– I –

O Thou that in the Heavens does dwell,
Wha, as it pleases best Thysel,
Sends ane to Heaven an' ten to Hell
    A' for Thy glory,

---

[1] In a headnote to a manuscript copy of this poem, Burns explained the occasion (see HH, II, 321): "Holy Willie was a rather oldish bachelor elder, in the parish of Mauchline, and much and justly famed for that polemical chattering which ends in tippling orthodoxy, and for that spiritualized bawdry which refines to liquorish devotion. In a sessional process with a gentleman in Mauchline—a Mr. Gavin Hamilton—*Holy Willie* and his priest, Father Auld, after full hearing in the Presbytery of Ayr, came off but second best, owing partly to the oratorical powers of Mr. Robert Aiken, Mr. Hamilton's counsel; but chiefly to Mr. Hamilton's being one of the most irreproachable and truly respectable characters in the country. On losing his process, the muse overheard him [Holy Willie] at his devotions, as follows."

Gavin Hamilton (1751–1805), a lawyer in Mauchline, was Burns's landlord and patron and the person to whom Burns dedicated his *Poems* (1786). The Kirk Session of Mauchline (the minister and his elders, the judicial body of the parish kirk) prosecuted him in the autumn of 1784 for failure in attendance at church and in family worship and for travelling on Sunday. Hamilton won an appeal to the next highest ecclesiastical court, the Presbytry of Ayr, in spite of the Session's appeal to the Synod, the court above that. Robert Aiken (1739–1807), a lawyer in Ayr and also since 1783 Burns's friend and patron (see dedicatory stanza of "The Cotter's Saturday Night"), represented Hamilton before the Synod. Holy Willie was William Fisher, since 1772 an elder in the Mauchline Kirk, under its minister William Auld, "God's ain Priest" in stanza 12 of this poem.

[2] Before the recent discovery of a pamphlet of 1789 (see Egerer, p. 32), with which Burns probably had nothing to do, the first publication was thought to be in a chapbook of 1799. At least six contemporary manuscripts survive.

[3] Alexander Pope, "Rape of the Lock," IV, 64.

And no for onie guid or ill
    They've done before Thee!

- 2 -

I bless and praise Thy matchless might,
When thousands Thou hast left in night,
That I am here before Thy sight,
    For gifts an' grace
A burning and a shining light[4]
    To a' this place.

- 3 -

What was I, or my generation,
That I should get sic exaltation?
I, wha deserv'd most just damnation
    For broken laws
Sax thousand years ere my creation,[5]
    Thro' Adam's cause!

- 4 -

When from my mither's womb I fell,
Thou might hae plung'd me deep in hell
To gnash my gooms, and weep, and wail
    In burning lakes,[6]
Whare damned devils roar and yell,
    Chain'd to their stakes.

---

[4] "He was a burning and a shining light . . ." (John 5:35). This and the other Biblical echoes from the Authorized Version given in these footnotes can be found conveniently listed, with some others, in T. Crawford, *Burns,* pp. 363–364 (see Bibliography).

[5] Burns conceived the ecclesiastical calendar as placing the Creation 5790 years before 1786 (see dateline to "Address of Beelzebub"). Holy Willie is rounding off.

[6] ". . . and shall cast them into a furnace of fire: there shall be wailing and gnashing of teeth" (Matthew 13:42).

- 5 -

Yet I am here, a chosen sample,
To show Thy grace is great and ample:
I'm here a pillar o' Thy temple,[7]
    Strong as a rock,
A guide, a buckler, and example
    To a' Thy flock!

- 6 -

O Lord, Thou kens what zeal I bear
When drinkers drink, an' swearers swear,
An' singin hear and dancin there   *here*
    Wi' great an sma';   *small*
For I am keepit by Thy fear
    Free frae them a'.[8]

- 7 -

But yet, O Lord! 'confess I must:
At times I'm fash'd wi' fleshly lust;   *troubled*
An' sometimes, too, in wardly trust,   *worldly*
    Vile self gets in;
But Thou remembers we are dust,[9]
    Defiled wi' sin.

- 8 -

O Lord! yestreen, Thou kens, wi' Meg—   *last night*
Thy pardon I sincerely beg—
O, may't ne'er be a living plague
    To my dishonour!

---

[7] "Him that overcometh will I make a pillar in the temple of my God ..." (Revelations 3:12).

[8] This stanza is only found in the manuscript used by *Stewart's Edition* of 1802 (see Egerer, p. 100). HH does not include the stanza in the text but gives it in a footnote (II, 322), which supplies the present text.

[9] "... he remembereth that we are dust" (Psalms 103:14).

An' I'll ne'er lift a lawless leg
Again upon her.

– 9 –

must Besides, I farther maun avow—
Wi' Leezie's lass, three times, I trow—
drunk But, Lord, that Friday I was fou,
When I cam near her,
Or else, Thou kens, Thy servant true
meddle with, injure Wad never steer her.

– 10 –

Maybe Thou lets this freshly thorn
evening Buffet Thy servant e'en and morn,
Lest he owre proud and high should turn
That he's sae gifted:[10]
hand must even If sae, Thy han' maun e'en be borne
Until Thou lift it.

– 11 –

Lord, bless Thy chosen in this place,
For here Thou has a chosen race!
But God confound their stubborn face
An' blast their name,
Wha bring Thy elders to disgrace
An' open shame!

– 12 –

Lord, mind Gau'n Hamilton's deserts:
cards He drinks, an' swears, an' plays at cartes,
Yet has sae monie takin arts
small Wi' great and sma',

---

10 ". . . there was given to me a thorn in the flesh, the messenger of Satan to buffet me, lest I should be exalted above measure" (II Corinthians 12:7).

Frae God's ain Priest the people's hearts
    He steals awa.   *away*

– 13 –

And when we chasten'd him therefore,
Thou kens how he bred sic a splore,   *row*
And set the warld in a roar
    O' laughin at us:
Curse Thou his basket and his store,[11]
    Kail an' potatoes!   *cabbage*

– 14 –

Lord, hear my earnest cry and pray'r
Against that Presbyt'ry of Ayr!
Thy strong right hand, Lord, mak it bare
    Upo' their heads![12]
Lord, visit them, an' dinna spare,   *do not*
    For their misdeeds!

– 15 –

O Lord, my God! that glib-tongu'd Aiken,
My vera heart and flesh are quakin   *very*
To think how we stood sweatin, shakin,
    An' pish'd wi' dread,
While he, wi' hingin lip an' snakin,   *exulting*
    Held up his head.

– 16 –

Lord, in Thy day o' vengeance try him!
Lord, visit him wha did employ him!

---

[11] "Cursed shall be thy basket and thy store . . ." (Deuteronomy 28:17).
[12] "The Lord hath made bare his holy arm in the eyes of all the nations" (Isaiah 52:10).

And pass not in Thy mercy by them,
  Nor hear their pray'r,
But for Thy people's sake destroy them,
  An' dinna spare!

– 17 –

But, Lord, remember me and mine
Wi' mercies temporal and divine,
possessions That I for grace an' gear may shine
  Excell'd by nane;
And a' the glory shall be Thine—
  Amen, Amen!

ADDRESS TO THE DEIL *devil*

(1785 or 1786, 1786)

O Prince! O chief of many throned pow'rs,
That led th' embattl'd Seraphim to war—
MILTON[1]

- 1 -

O Thou, whatever title suit thee!
Auld Hornie, Satan, Nick, or Clootie,   *or Cloven-hoofed*
Wha in yon cavern grim an' sootie,
    Clos'd under hatches,
Spairges about the brunstane cootie,   *Splashes; brimstone basin*
    To scaud poor wretches!   *scald*

- 2 -

Hear me, auld Hangie, for a wee,   *Hangman (the devil)*
An' let poor damned bodies bee;
I'm sure sma' pleasure it can gie   *give*
    Ev'n to a deil,
To skelp an' scaud poor dogs like me,   *slap; scald*
    An' hear us squeel!

- 3 -

Great is thy pow'r, an' great thy fame;
Far kend an' noted is thy name;

---

[1] *Paradise Lost,* I, 128–129. Because he identified with the proud defiance of Milton's character and because he reacted to the Evangelical party's constant use of the Calvinist devil as a ubiquitous enemy, Burns considered Milton's Satan his "favorite hero" (see *Letters,* I, 95, 156). There is an intentional contrast in this poem, of course, between Milton's noble creation and the Scots devil—sly, sneeking, "hamely." Burns, incidentally, predated William Blake in taking Satan to be the true hero of *Paradise Lost.*

burning pit An' tho' yon lowan heugh's thy hame,
　　　　Thou travels far;
backward An' faith! thou's neither lag, nor lame,
bashful; afraid 　　　　Nor blate nor scaur.

- 4 -

Sometimes Whyles, ranging like a roaran lion,
　　　For prey, a' holes an' corners tryin;
　　　Whyles, on the strong-wing'd tempest flyin,
unroofing; churches 　　　　Tirlan the kirks;
　　　Whyles, in the human bosom pryin,
　　　　Unseen thou lurks.

- 5 -

Granny I've heard my rev'rend Graunie say,
　　　In lanely glens ye like to stray;
　　　Or, where auld ruin'd castles grey
　　　　Nod to the moon,
　　　Ye fright the nightly wand'rer's way
unearthly wail 　　　　Wi' eldritch croon.

- 6 -

　　　When twilight did my Graunie summon,
sedate To say her pray'rs, douse, honest woman!
Oft beyond; wall; humming Aft 'yont the dyke she's heard you bumman,
droning 　　　　Wi' eerie drone;
elders Or, rustlin, thro' the boortrees coman,
　　　　Wi' heavy groan.

- 7 -

　　　Ae dreary, windy, winter night,
slanting The stars shot down wi' sklentan light,

Wi' you, mysel, I gat a fright:
    Ayont the lough;   *Beyond; pond*
Ye, like a rash-buss, stood in sight,   *clump of rushes (rush-bush)*
    Wi' waving sugh.   *moan*

– 8 –

The cudgel in my nieve did shake,   *fist*
Each bristl'd hair stood like a stake;
When wi' an eldritch, stoor 'quaick, quaick,'   *harsh*
    Amang the springs,
Awa ye squatter'd like a drake,   *flapped*
    On whistling wings.

– 9 –

Let Warlocks grim, an' wither'd Hags,
Tell how wi' you on ragweed nags,   *ragwort*
They skim the muirs an' dizzy crags,   *moors*
    Wi' wicked speed;
And in kirk-yards renew their leagues,
    Owre howcket dead.   *Over exhumed*

– 10 –

Thence, countra wives, wi' toil an' pain,
May plunge an' plunge the kirn in vain;   *churn*
For Oh! the yellow treasure's taen   *taken*
    By witching skill;
An' dawtit, twal-pint Hawkie's gane   *petted; twelve-*
    As yell's the Bill.   *dry as; Bull*

– 11 –

Thence, mystic knots mak great abuse
On young guidmen, fond, keen an' croose;   *husbands; confident*

work-loom   When the best wark-lume i' the house,
magic   By cantraip wit,
        Is instant made no worth a louse,
decisive moment   Just at the bit.[2]

– 12 –

thaws   When thowes dissolve the snawy hoord,
surface   An' float the jinglan icy boord,
        Then, Water-kelpies haunt the foord,
        By your direction,
        An' nighted trav'llers are allur'd
        To their destruction.

– 13 –

bog-; Will-o'-the-wisps   And aft your moss-traversing Spunkies
        Decoy the wight that late an' drunk is:
        The bleezan, curst, mischievous monkies
        Delude his eyes,
        Till in some miry slough he sunk is,
        Ne'er mair to rise.

– 14 –

        When Masons' mystic word an' grip,
        In storms an' tempests raise you up,
        Some cock or cat your rage maun stop,
        Or, strange to tell!
        The youngest Brother ye wad whip
        Aff straught to Hell.

– 15 –

garden   Lang syne in Eden's bonie yard,
        When youthfu' lovers first were pair'd,

---

[2] Since *lume* in Scots also means "utensil" or "tool," this stanza has a bawdy double meaning.

An' all the Soul of Love they shar'd,
    The raptur'd hour,
Sweet on the fragrant flow'ry swaird,
    In shady bow'r.

– 16 –

Then you, ye auld, snick-drawing dog!   *latch-lifting*
Ye cam to Paradise incog,
An' play'd on man a cursed brogue,   *trick*
    (Black be your fa'!),   *fall*
An' gied the infant warld a shog,   *gave; shake*
    'Maist ruin'd a'.   *Almost*

– 17 –

D' ye mind that day, when in a bizz,   *remember; flurry*
Wi' reeket duds, an' reestet gizz,   *smoky clothes: scorched wig*
Ye did present your smoutie phiz,   *smutty*
    'Mang better folk,
An' sklented on the man of Uzz,[3]   *cast obliquely*
    Your spitefu' joke?

– 18 –

An' how ye gat him i' your thrall,
An' brak him out o' house an' hal',
While scabs an' botches did him gall,
    Wi' bitter claw,
An' lows'd his ill-tongu'd wicked Scawl   *loosed; Scold*
    Was warst ava?   *of all*

– 19 –

But a' your doings to rehearse,
Your wily snares an' fechtin fierce,   *fighting*

[3] Job.

Sin' that day Michael did you pierce[4]
Down to this time,
Would beat; Lowland Wad ding a Lallan tongue, or Erse,
In prose or rhyme.

– 20 –

Hoofs An' now, auld Cloots, I ken ye're thinkan,
A certain Bardie's rantin, drinkin,
hurrying Some luckless hour will send him linkan,
To your black pit;
dodging But, faith! he'll turn a corner jinkan,
An' cheat you yet.

– 21 –

But fare-you-weel, auld Nickie-ben!
mend O, wad ye tak a thought an' men'!
perhaps; don't know Ye aiblins might—I dinna ken—
Still hae a stake—
woeful I'm wae to think upo' yon den,
Ev'n for your sake!

---

[4] Burns's note (1786): "Vide Milton, Book 6th." The reference is to the war in heaven, *Paradise Lost,* VI, 320–334.

THE ORDINATION

(1785–1786, 1787)

For sense they little owe to frugal Heav'n—
To please the mob they hide the little giv'n.[1]

– 1 –

Kilmarnock wabsters, fidge an' claw,	*weavers, fidget*
An' pour your creeshie nations;	*greasy*
An' ye wha leather rax an' draw,	*stretch*
Of a' denominations;	
Swith to the Laigh Kirk, ane an' a',	*Hurry*
An' there tak up your stations;	
Then aff to Begbie's[2] in a raw,	*row*
An' pour divine libations	
For joy this day.	

– 2 –

Curst Common-sense, that imp o' hell,
    Cam in wi' *Maggie Lauder:*[3]

---

[1] The motto is of Burns's authorship; in one manuscript he signed it with *Ruisseaux,* French for *burns* (Scots for *streams*).

[2] A tavern near the Laigh Kirk across a bridge so narrow as to require people to go in single file.

[3] Common sense, the leading quality of the Moderate faction, had ruled in the second charge of Laigh Kirk for twenty-one years. Burns's note (1787): "Alluding to a scoffing ballad which was made on the admission of the late Reverend and worthy Mr. L[indsay] to the Laigh Kirk." William Lindsay, whose wife's name was Margaret Lauder, was ordained in the second charge of the Laigh Kirk in 1764. He died in 1775 and was succeeded by another Moderate, John Multrie (see stanza 10), whose death in June 1785 created the opportunity for the presentation, at long last, of an Evangelical minister, whose future ordination is ironically celebrated in this poem.

But Oliphant aft made her yell,
strongly abused   An' Russell sair misca'd her:[4]
This day Mckinlay taks the flail,[5]
slap   An' he's the boy will blaud her!
cleft stick (used with dogs) He'll clap a shangan on her tail,
children; pelt   An' set the bairns to daud her
       Wi' dirt this day.

- 3 -

Mak haste an' turn King David owre,
     An' lilt wi' holy clangor;
give O' double verse come gie us four,[6]
shriek, yell   An' skirl up the Bangor:[7]
dust This day the Kirk kicks up a stoure:
     Nae mair the knaves shall wrang her,
For Heresy is in her pow'r,
     And gloriously she'll whang her
       Wi' pith this day.

- 4 -

Come, let a proper text be read,
     An' touch it aff wi' vigour,
How graceless Ham leugh at his Dad,[8]
     Which made Canaan a nigger;

---

4 James Oliphant and John Russell (see p. 153, note 14), both Evangelicals and, in sequence, ministers of another church in Kilmarnock.

5 James MacKinlay, an Evangelical, presented to the second charge of the Laigh Kirk late in 1785, but not ordained there until April of the next year. Burns wrote this ironic jubilation for his ordination at least two months before that event.

6 Two stanzas, of two quatrains each ("double verse"), in the Scottish *Metrical Psalms* was customary.

7 A popular hymn melody.

8 Variant in manuscript for lines 1 and 3 of this stanza:

choose   Come wale a text a proper verse
. . . .
laughed   How Ham leugh at his father's arse.

Or Phineas drove the murdering blade
  Wi' whore-abhorring rigour;
Or Zipporah, the scauldin jad,   *scolding shrew*
  Was like a bluidy tiger
    I' th' inn that day.[9]

– 5 –

There, try his[10] mettle on the creed,
  And bind him down wi' caution,
That Stipend is a carnal weed
  He taks but for the fashion;
And gie him o'er the flock, to feed,
  And punish each transgression;
Especial, rams that cross the breed,
  Gie them sufficient threshin:
    Spare them nae day.

– 6 –

Now auld Kilmarnock, cock thy tail,
  An' toss thy horns fu' canty;   *merrily*
Nae mair thou'lt rowte out-owre the dale,   *low all over*
  Because thy pasture's scanty;
For lapfu's large o' gospel kail   *armfuls; cabbage*
  Shall fill thy crib in plenty,
An' runts o' grace, the pick an' wale,   *stalks; choice*
  No gi'en by way o' dainty,   *Not given*
    But ilka day.   *every*

– 7 –

Nae mair by Babel's streams we'll weep
  To think upon our Zion;

---

[9] Burns gave (1787) these references to allusions in this stanza: Genesis ix.22, Numbers xxv.8, Exodus iv.25.

[10] I.e., MacKinlay, the new minister.

And hing our fiddles up to sleep,

-clothes   Like baby-clouts a-dryin:

Come, screw the pegs wi' tunefu' cheep,

strings   And o'er the thairms be tryin;

elbows jerk   O, rare! to see our elbucks wheep,

And a' like lamb-tails flyin

Fu' fast this day!

– 8 –

Long; iron   Lang, Patronage,[11] wi' rod o' airn,

threatened   Has shor'd the Kirk's undoin;

sorely distressed   As lately Fenwick,[12] sair forfairn,

Has proven to its ruin:

Our Patron, honest man! Glencairn,[13]

He saw mischief was brewin;

child   An' like a godly, elect bairn,

chose   He's wal'd us out a true ane,

And sound this day.

– 9 –

Now Robertson[14] harangue nae mair,

shut; mouth   But steek your gab for ever;

Or try the wicked town of Ayr,

For there they'll think you clever;

---

[11] Patronage, here personified, is the practice of the local landowner (called the patron) making the appointment or presentation of a minister rather than the elders of a kirk electing one. The wealthy patrons were inclined to the Moderate party and thus were opposed by the more orthodox masses.

[12] A congregation in this town in 1780 by opposing a presentation delayed the ordination by two years.

[13] James Cunningham, 14th Earl of Glencairn, who had made the presentation of MacKinlay. He later became Burns's patron.

[14] John Robertson, a Moderate, the minister of the first charge in the Laigh Kirk since 1765.

Or, nae reflection on your lear,   *learning*
   Ye may commence a Shaver;   *Barber*
Or to the Netherton[15] repair,
   An' turn a Carpet-weaver
     Aff-hand this day.   *At once*

- 10 -

Multrie[16] and you were just a match,
   We never had sic twa drones:
Auld Hornie did the Laigh Kirk watch,   *The Devil*
   Just like a winkin baudrons,   *cat*
And ay he catch'd the tither wretch,   *another*
   To fry them in his caudrons;   *caldrons*
But now his Honor maun detach,
   Wi' a' his brimstone squadrons,
     Fast, fast this day.

- 11 -

See, see auld Orthodoxy's faes   *foes*
   She's swingein thro' the city!   *flogging*
Hark, how the nine-tail'd cat she plays!
   I vow it's unco pretty: *very*
There, Learning, with his Greekish face,
   Grunts out some Latin ditty;
And Common Sense is gaun, she says,   *going*
   To mak to Jamie Beattie[17]
     Her plaint this day.

- 12 -

But there's Morality himsel,
   Embracing all opinions;

---

[15] Carpet-weaving district in Kilmarnock.
[16] See note 3.
[17] A Scottish author with Moderate religious persuasions; see p. 12, note 3.

gives another   Hear, how he gies the tither yell
            Between his twa companions!
subcutaneous tissue   See, how she peels the skin an' fell,
As if one   As ane were peelin onions!
            Now there, they're packed aff to hell,
            An' banish'd our dominions,
                Henceforth this day.

– 13 –

            O happy day! rejoice, rejoice!
                Come bouse about the porter!
            Morality's demure decoys
                Shall here nae mair find quarter:
            Mckinlay, Russell, are the boys
                That Heresy can torture;
give; rope; hoist   They'll gie her on a rape a hoyse,
cut   And cowe her measure shorter
                By th' head some day.

– 14 –

another pint-measure of whisky   Come, bring the tither mutchkin in,
                And here's, for a conclusion,
            To ev'ry New-light[18] mother's son,
                From this time forth, Confusion!
deafen   If mair they deave us wi' their din,
                Or patronage intrusion,
match   We'll light a spunk, and ev'ry skin,
                We'll run them aff in fusion,
                Like oil some day.

---

[18] Burns's note (1787): *"New-licht* is a cant phrase, in the West of Scotland, for those religious opinions Dr. Taylor of Norwich has defended so strenuously." John Taylor in *The Scripture Doctrine of Original Sin* (1740) argued that "the consequences of Adam's first transgression upon us are labour, sorrow, and mortality" but not our total depravity and damnation irrespective of good deeds.

THE TWA HERDS: OR, THE HOLY TULYIE
An Unco Mournfu' Tale[1]

two shepherds;
squabble, brawl
very

(1785, 1796)

Blockheads with reason wicked wits abhor,
But fool with fool is barbarous civil war.

POPE[2]

– 1 –

O a' ye pious godly flocks,
Weel fed on pastures orthodox,
Wha now will keep you frae the fox
    Or worrying tykes?   *dogs*
Or wha will tent the waifs an' crocks   *tend; stragglers; old ewes*
    About the dykes?   *stone fences*

– 2 –

The twa best herds in a' the wast,   *shepherds; west*
That e'er gae gospel horn a blast   *gave*
These five an' twenty simmers past—
    O, dool to tell!—   *sad*
Hae had a bitter, black out-cast   *quarrel*
    Atween themsel.

---

[1] Burns's note in the manuscript copy of the poem in the British Museum: "The following was the first of my poetical productions that saw the light. . . . The occasion was a bitter and shameless quarrel between two Rev. gentlemen, Moodie of Riccarton and Russell of Kilmarnock. It was at the time when the hue and cry against patronage was at its worst." A similar account is in the autobiographical letter (see Appendix B). The poem ridicules the Evangelical faction by ironically calling for an end to the dispute between the two orthodox ministers.

[2] Alexander Pope, *Dunciad,* III, 175–176.

175

– 3 –

O Moodie, man an' wordy Russell,[3]
How could you raise so vile a bustle?
Ye'll see how New-Light herds will whistle,
    An' think it fine!
got no such sprain The Lord's cause gat na sic a twistle
have mind (remember)   Sin' I hae min'.

– 4 –

O Sirs! whae'er wad hae expeckit
would have so Your duty ye wad sae negleckit?
landowners; esteemed fit Ye wha were no by lairds respeckit
    To wear the plaid,
But by the brutes themselves eleckit
    To be their guide![4]

– 5 –

What flock wi' Moodie's flock could rank,
Sae hale an' hearty every shank?
sour; standing pool Nae poison'd, soor Arminian[5] stank
    He let them taste;
But Calvin's fountainhead they drank—
    O, sic a feast!

– 6 –

polecat; badger; fox The thummart, wilcat, brock, an' tod
Weel kend his voice thro' a' the wood;
every He smell'd their ilka hole an' road,
    Baith out and in;

---

[3] Both ministers appear in "The Holy Fair;" see pp. 150, 153.

[4] The allusion; here, as in stanza 15, is to the patronage controversy (see Introduction, p. xxii): Moodie and Russell were both elected by the representatives of the congregation, not presented by a patron.

[5] Beliefs hostile to Calvinistic doctrines of predestination.

An' weel he lik'd to shed their bluid
    An' sell their skin.

– 7 –

What herd like Russell tell'd his tale?   *spoke*
His voice was heard thro' muir and dale;   *moor*
He kend the Lord's sheep, ilka tail,   *each*
    O'er a' the height;
An tell'd gin they were sick or hale   *said if*
    At the first sight.

– 8 –

He fine a mangy sheep could scrub;
Or nobly swing the gospel club;
Or New-Light herds could nicely drub   *shepherds*
    And pay their skin;   *beat*
Or hing them o'er the burning dub   *hang; pool*
    Or heave them in.

– 9 –

Sic twa—O, do I live to see't?—
Sic famous twa sud disagree't,   *should have*
An' names like villain, hypocrite,
    Ilk ither gi'en,   *each other have given*
While New-Light herds wi' laughin spite   *shepherds*
    Say neither's liein!

– 10 –

A' ye wha tent the gospel fauld,   *tend; fold*
Thee Duncan deep, an' Peebles shaul',   *shallow*
But chiefly great apostle Auld,[6]

---

[6] Three Evangelicals: Robert Duncan, minister at Dundonald since 1783; for Peebles
see "The Holy Fair" (p. 152, note 11); William Auld, Burns's own minister at Mauchline, where he had been since 1742.

We trust in thee,
That thou wilt work them hot an' cauld
Till they agree!

– 11 –

Consider, sirs, how we're beset:
shepherd There's scarce a new herd that we get
But comes frae 'mang that cursed set
I winna name:
I hope frae heav'n to see them yet
In fiery flame!

– 12 –

foe Dalrymple has been lang our fae,
a great deal of woe M'Gill has wrought us meikle wae,
An' that curs'd rascal ca'd M'Quhae,
An' baith the Shaws,[7]
That aft hae made us black an' blae
Wi' vengefu' paws.

– 13 –

always Auld Wodrow[8] lang has hatch'd mischief:
We thought ay death wad bring relief,
But he has gotten to our grief
Ane to succeed him,[9]

---

[7] A group of learned Moderates, all at this time or later doctors of divinity: William Dalrymple, minister at Ayr since 1746, Moderator of the General Assembly (the highest body of the Kirk of Scotland) in 1781, baptized Burns (see Burns's eulogy in "The Kirk's Alarm"); William M'Gill, colleague of Dalrymple in the second charge at Ayr, whose prosecution for heterodoxy was the occasion for "The Kirk's Alarm"; William M'Quhae, minister at St. Quivox since 1764; Andrew Shaw, son of a professor of divinity at St. Andrew University, minister at nearby Craigie since 1765; David Shaw, minister at Coylton since 1749 and Moderator of the General Assembly in 1775.

[8] Patrick Wodrow, minister at Tarbolton since in 1738.

[9] Rev. John M'Math, assistant and successor (1789) to Wodrow at Tarbolton; Burns thought him so tolerant that he wrote him a verse epistle to accompany a presentation copy of the fiery "Holy Willie's Prayer" (HH, II, 76–81).

A chield wha'll soundly buff our beef—   *fellow; whack*
    I meikle dread him.   *greatly*

– 14 –

An' monie mae that I could tell,   *more*
Wha fain would openly rebel,
Forby turn-coats amang oursel: *Besides*
    There's Smith[10] for ane—
I doubt he's but a greyneck still,   *suspect; trimmer, time-server*
    An' that ye'll fin'!   *find*

– 15 –

O a' ye flocks o'er a' the hills,
By mosses, meadows, moors, an' fells,   *bogs; hillsides*
Come, join your counsel and your skills
    To cowe the lairds,   *humble; landowners (patrons)*
An' get the brutes the power themsels
    To chuse their herds!   *shepherds*

– 16 –

Then Orthodoxy yet may prance,
An' Learning in a woody dance,   *hangman's noose*
An' that fell cur ca'd Common-sense,   *dangerous; called*
    That bites sae sair,   *sorely*
Be banish'd o'er the sea to France—
    Let him bark there!

– 17 –

Then Shaw's an' D'rymple's eloquence,
M'Gill's close, nervous excellence,
M'Quhae's pathetic, manly sense,
    An' guid M'Math
Wha thro' the heart can brawly glance,   *very well*
    May a' pack aff!

---

[10] Rev. George Smith appears in "The Holy Fair;" see p. 151, note 10.

THE KIRK'S ALARM[1]

(1789; 1789? 1799, 1903)[2]

- I -

Orthodox! orthodox!—

Wha believe in John Knox—

Let me sound an alarm to your conscience:

A heretic blast

Has been blawn i' the Wast,

That what is not sense must be nonsense—

Orthodox!

That what is not sense must be nonsense.

---

[1] This poem satirizes the opponents of William M'Gill ("Dr. Mac" of stanza 2), minister in the second charge at Ayr since 1761. M'Gill's *Practical Essay on the Death of Christ* in 1786 (the "heretic blast" of stanza 1) had aroused a storm against him. The orthodox considered his beliefs Socinian. The particular occasion was the Presbytry's complaint against M'Gill's doctrines presented to the Synod in July, 1789. Burns composed eleven stanzas of the poem within two days of this event and commented on them in a letter: "You know my sentiments respecting the present two great Parties that divide our Scots Ecclesiastics.—I do not care three farthings for Commentators & authorities.—An honest candid enquirer after truth, I revere; but illiberality & wrangling I equally detest.—You will be well acquainted with the persecutions that my worthy friend, Dr Mcgill, is undergoing among your Divines.—Several of these reverend lads, his opponents, have come thro' my hands before; but I have some thoughts of serving them up again in a different dish.—I have just sketched the following ballad, & as usual I send the first rough-draught to you.—I do not wish to be known in it, tho' I know, if ever it appear, I shall be suspected.—If I finish it, I am thinking to throw off two or three dozen copies at a Press in Dumfries, & send them, as from Edinr to some Ayr-shire folks on both sides of the question.—If I should fail of rendering some of the Doctor's foes ridiculous, I shall at least gratify my resentment in his behalf."

The "reverend lads" who, by the time he had written all the stanzas, had already "come through my hands," besides the Moderates M'Gill and Dalrymple (see "The

- 2 -

Dr. Mac! Dr. Mac!
You should stretch on a rack,
To strike wicked Writers wi' terror:
To join faith and sense,
Upon onie pretence,
Was heretic, damnable error—
Dr. Mac!
'Twas heretic, damnable error.

- 3 -

Town of Ayr! Town of Ayr!
It was rash, I declare,
To meddle wi' mischief a-brewing:
Provost John[3] is still deaf
To the church's relief,

Twa Herds," p. 178, note 7), both of whom, of course, Burns admired, are all
Evangelicals:

"Rumble John" (stanza 6: John Russell, see "The Holy Fair," p. 153, note 14),
"Simper James" (stanza 7: James MacKinlay, see "The Ordination," p. 170, note 5),
"Singet Sawnie" (stanza 8: Alexander Moodie, see "The Holy Fair," p. 150, note 8),
"Daddie Auld" (stanza 9: William Auld, see "The Twa Herds," p. 177, note 6),
"Poet Willie" (stanza 12: William Pebbles, see "The Holy Fair," p. 152, note 11),
"Irving-side" (stanza 15: George Smith, see "The Holy Fair," p. 151, note 10), and
"Holy Will" (stanza 17: William Fisher, the hero of "Holy Willie's Prayer,"
p. 157, note 1).

The poem was intended to be sung; for the complicated question of the tune, see Dick, p. 485.

[2] Thirteen stanzas appeared in a broadside, published anonymously probably in 1789 in Dumfries by Burns himself, the fuller version appearing after his death (see Egerer, pp. 31, 61), and with music only in Dick (pp. 308-311).

[3] John Ballantine (1743-1812), merchant and banker in Ayr, who in 1787 became the Provost. The officials of the town of Ayr, under his leadership, supported M'Gill.

And Orator Bob[4] is its ruin—
Town of Ayr!
And Orator Bob is its ruin.

– 4 –

D'rymple mild! D'rymple mild!
Tho' your heart's like a child,
An' your life like the new-driven snaw,
will not   Yet that winna save ye:
Auld Satan must have ye,
For preaching that three's ane and twa—
D'rymple mild!
For preaching that three's ane and twa.[5]

– 5 –

Calvin's sons! Calvin's sons!
Seize your sp'ritual guns,
Ammunition you never can need:
Your hearts are the stuff
Will be powther enough,
And your skulls are store-houses o' lead—
Calvin's sons!
Your skulls are store-houses o' lead.

– 6 –

Rumble John! Rumble John!
Mount the steps with a groan,
Cry:-"The book is wi' heresy cramm'd";
Then lug out your ladle,
the urine of cattle   Deal brimstone like adle,
And roar every note o' the damn'd—

---

[4] Robert Aiken (see p. 46, note 1) argued M'Gill's case in the ecclesiastical courts.
[5] Dalrymple had commended in print his colleague M'Gill's *Essay.*

Rumble John!
And roar every note o' the damn'd.

– 7 –

Simper James! Simper James!
Leave the fair Killie dames—   *Kilmarnock*
There's a holier chase in your view;
I'll lay on your head
That the pack ye'll soon lead,
For puppies like you there's but few—
Simper James!
For puppies like you there's but few.

– 8 –

Singet Sawnie! Singet Sawnie!   *Shrivelled*
Are ye herding the penny,   *hoarding*
Unconcious what evils await?
Wi' a jump, yell, and howl
Alarm every soul,
For the Foul Thief is just at your gate—
Singet Sawnie!
The Foul Thief is just at your gate.

– 9 –

Daddie Auld! Daddie Auld!
There's a tod in the fauld,   *fox; fold*
A tod meikle waur than the clerk:[6]   *much worse*
Tho' ye can do little skaith,   *damage*
Ye'll be in at the death,
And gif ye canna bite, ye may bark—   *if*
Daddie Auld!
For gif ye canna bite ye may bark.

---

[6] Gavin Hamilton (see p. 157, note 1).

– 10 –

Davie Rant! Davie Rant![7]

saint   In a face like a saunt

And a heart that would poison a hog,

Raise an impudent roar,

blown toward the shore   Like a breaker lee-shore,

lost   Or the Kirk will be tint in a bog—

Davie Rant!

Or the Kirk will be tint in a bog.

– 11 –

Jamie Goose! Jamie Goose![8]

an empty boast   Ye hae made but toom roose

In hunting the wicked lieutenant;

But the Doctor's[9] your mark,

For the Lord's haly ark,

repaired (used for barrels); knocked   He has cooper'd, and ca'd a wrang pin in't—

Jamie Goose!

He has copper'd and ca'd a wrang pin in't.

– 12 –

Poet Willie! Poet Willie![10]

Give   Gie the Doctor a volley,

Wi' your "Liberty's chain" and your wit:

O'er Pegasus' side

Ye ne'er laid a stride,

---

[7] David Grant, minister of Ochiltree since 1786, very active in the prosecution of M'Gill.

[8] Burns's note in a manuscript: "James Young of Cumnock, who had lately been foiled in an ecclesiastical prosecution against a Lieutenant Mitchell."

[9] M'Gill.

[10] Burns's note in a manuscript: "William Peebles in Newton-on-Ayr, a poetaster who, among other things, published an ode on the centenary of the Revolution in which was the line:—'And bound in Liberty's endearing chain,'"

Ye but smelt, man, the place where he shit—
    Poet Willie!
Ye smelt but the place where he shit.

– 13 –

Andro' Gowk! Andro' Gowk![11]   *Cuckoo*
  Ye may slander the Book,
And the Book not the waur, let me tell ye: *worse*
  Ye are rich, and look big,
  But lay by hat and wig,
And ye'll hae a calf's head o' sma' value—
    Andro Gowk!
'Ye'll hae a calf's head o' sma' value.

– 14 –

Barr Steenie! Barr Steenie![12]
  What mean ye? what mean ye?
If ye'll meddle nae mair wi' the matter,
  Ye may hae some pretence
  To havins and sense   *manners*
Wi' people wha ken ye nae better—
    Barr Steenie!
Wi' people wha ken ye nae better.

– 15 –

Irvine-side! Irvine-side!
  Wi' your turkey-cock pride,
Of manhood but sma' is your share:
  Ye've the figur, 'tis true,
  Even your faes will allow,   *foes*
And your friends daurna say ye hae mair—   *do not dare; more*

---

[11] Andrew Mitchell, minister of Monkton since 1774.
[12] Stephen Young, minister of Barr since 1780.

Irvine-side!
Your friends daurna say ye hae mair.

– 16 –

Muirland Jock![13] Muirland Jock!
Whom the Lord gave a stock

Would; tinker Wad set up a tinkler in brass,
If ill manners were wit,
There's no mortal so fit
To prove the poor Doctor an ass—
Muirland Jock!
To prove the poor Doctor an ass.

– 17 –

Holy Will! Holy Will!
There was wit i' your skull,
When ye pilfer'd the alms o' the poor:

supply (timber) The timmer is scant,
taken; saint When ye're taen for a saunt
rope Wha should swing in a rape for an hour—
Holy Will!
Ye should swing in a rape for an hour.

– 18 –

Poet Burns! Poet Burns!
-spanking Wi' your priest-skelping turns,
Why desert ye your auld native shire?
Your Muse is a gipsy,
Yet were she ev'n tipsy,
call; worse She could ca' us nae waur than we are—
Poet Burns!
Ye could ca' us nae waur than we are.

---

[13] John Shepherd, minister of Muirkirk since 1775.

Elegies

These two elegies stand out among those new kinds of poems with which Burns experimented after the Kilmarnock edition. They both are reactions to the death of older friends. They both are written in Scots-English, that is with a sprinkling of Scots among a preponderance of words spelled like English but pronounced like Scots. And they are both formal and studied productions.

In "Elegy to Captain Matthew Henderson" Burns adapts the stanza form and something of the manner associated with the Scots comic elegy (compare stanza 1, for instance, with "Tam Samson's Elegy") to the European tradition of the serious pastoral elegy, with its lament, its call to nature to mourn, its critical comment on an aspect of contemporary society (see stanza 16), and its account of the translation of the departed one to the heavens (stanza 14). These traditional features, the poem's relation to Milton's "Lycidas" and to Robert Fergusson's "Elegy on the Death of Scots Music," besides its clear echoes of Gray's "Elegy" (see stanza 16) and of William Collins' "Ode to Evening" (see stanzas 12 and 13), show it to be very literary and formal, qualities not often associated with Burns's poetry.

Burns describes an old bard and his surroundings in the first two stanzas of "Lament for James Earl of Glencairn" and in the rest presents the bard's song of lamentation, with only some particulars relevant to Burns's personal relation to his subject. The poem shows that Burns could adapt his Scots idiom to the most dignified and serious of the English tradition of his time, to the high artifice of pastoral elegy.

ELEGY ON CAPTAIN MATTHEW HENDERSON[1]

A Gentleman Who Held the Patent for His Honours
Immediately from Almighty God!

(1790; 1790, 1793)[2]

But now his radiant course is run,
For Matthew's course was bright:
His soul was like the glorious sun
A matchless, Heavenly light.

– I –

                    O Death! thou tyrant fell and bloody!

great; halter   The meikle Devil wi' a woodie

Drag; smithy   Haurl thee hame to his black smiddie

hedgehog   O'er hurcheon hides,

---

[1] Burns had met Matthew Henderson (1737-1788) in Edinburgh, where the latter, an impecunious landowner, pensioner, and former soldier, led a convivial club life. Burns wrote in 1790 to a professor friend who had once lent him a book of literary criticism which had influenced this poem: "I dare say if you have not met with Captn Matthew Henderson about Edinr, you must have heard of him.—He was an intimate acquaintance of mine; & of all Mankind I ever knew, he was one of the first for a nice sense of honor, a generous contempt of the adventitious distinctions of Men, and sterling tho' sometimes outré Wit.... It is ... ever since I read your [John] Aiken on the poetical use of Natural history, a favorite study of mine, the characters of the Vegetable & the manners of the Animal kingdoms.... How I have succeeded on the whole—if there is any incongruity in the imagery—or whether I have not omitted some apt rural paintings altogether.—I will not pretend to say ..." (*Letters*, II, 33).

[2] Burns wrote two stanzas of this elegy at the time of Henderson's death in late 1788 and all the others almost two years later. It was published, probably without his authority, in *The Edinburgh Magazine* of Aug. 1790 but inserted in his *Poems* of 1793 (Egerer, p. 39), from which this text is taken.

And like stock-fish come o'er his studdie   *haddock strike; anvil*
    Wi' thy auld sides!3

– 2 –

He's gane, he's gane! he's frae us torn,   *gone*
The ae best fellow e'er was born!   *one*
Thee, Matthew, Nature's sel shall mourn,
    By wood and wild,
Where, haply, Pity strays forlorn,   *perhaps*
    Frae man exil'd.

– 3 –

Ye hills, near neebors o' the starns,   *neighbors; stars*
That proudly cock your cresting cairns;   *heaps of rocks*
Ye cliffs, the haunts of sailing yearns,   *eagles*
    Where Echo slumbers,
Come join, ye Nature's sturdiest bairns,   *offspring*
    My wailing numbers.

– 4 –

Mourn, ilka grove the cushat kens;   *each; pigeon knows*
Ye hazly shaws and briery dens;   *hazel woods; lushly foliaged*
Ye burnies, wimplin down your glens,   *little streams; winding*
    Wi' toddlin din,   *murmuring sound*
Or foaming, strang, wi' hasty stens,   *strong; quick leaps*
    Frae lin to lin!   *waterfall*

– 5 –

Mourn, little harebells o'er the lea;
Ye stately foxgloves, fair to see;

---

3 The image is of a split haddock being beaten flat, and smoked or dried in the sun (like finnan haddie), in this case Death's body beaten on the Devil's anvil in hot and smoky hell.

Ye woodbines, hanging bonnilie,
 In scented bowers;
Ye roses on your thorny tree,
 The first o' flowers.

– 6 –

At dawn, when every grassy blade
Droops with a diamond at his head,
At even, when beans their fragrance shed,
 I' th' rustling gale,
rabbits; skipping Ye maukins whiddin thro' the glade,
 Come join my wail.

– 7 –

Mourn, ye wee songsters o' the wood;
crop Ye grouse that crap the heather bud;
cloud Ye curlews calling thro' a clud;
 Ye whistling plover;
partridge And mourn, ye whirring paitrick brood;
 He's gane for ever!

– 8 –

Mourn, sooty coots, and speckled teals;
Ye fisher herons, watching eels;
Ye duck and drake, wi' airy wheels
 Circling the lake:
Ye bitterns, till the quagmire reels,
Roar Rair for his sake!

– 9 –

corncrakes Mourn, clamouring craiks at close o' day,
clover 'Mang fields o' flowring claver gay;
And when you wing your annual way
 Frae our cauld shore,

Tell thae far warlds, wha lies in clay,   *those*
    Wham we deplore.

– 10 –

Ye houlets, frae your ivy bower,   *owls*
In some auld tree, or eldritch tower,   *unearthly, haunted*
What time the moon, wi' silent glowr,   *When; stare*
    Sets up her horn,
Wail thro' the dreary midnight hour
    Till waukrife morn.   *wakeful*

– 11 –

O rivers, forests, hills, and plains!
Oft have ye heard my canty strains: *cheerful*
But now, what else for me remains
    But tales of woe;
And frae my een the drapping rains   *eyes*
    Maun ever flow.   *Must*

– 12 –

Mourn, Spring, thou darling of the year;
Ilk cowslip cup shall kep a tear: *Each; catch*
Thou, Simmer, while each corny spear   *grain-ladened*
    Shoots up its head,
Thy gay, green, flowery tresses shear
    For him that's dead!

– 13 –

Thou, Autumn, wi' thy yellow hair,
In grief thy sallow mantle tear;
Thou, Winter, hurling thro' the air
    The roaring blast,
Wide o'er the naked world declare
    The worth we've lost!

– 14 –

Mourn him thou Sun, great source of light;
Mourn, Empress of the silent night;
little stars And you, ye twinkling starnies bright,
My Matthew mourn;
taken For through your orbs he's taen his flight,
Ne'er to return.

– 15 –

O Henderson! the man! the brother!
And art thou gone, and gone for ever!
And hast thou crost that unknown river,
Life's dreary bound!
Like thee, where shall I find another,
The world around?

– 16 –

Go to your sculptur'd tombs, ye Great,
In a' the tinsel trash o' state!
But by thy honest turf I'll wait,
Thou man of worth!
one And weep the ae best fellow's fate
E'er lay in earth!⁴

---

⁴ The poem contains an "Epitaph" of 8 quatrains (HH, I, 266–268), here omitted.

LAMENT FOR JAMES, EARL OF GLENCAIRN[1]
(1791, 1793)

– 1 –

The wind blew hollow frae the hills;
  By fits the sun's departing beam
Look'd on the fading yellow woods,
  That wav'd o'er Lugar's winding stream.
Beneath a craigy steep, a Bard,
  Laden with years and meikle pain,   *much*
In loud lament bewail'd his lord,
  Whom Death had all untimely taen.   *taken*

– 2 –

He lean'd him to an ancient aik,   *oak*
  Whose trunk was mould'ring down with years;
His locks were bleached white with time,
  His hoary cheek was wet wi' tears;
And as he touch'd his trembling harp,
  And as he tun'd his doleful sang,
The winds, lamenting thro' their caves,
  To echo bore the notes alang.

---

[1] James Cunningham (1749–1791), after 1775 the 14th Earl of Glencairn, was Burns'
most influential patron. After meeting Burns in Edinburgh in 1786, he vigorously urged
the sale of the first Edinburgh edition and later helped Burns get a position as a tax
collector. Burns wrote in a letter soon after Glencairn's death: "From him all my fame
and fortune took its rise: to him I owe every thing that I am or have, & for his Sake I
wear these Sables with as much devout sincerety as ever bleeding Gratitude did for
departed Benevolence" (*Letters,* II, 60–61).

– 3 –

"Ye scatter'd birds that faintly sing,
    The reliques of the vernal quire;
Ye woods that shed on a' the winds
    The honours of the aged years,
A few short months, and glad and gay,
eye   Again ye'll charm the ear and e'e;
nought But nocht in all-revolving time
    Can gladness bring again to me.

– 4 –

"I am a bending aged tree,
    That long has stood the wind and rain;
But now has come a cruel blast,
gone   And my last hold of earth is gane:
Nae leaf o' mine shall greet the spring,
summer   Nae simmer sun exalt my bloom;
must But I maun lie before the storm,
others   And ithers plant them in my room.

– 5 –

so many "I've seen sae monie changefu' years,
    On earth I am a stranger grown:
I wander in the ways of men,
    Alike unknowing and unknown:
Unheard, unpitied, unreliev'd,
alone; load   I bear alane my lade o' care,
For silent, low, on beds of dust,
    Lie a' that would my sorrows share.

– 6 –

"And last (the sum of a' my griefs!)
    My noble master lies in clay;
The flow'r amang our barons bold,

His country's pride, his country's stay:
In weary being now I pine,
    For all the life of life is dead,
And hope has left my aged ken,   *consciousness*
    On forward wing for ever fled.

- 7 -

"Awake thy last sad voice, my harp!
    The voice of woe and wild despair!
Awake, resound thy latest lay,
    Then sleep in silence evermair!
And thou, my last, best, only friend,
    That fillest an untimely tomb,
Accept this tribute from the Bard
    Thou brought from Fortune's mirkest gloom.

- 8 -

"In Poverty's low barren vale,
    Thick mists obscure involv'd me round;
Though oft I turn'd the wistful eye,
    Nae ray of fame was to be found;
Thou found'st me, like the morning sun
    That melts the fogs in limpid air:
The friendless Bard and rustic song
    Became alike thy fostering care.

- 9 -

"O! why has Worth so short a date!
    While villains ripen grey with time!
Must thou, the noble, gen'rous, great,
    Fall in bold manhood's hardy prime!
Why did I live to see that day?
    A day to me so full of woe?
O! had I met the mortal shaft
    Which laid my benefactor low!

– 10 –

"The bridegroom may forget the bride,

last night   Was made his wedded wife yestreen;

The monarch may forget the crown

That on his head an hour had been;

The mother may forget the child

That smiles sae sweetly on her knee;

But I'll remember thee, Glencairn,

And a' that thou hast done for me!"

Shorter Occasional Pieces

EPITAPH ON A HENPECKED SQUIRE

(? , 1786)

As father Adam first was fool'd,
  A case that's still too common,
Here lyes a man a woman rul'd:
  The devil rul'd the woman.

EPIGRAM ON SAID OCCASION

(? , 1786)

O Death, had'st thou but spar'd his life,
   Whom we this day lament!
We freely wad exchang'd the wife,
   An' a' been weel content.

Ev'n as he is, cauld in his graff,   *grave*
   The swap we yet will do't;
Tak thou the carlin's carcase aff,   *old hag's*
   Thou'se get the saul o' boot.   *Thou shalt; soul besides*

THE TOADEATER

(? , 1829)

Of lordly acquaintance you boast,

last night   And the Dukes that you dined with yestreen;

Yet an insect's an insect at most,

    Tho' it crawl on the curl of a Queen!

AGAINST THE EARL OF GALLOWAY[1]

(1793, 1808)

What dost thou in that mansion fair?
   Flit, Galloway, and find
Some narrow, dirty, dungeon cave,
   The picture of thy mind.

---

[1] The occasion for these four squibs is given by John Syme, who accompanied Burns on a tour of Galloway in the summer of 1793. Awakening one morning on the trip with a hangover, Burns tore his wet boots to shreds in attempting to put them on. "Mercy on us," Syme wrote, "how he did fume and rage! Nothing could reinstate him in temper. I tried various expedients, and at last hit on one that succeeded. I showed him the house of Garlieston [residence of the son of the Earl], across the bay of Wigton. Against the Earl of Galloway, with whom he was offended, he expectorated his spleen, and regained a most agreeable temper." Burns probably hated John Stewart (1736–1806), 7th Earl of Galloway, because of the latter's puritanical and Tory principles.

ON THE SAME

(1793, 1808)

No Stewart art thou, Galloway:
　The Stewarts all were brave.
Besides, the Stewarts were but fools,
　Not one of them a knave.

ON THE SAME
(1793, 1808)

Bright ran thy line, O Galloway,
   Thro' many a far-famed sire!
So ran the far-famed Roman way,
   And ended in a mire.

ON THE SAME, ON THE AUTHOR BEING THREATENED WITH VENGEANCE

(1793?, 1808)

Spare me thy vengeance, Galloway!
  In quiet let me live:
I ask no kindness at thy hand,
  For thou hast none to give.

GRACE
AT THE GLOBE TAVERN
AFTER MEAT

(? , 1801)

O Lord, we do Thee humbly thank
  For that we little merit: *what*
Now Joan may tak the flesh away, *meat*
  And Will bring in the spirit.

ON A WAG IN MAUCHLINE

(1786?, 1801)

– 1 –

Lament him, Mauchline husbands a',
    He aften did assist ye;
whole For had ye staid hale weeks awa',
    Your wives they ne'er had missed ye!

– 2 –

Ye Mauchline bairns, as on ye pass
    To school in bands thegither,
O, tread ye lightly on his grass—
    Perhaps he was your father!

Masterpieces

Burns wrote "The Jolly Beggars" almost a year before the Kilmarnock edition but never published it, undoubtedly because he thought that its occasional bawdry and its nihilistic view would do his reputation a disservice. The world has judged otherwise about this single attempt by Burns to create a number of characters, put them in a whole imaginative world, and manipulate them dramatically in a formal plot.

The poem must be read as a miniature comic opera. It has three parts: an overture (the maimed veteran and the campfollower), an action (the rivalry between the fiddler and the tinker for the favors of the widowed pickpocket, with the resolution provided by the bard, who relinquishes one of his three women to the disappointed lover), and a finale (the bard's second, climactic song).

After the veteran begins the show, each character has a dramatic reason for coming forward to sing. The characters' views of and positions in life are not exactly the same. The veteran is still loyal to the military establishment, but has been forced out of it by its own evils. His companion embodies total sexual permissiveness and contempt for respectability. Both have found a present substitute in vagabondage for a better life during war times. But the widowed pickpocket has found no satisfactory substitute for a life in which as a thief and a wife of an outlaw she was never accepted by society. She is the only dissatisfied one, but her dissatisfaction is mitigated by the obvious pleasure she takes in singing of her lost love, and later, as part of the dramatic resolution, by her love match with the tinker. Her hatred of Lowland law and the campfollower's contempt for hypocritical sanctity are preludes to the bard's final devastating dismissal of the official and respectable world.

The fiddler is more vulnerable than the rest, but his pluck and resilience save him from pathos; he just wants to be left alone to enjoy himself in his tiny way, and his ideal of the carefree life is a dainty anticipation of the bard's more robust hedonism. The tinker presents another contrast: he is a hulking and bullying amoral materialist who vaunts the security his occupation gives him.

The bard, who rises to give his magnanimous approval to the fiddler's timely seduction of one of his three women, also has an occupation, but his is not to gain security but to celebrate the compensatory pleasures of a life of insecurity. After his first song, in which he divorces himself from the genteel world and declares himself for a life of indulgence in sex and art, he is then led by acclamation to sum up in his second song the common attitudes of all who have gone before him in the drama: their animal joy in the outcast's life, their jaunty and pugnacious *joie de vivre,* their belief in making the best of the moment.

But in the excitement of the occasion he takes them along with him to a position more radical and explicit than their previous ones, by comparing the pale pleasures of the artificial world to the scarlet pleasures of the natural one. The artificial world, however, is only attacked by being contemned and not by charging that it is productive of involuntary miseries. These are voluntary beggars, whose attitudes are emotional, not intellectual. The beggars do not express any direct attack on the evils of society. The social criticism emerges indirectly, in the manner of burlesque, from the ironic language of gallantry and elegant sentiment put into their unconscious mouths and used to describe their actions.

"Tam o' Shanter" is the only longer poem of quite obvious superior merit that Burns wrote after the year of the Kilmarnock volume. Unlike his attitude toward his other masterpiece, he soon recognized its merit, calling it within six months of its composition his "standard performance in the Poetical line" and his "favorite poem" among his own productions (*Letters,* II, 68, 69).

Much of the humor comes from the mock heroic quality of the tale, that is, the use of an epic style for a low subject: the epithets, the sober moral commentary, the portentous tone, the piling on of similes, the details of horror exaggerated to the point of burlesque, the formal statement of the obviously inadequate moral at the end. Chaucer's "Nun's

Priest's Tale" invites comparison. Humor also derives from the character and actions of Tam, a simple male animal, responsive to the pleasures of tavern camaraderie, happily indifferent to danger in his tipsy condition. We are also amused by the errors of the narrator, who, for example, accuses Tam of ogling at old witches and then discovers the pretty Nannie, and who predicts Tam's capture and damnation, which never take place.

The poem alternates passages of narrative and of moral commentary. The voice of the former passages is sympathetic to Tam and to what he likes—ale, social pleasures, women, dancing, and song. The voice of the later is sympathetic to Tam's wife Kate and what she stands for—responsibility, duty, reason and resistence to sin. If we distinguish these two voices of the narrator, perhaps we can see the poem as a burlesque of Burns's divided self (and by extension Scotland's and the world's), torn between feeling and reason, pleasure and duty, romance and practicality.

THE JOLLY BEGGARS

A Cantata[1]

(1785, 1799)[2]

– I –

RECITATIVO[3]

grey; ground	When lyart leaves bestrow the yird,
Bat	Or, wavering like the Bauckie-bird,
	Bedim cauld Boreas' blast;
slanting stroke	When hailstanes drive wi' bitter skyte,
	And infant Frosts begin to bite,
hoarfrost	In hoary cranreuch drest;
One; evening	Ae night at e'en a merry core
careless; vagrant	O' randie, gangrel bodies
riotous frolic	In Poosie-Nansie's[4] held the splore,

---

[1] In The Library, University of Edinburgh, there is a manuscript in Burns's hand of an early version of this poem entitled "Love and Liberty."

[2] The copy-text for this printing of "The Jolly Beggars" is the *original* holograph manuscript (i.e., without the single sheet inserted in about 1800 after the second sheet of the original) at the Burns Museum at Alloway, Ayrshire, the manuscript used as the source for the first printing in 1799 (Egerer, p. 60) and clearly a later version than the manuscript entitled "Love and Liberty." The recitative and the song of the Merry Andrew, traditionally placed after the second song, is not included in this text, because it is a fragment of an earlier version whose inclusion was never authorized by Burns (see John C. Weston, "The Text of Burns' 'The Jolly Beggars'," *Studies in Bibliography*, XIII (1960), 239–248).

[3] The two stanzas of this recitative are in an old Scots verse form dating back to the sixteenth century and generally called "The Cherry and the Slae" from its use by Alexander Montgomerie late in that century. The last recitative is cast in the same stanza, the only exact repetition of a verse form in this metrically diversified poem.

[4] Burns's note in manuscript called "Love and Liberty": "The Hostess of a noted Caravansary in M[auchline], well known to and much frequented by the lowest orders

To drink their orra duddies: *extra rags*
Wi' quaffing and laughing,
    They ranted an' they sang;
Wi' jumping an' thumping
    The vera girdle rang.   *griddle*

First, niest the fire, in auld, red rags,[5]   *next*
Ane sat;[6] weel brac'd wi' mealy bags,[7]   *One*
    And knapsack a' in order;
His doxy lay within his arm;   *hussy*
Wi' usquebae an' blankets warm,   *whisky*
    She blinket on her Sodger.
An' ay he gies the tozie drab   *tipsy harlot*
    The tither skelpan kiss,   *Another smacking*
While she held up her greedy gab,   *mouth*
    Just like an aumous dish:[8]   *alms*

---

of Travellers and Pilgrims." Concerning the origin of the poem, Robert Chambers wrote an account of what he learned from an eyewitness: "In the company of John Richmond and James Smith, [Burns] dropped accidentally at a late hour into the humble hostelry of Mrs. [Agnes] Gibson. . . . After witnessing much jollity among a company who by day appeared as miserable beggars, the three young men came away, Burns professing to have been greatly amused by the scene, but particularly with the gleesome behavior of an old maimed soldier. In the course of a few days, he recited a part of the poem to Richmond, who informed me that . . . it contained, in its original complete form, songs by a sweep and a sailor, which did not afterward appear" (Robert Chambers, ed., *The Life and Works of Robert Burns*, 1851, I, 181).

[5] The remains of his "scarlet" uniform, his "rags regimental" (Song 1, line 16 and Song 2, line 19).

[6] A beggar soldier appears in a poem in Allan Ramsay's *The Tea-Table Miscellany* (1724–1732)—"The Merry Beggars." This poem and its companion, "The Happy Beggars," in the same collection, are probably Burns's main literary sources.

[7] Meal was the main alms given to beggars, who carried bags to collect it in; at the end of the poem, the company empties the meal from their bags to exchange it, like their clothes, for drink (see Recitative 7, line 4).

[8] This is another piece of standard equipment for beggars, a large wooden dish held up in supplication for the reception of scraps of food given as alms.

Ilk smack still, did crack still,
horse-driver's   Just like a cadger's whip;
Then staggering, an' swaggering,
He roar'd this ditty up—

– I –

Song
Tune: *Soldier's Joy*

I am a Son of Mars who have been in many wars,
And show my cuts and scars wherever I come;
This here was for a Wench, and that other in a
trench,
When welcoming the French at the sound of the
drum.
Lal de daudle, &c.

My Prenticeship I past, where my Leader[9] breath'd
his last,
When the bloody die was cast on the heights of
Abram;[10]
And I served out my Trade when the gallant game
was play'd,
And the Moro[11] low was laid at the sound of the
drum.

I lastly was with Curtis among the floating
batt'ries,[12]
And there I left for witness, an arm and a
limb;

---

[9] General James Wolfe (1727–1759).

[10] The heights of Abraham at Quebec.

[11] El Moro, the fortress which defended the harbor of Santiago in Cuba, taken by the British in 1762.

[12] Sir Roger Curtis (1746–1816) destroyed the French battering boats before Gibraltar in 1782.

Yet let my Country need me, with Eliott[13] to
   head me
  I'd clatter on my stumps at the sound of the
   drum.

And now tho' I must beg, with a wooden arm
   and leg,
  And many a tatter'd rag hanging over my
   bum,
I'm as happy with my wallet, my bottle, and my
   Callet   *woman*
  As when I us'd in scarlet to follow a drum.

What tho', with hoary locks, I must stand the
   winter shocks,
  Beneath the woods and rocks, oftentimes for a
   home,
When the tother bag I sell and the tother bottle
   tell,
  I could meet a troop of Hell at the sound
   of a drum.

– 2 –

RECITATIVO[14]

He ended; and the kebars sheuk,   *rafters shook*
  Aboon the chorus roar;   *Above*

---

[13] The governor of Gibraltar, General George Augustus Eliott (1717–1790), later
Lord Heathfield, who defended the fortress against the Spanish and French for more than
three years, 1779–1783, during which time the veteran became maimed; since the poem
was written in 1785, he has thus been a beggar for at least two years, long enough for
his uniform to become ragged.

[14] This very old Scots stanza form runs on two rimes only, unlike the less classic but
metrically similar octave of "The Holy Fair." Recitative 6 differs only in having a kind
of refrain line which suggests the bobwheel at the end of the stanza of the ancient
"Christ's Kirk on the Green." The "Christ-Kirk" stanza without its three-line bobwheel is the same as the stanza Burns uses here.

rats; look	While frighted rattons backward leuk,
inmost hole	An' seek the benmost bore:
from the corner	A fairy fiddler frae the neuk,
cried out shrilly	He skirl'd out, Encore,
Woman	But up arose the martial Chuck,
	An' laid the loud uproar—

– 2 –

Song

Tune: *Sodger Laddie*

I once was a Maid tho' I cannot tell when,
And still my delight is in proper[15] young men:
Some one of a troop of Dragoons was my dadie:
No wonder I'm fond of a Sodger laddie.

    Sing, lal de dal, &c.

The first of my Loves was a swaggering blade:[16]
To rattle the thundering drum was his trade;
His leg was so tight and his cheek was so ruddy,
Transported I was with my Sodger laddie.

But the godly old Chaplain left him in the lurch;[17]
The sword I forsook for the sake of the church;

---

[15] The word in context has both the archaic meaning of "handsome" and the ironic meaning of "polite"; this instance of ironic ambiguity illustrates the basic contrast in the poem, ironically expressed in its diction from the polite world, sometimes from the sentimental novel: the contrast between the decorous life of respectability and the permissive life of social deviation. See, for instance, the contrast in the brilliant "rags regimental" (Song 2, line 19).

[16] The priapean imagery of this and the following two stanzas, particularly line 15, suits the sexual preoccupation of the campfollower.

[17] The camp follower here assigns the fault for the desertion (line 12) of her first love, the drummer, to the chaplain, who evidently betrayed his rival somehow; this is part of her attack on the churchly, as is her suggestion that he had venereal disease (line 11) and was a drunkard (line 13).

He ventur'd the Soul, and I risked the Body:
'Twas then I prov'd false to my Sodger laddie.

Full soon I grew sick of my sanctified Sot;
The Regiment at large for a husband I got;
From the gilded Spontoon to the Fife I was   *pike*
   ready:
I asked no more but a Sodger laddie.

But the Peace[18] it reduc'd me to beg in despair,
Till I met my old boy in a Cunningham[19] Fair;
His rags regimental they flutter'd so gaudy:
My heart it rejoic'd at a Sodger laddie.

And now I have lived—I know not how long,
But still I can join in a cup and a song;
And whilst with both hands I can hold the glass
   steady,
Here's to thee, my hero, my Sodger laddie!

– 3 –

RECITATIVO

Then niest outspak a raucle Carlin,[20]   *next; sturdy Old Girl*
Wha ken't fu' weel to cleek the Sterlin;   *snatch the Sterling*
For monie a pursie she had hooked,   *stolen*
An' had in monie a well been douked: *ducked*

---

[18] The Peace of Versailles, 1783.

[19] A district in Ayr.

[20] The widowed pickpocket rises to protest that she, unlike the previous singer, has *not* found a substitute for her former life. The erroneous intrusion of the Merry Andrew in the traditional text between these songs (see note 2, p. 210), blunts the dramatic effect of this reaction and obscures her motive for singing her song at just this time. The octosyllabic couplet used in this recitative is a classic Scots verse form for narrative, going back to Barbour's *Bruce* in the fourteenth century.

Her Love had been a Highland laddie,

a curse upon the woeful noose But weary fa' the waefu' woodie!

Wi sighs an' sobs she thus began

handsome To wail her braw John Highlandman—

− 3 −

Song

Tune: *O, An' Ye Were Dead, Gudeman*[21]

A highland lad my love was born,

Lowland The lalland laws he held in scorn:

But he still was faithfu' to his clan,[22]

My gallant, braw John Highlandman.

Chorus

Sing hey my braw John Highlandman!

Sing ho my braw John Highlandman!

There's not a lad in a' the lan'

Was match for my John Highlandman!

kilt With his philibeg, an' tartan plaid,

good Highland sword An' guid Claymore down by his side,

ensnare The ladies' hearts he did trepan,

---

[21] As shown by Dick, p. 224, the tune is from a lively folk ballad to be sung "cheerily." One set for this tune (David Herd, *Scots Songs,* 1769) shows its rollicking irreverence:

> I wish that you were Dead, goodman,
>
> And a green sod on your Head, goodman,
>
> *bestow* That I might ware my widowhead
>
> Upon a ranting Highlandman!

That the widow should sing her lament to this tempo and in this mood shows that the "hearty can" has provided the comfort desired (stanza 6 of her song) and that Burns wanted no genteel sentimentality to detract from the riotous spirit of this poem.

[22] A reference evidently to the English laws enacted after the uprising of 1745–1746 to break up the clans. The outlaw's continuing to wear the clan dress (see the next stanza) was itself against the law.

My gallant, braw John Highlandman.
    Sing hey &c.

We ranged a' from Tweed to Spey,[23]
An' liv'd like lords an' ladies gay:
For a lalland face he feared none,
My gallant, braw John Highlandman.
    Sing hey &c.

They banish'd him beyond the sea,
But ere the bud was on the tree,
Adown my cheeks the pearls ran,
Embracing my John Highlandman.
    Sing hey &c.

But, Och! they catch'd him at the last,
And bound him in a dungeon fast.
My curse upon them every one,
They've hang'd my braw John Highlandman!
    Sing hey &c.

And now a widow I must mourn
The pleasures that will ne'er return;
No comfort but a hearty can   *cup*
When I think on John Highlandman.
    Sing hey &c.

- 4 -

RECITATIVO[24]

A pigmy Scraper on a Fiddle,
Wha us'd to trystes an' fairs to driddle,   *cattle markets; totter*

---

[23] The first is a river on the border between Northumberland and Berwick; the second is a river in Inverness—in other words, "from the south to the north of Scotland."

[24] The two stanzas of this recitative are in Burns' favorite verse form, the famous Habbie Simson, Standard Scots, Standard Habbie, or simply the Burns Stanza, which has

buxom　　Her strappan limb an' gausy middle,
　　　　　　(He reach'd nae higher)
pierced; sieve　Had hol'd his heartie like a riddle,
　　　　　　An' blawn't on fire.

haunch; eye　Wi' hand on hainch and upward e'e
hummed his scale　He croon'd his gamut, one, two, three,
　　　　　　Then in an arioso key,
　　　　　　　The wee Apollo
　　　　　　Set off wi' allegretto glee
jig-song alone　　His giga solo—

- 4 -

Song

Tune: *Whistle owre the lave o't*

reach; wipe　Let me ryke up to dight that tear,
　　　　　　An' go wi' me an' be my Dear,
　　　　　　An' then your every care an' fear
over the rest of it　May whistle owre the lave o't.[25]

Chorus

　　　　　　I am a Fiddler to my trade,
　　　　　　An' a' the tunes that e'er I play'd,
　　　　　　The sweetest still to wife or maid
　　　　　　　Was Whistle owre the lave o't.

harvest feasts; we'll　At kirns an' weddins we'se be there,
so nicely as　An' O sae nicely's we will fare!

---

very ancient Scots progenitors but became very popular after an early eighteenth-century printing of "The Piper of Kilbarchan, or, The Epitaph of Habbie Simson" by Robert Sempill of Beltree.

[25] The refrain here and in its source has a connotation of "fornification," or "loss of maidenhead" (chorus and stanza 3). But in other lines of this song, it means something like, "we won't give a damn" or "can go to the devil."

We'll bowse about till Dadie care   *booze*
   Sing Whistle owre the lave o't.
     I am &c.

Sae merrily's the banes we'll pyke,   *So merrily as; bones; pick*
An' sun oursels about the dyke;   *wall*
An' at our leisure when ye like
   We'll whistle owre the lave o't!
     I am &c.

But bless me wi' your heav'n o' charms,
An' while I kittle hair on thairms,[26]   *tickle; catgut*
Hunger, cauld, an' a' sic-harms
   May whistle owre the lave o't.
     I am &c.

– 5 –

RECITATIVO

Her charms had struck a sturdy Caird,   *Tinker*
   As weel as poor gutscraper;
He taks the Fiddler by the beard,
   An' draws a roosty rapier—   *rusty*
He swoor by a' was swearing worth
   To speet him like a Pliver,   *spit; Plover*
Unless he would from that time forth
   Relinquish her for ever.
Wi' ghastly e'e poor Tweedledee   *eye*
   Upon his hunkers bended,   *haunches*
An' pray'd for grace wi' ruefu' face,
   An' sae the quarrel ended.
But tho' his little heart did grieve,
   When round the Tinkler prest her,   *Tinker*

---

[26] Since "thairms" also means in Scots the human belly, Burns probably intended a sexual double meaning.

219

snigger He feign'd to snirtle in his sleeve
          When thus the Caird address'd her—

- 5 -

Song

Tune: *Clout the Caudron*

My bonie lass I work in brass,
    A Tinkler is my station;
I've travell'd round all Christian ground
    In this my occupation;
I've taen the gold an' been enrolled
    In many a noble squadron;
But vain they search'd when off I march'd[27]
mend the cauldron   To go an' clout the cauldron.[28]
    I've ta'en the gold &c.

Despise that shrimp, that wither'd imp,
capering   With a' his noise an' cap'rin,
An' take a share wi' those that bear
tinker's bag of tools   The budget and the apron!
cup; hope   And by that stowp, my faith an' houpe!
whisky   And by that dear Keilbaigie,[29]
If e'er ye want, or meet wi' scant,
wet my throat   May I ne'er weet my craigie!
    And by that Stowp, &c.

---

[27] The tinker is a "bounty-jumper."

[28] To those who know the old ballads set to this tune and indeed the widespread use of receptacles as symbols of female sexual organs, this phrase has bawdy overtones. In at least three English seventeenth-century versions, a lady persuades her lover to disguise himself as a tinker so that he can come to "clout her cauldron" or "mend both pot and pan." Burns used the tune for a bawdy poem, "The Fornicator," found on p. 286.

[29] Burns's note in the manuscript: "A peculiar sort of Whiskie so called: favorite with Poosie Nansie's Clubs."

RECITATIVO

The Caird prevail'd—th' unblushing fair
  In his embraces sunk,
Partly wi' Love o'ercome sae sair,   *sore*
  An' partly she was drunk:
Sir Violino with an air
  That show'd a man o' spunk,
Wish'd unison between the pair,
  An' made the bottle clunk
    To their health that night.

But hurchin Cupid shot a shaft,   *urchin*
  That play'd a dame[30] a shavie—   *trick*
The fiddler rak'd her fore and aft,[31]
  Behint the chicken cavie: *coop*
Her lord, a Wight of Homer's craft,[32]
  Tho' limpan wi' the Spavie,   *limping; spavin*
He hirpl'd up an' lap like daft,   *limped; leapt*
  An' shor'd them Dainty Davie[33]   *offered*
    O' boot that night.   *besides (to boot)*

---

[30] One of the three doxies in the bard's entourage (see chorus of Song 6 and Recitativo 7, line 12).

[31] The earlier version called "Love and Liberty" has "A Sailor" instead of "The fiddler." When he decided to resolve the rivalry between the caird and the fiddler by giving the latter one of the bard's women, he left the nautical imagery in the line originally intended for the sailor.

[32] Burns's manuscript note: "Homer is allowed to be the eldest Ballad-singer on record."

[33] Burns alludes to the old ballad called "Dainty Davie" about a young Scots lad named David; a woman sends him to bed with her daughter to prevent his detection by pursuing soldiers. The girl, of course, proves to be with child. Burns merely means that the bard is, like the mother in the ballad, willing to offer up a female. He also suggests by this allusion that the bard has caught the fiddler and the woman who has jilted him in the act of fornication. For the tune, see p. 283.

He was a care-defying blade,
enlisted   As ever Bacchus listed!
Tho' Fortune sair upon him laid,
      His heart, she ever miss'd it.
He had no wish but—to be glad,
thirsted   Nor want but—when he thristed;
He hated nought but—to be sad,
      An' thus the Muse suggested
song   His sang that night.

– 6 –

Song
Tune: *For a' that, an' a' that*[34]
I am a bard of no regard
      Wi' gentle folks an' a' that,
staring crowd   But Homer like the glowran byke,
      Frae town to town I draw that.

Chorus
For a' that, an' a' that,
much as   An' twice as muckle's a' that,
I've lost but ane, I've twa behin',
      I've wife eneugh for a' that.

pond   I never drank the Muses' stank,
      Castalia's burn, an' a' that;
froths   But there it streams an' richly reams,
      My Helicon I ca' that.
      For a' that &c.

Great love I bear to a' the fair,
      Their humble slave an' a' that;

---

[34] For this tune, see p. 280.

But lordly will, I hold it still
  A mortal sin to thraw that.   *thwart*
    For a' that &c.

In raptures sweet this hour we meet
  Wi' mutual love an' a' that;
But for how lang the flie may stang,   *fly; sting*
  Let inclination law that!   *determine*
    For a' that &c.

Their tricks an' craft hae put me daft,
  They've ta'en me in, an' a' that,
But clear your decks, an' here's the Sex
  I like the jads for a' that.   *jades*
    For a' that, an' a' that.
      An' twice as muckle's a' that,
    My dearest bluid to do them guid,
     They're welcome till't for a' that.   *to it*

– 7 –

RECITATIVO

So sung the bard, and Nansie's waws   *walls*
Shook with a thunder of applause,
  Re-echo'd from each mouth!
They toom'd their pocks, they pawn'd their duds, *emptied their bags*
They scarcely left to coor their fuds,   *cover their buttocks*
  To quench their lowan drouth.   *burning thirst*
Then owre again the jovial thrang   *throng*
  The Poet did request
To lowse his pack an' wale a sang,   *loose; choose a song*
  A ballad o' the best.
    He, rising, rejoicing,
     Between his twa Deborahs,
    Looks round him an' found them
     Impatient for the Chorus:—

223

– 7 –

Song

Tune: *Jolly Mortals, fill your glasses*

See the smoking bowl before us!
Mark our jovial ragged ring!
Round and round take up the Chorus,
And in raptures let us sing—

Chorus

A fig for those by law protected!
Liberty's a glorious feast!
Courts for cowards were erected,
Churches built to please the priest.

What is title, what is treasure,
What is reputation's care?
If we lead a life of pleasure,
'Tis no matter how or where!
A fig &c.

With the ready trick and fable
Round we wander all the day;
And at night, in barn or stable,
Hug our doxies on the hay.
A fig &c.

Does the train-attended carriage
Thro' the country lighter rove?
Does the sober bed of marriage
Witness brighter scenes of love?
A fig for &c.

Life is all a variorum,
We regard not how it goes;

Let them prate about decorum,
  Who have character to lose.
    A fig for &c.

Here's to budgets, bags, and wallets!
  Here's to all the wandering train!
Here's our ragged brats and callets!
  One and all cry out, Amen!
      A fig for those by law protected!
       Liberty's a glorious feast!
      Courts for Cowards were erected,
       Churches built to please the priest.

TAM O' SHANTER[1]

A Tale

(1790, 1791)[2]

Of Brownyis and of Bogillis full is this Buke.

GAWIN DOUGLAS[3]

market-stall keepers	When chapman billies leave the street,
thirsty (droughty)	And drouthy neebors neebors meet;
	As market-days are wearing late,
road	An' folk begin to tak the gate;
ale	While we sit bousing at the nappy,

---

[1] Burns's prose version of this tale, written before he wrote the poem, presents the folk tale associated with the ruins of Kirk Alloway ("well known to be a favorite haunt of the devil and the devil's friends and emissaries," *Letters,* II, 22), which lies on the road from Ayr to Maypole, less than a mile south of Burns's birthplace (see Map). "On a market day in the town of Ayr, a farmer from Carrick, and consequently whose way lay by the very gate of Aloway kirk-yard, in order to cross the river Doon at the old bridge, which is about two or three hundred yards farther on than the said gate, had been detained by his business till by the time he reached Aloway it was the wizard hour, between night and morning.

"Though he was terrified with a blaze streaming from the kirk, yet as it is a well known fact, that to turn back on these occasions is running by far the greatest risk of mischief, he prudently advanced on his road. When he had reached the gate of the kirk-yard, he was surprised and entertained, through the ribs and arches of an old gothic window which still faces the highway, to see a dance of witches merrily footing it round their old sooty blackguard master, who was keeping them all alive with the power of his bagpipe. The farmer stopping his horse to observe them a little, could plainly descry the faces of many old women of his acquaintance and neighbourhood. How the gentleman was dressed, tradition does not say; but the ladies were all in their smocks; and one of them happening unluckily to have a smock which was considerably too short to answer all the purpose of that piece of dress, our farmer was so tickled that he involuntarily burst out, with a loud laugh, 'Weel luppen, Maggy wi' the short sark!' and recollecting himself, instantly spurred his horse to the top of his speed. I need not mention the

An' getting fou and unco happy,   *drunk (full); very*
We think na on the lang Scots miles,
The mosses, waters, slaps, and styles,   *bogs; pools; openings in*
That lie between us and our hame,   *a hedge or wall; stiles*
10 Whare sits our sulky, sullen dame,
Gathering her brows like gathering storm,
Nursing her wrath to keep it warm.

This truth fand honest Tam o' Shanter,[4]   *found*
As he frae Ayr ae night did canter: *one*
(Auld Ayr, wham ne'er a town surpasses,
For honest men and bonie lasses).

O Tam, had'st thou but been sae wise,
As taen thy ain wife Kate's advice!   *to have taken; own*
She tauld thee weel thou was a skellum,   *wretch*
20 A blethering, blustering, drunken blellum;   *A nonsense-talking; blabber-mouth*

---

universally known fact, that no diabolical power can pursue you beyond the middle of a running stream. Lucky it was for the poor farmer that the river Doon was so near, for notwithstanding the speed of his horse, which was a good one, against he reached the middle of the arch of the bridge, and consequently the middle of the stream, the pursuing, vengeful hags were so close at his heels, that one of them actually sprung to seize him: but it was too late; nothing was on her side of the stream but the horse's tail, which immediately gave way to her infernal grip, as if blasted by a stroke of lightning; but the farmer was beyond her reach. However, the unsightly, tailless condition of the vigorous steed was to the last hours of the noble creature's life, an awful warning to the Carrick farmers, not to stay too late in Ayr markets" (*Letters,* II, 23–24).

[2] First published in two Scottish periodicals in March 1791, then one month later as a footnote in *Antiquities of Scotland* by Francis Grose (for whom Burns had written it), and finally in the third edition of Burns's *Poems,* 1793, on which HH generally based their text (Egerer, pp. 35–36). The following text is taken from HH.

[3] Burns' epigraph is from one of the greatest achievements in the early renaissance of Scottish literature, Gavin Douglas' translation (1513) of Virgil's *Aeneid.* More particularly it comes from one of the original prologues which Douglas wrote for each book ("Proloug" VI, line 18).

[4] Tom of the farm of Shanter in Carrick, the Ayrshire district south of the River Doon.

That frae November till October,
Ae market-day thou was nae sober;
each meal-grinding That ilka melder wi' the miller,
silver Thou sat as lang as thou had siller;
shod That ev'ry naig was ca'd a shoe on,
drunk The smith and thee gat roaring fou on,
That at the Lord's house, even on Sunday,
Thou drank wi' Kirkton Jean till Monday.
She prophesied, that, late or soon,
30 Thou would be found deep drown'd in Doon,
wizards; dark Or catch'd wi' warlocks in the mirk
By Alloway's auld, haunted kirk.

makes; weep Ah! gentle dames, it gars me greet,
To think how monie counsels sweet,
How monie lengthen'd, sage advices
The husband frae the wife despises!

But to our tale:—Ae market-night,
just Tam had got planted unco right,
Right near a hearth Fast by an ingle, bleezing finely,
foaming ale 40 Wi' reaming swats, that drank divinely;
Cobbler And at his elbow, Souter Johnie,
thirsty His ancient, trusty, drouthy cronie:
loved Tam lo'ed him like a very brither;
drunk They had been fou for weeks thegither.
The night drave on wi' sangs and clatter;
still And ay the ale was growing better:
The landlady and Tam grew gracious
Wi' secret favours, sweet and precious:
funniest The Souter tauld his queerest stories;
50 The landlord's laugh was ready chorus:
roar The storm without might rair and rustle,
Tam did na mind the storm a whistle.

Care, mad to see a man sae happy,
E'en drown'd himsel amang the nappy.   *ale*
As bees flee hame wi' lades o' treasure,   *fly; loads*
The minutes wing'd their way wi' pleasure:
Kings may be blest but Tam was glorious,
O'er a' the ills o' life victorious!

But pleasures are like poppies spread:
60 You seize the flow'r, its bloom is shed;
Or like the snow falls in the river,[5]
A moment white—then melts for ever;
Or like the borealis race,
That flit ere you can point their place;
Or like the rainbow's lovely form
Evanishing amid the storm.
Nae man can tether time or tide;
The hour approaches Tam maun ride: *must*
That hour, o' night's black arch the key-stane,
70 That dreary hour Tam mounts his beast in;
And sic a night he taks the road in,
As ne'er poor sinner was abroad in.

The wind blew as 'twad blawn its last;   *if it would have blown*
The rattling showers rose on the blast;
The speedy gleams the darkness swallow'd;
Loud, deep, and lang the thunder bellow'd:
That night, a child might understand,
The Deil had business on his hand.   *Devil*

Weel mounted on his gray mare Meg,
80 A better never lifted leg,
Tam skelpit on thro' dub and mire,   *drove; puddle*

---

[5] An occasional Scots construction for "like the snow *that* falls in the river."

Despising wind, and rain, and fire;
Sometimes; good   Whiles holding fast his guid blue bonnet,
humming; song   Whiles croonin o'er some auld Scots sonnet,
gazing   Whiles glow'ring round wi' prudent cares,
ghosts   Lest bogles catch him unawares:
Kirk-Alloway was drawing nigh,
owls   Whare ghaists and houlets nightly cry.

By this time he was cross the ford,
peddler smothered   90   Whare in the snaw the chapman smoor'd;
birches; huge stone   And past the birks and meikle stane,
broke his   Whare drunken Charlie brak's neck-bane;
gorse   And thro' the whins, and by the cairn,
child   Whare hunters fand the murder'd bairn;
hawthorn; above   And near the thorn, aboon the well,
Whare Mungo's mither hang'd hersel.
Before him Doon pours all his floods;
The doubling storm roars thro' the woods;
The lightnings flash from pole to pole;
100   Near and more near the thunders roll:
When, glimmering thro' the groaning trees,
blaze   Kirk-Alloway seem'd in a bleeze,
each crevice   Thro' ilka bore the beams were glancing,
And loud resounded mirth and dancing.

Inspiring bold John Barleycorn,
What dangers thou canst make us scorn!
weak beer   Wi' tippenny, we fear nae evil;
whisky   Wi' usquabae, we'll face the Devil!
ale so foamed   The swats sae ream'd in Tammie's noddle,
not a quarter-penny about devils   110   Fair play, he car'd na deils a boddle.
very sorely   But Maggie stood, right sair astonish'd
Till, by the heel and hand admonish'd,
She ventur'd forward on the light;
uncommon   And, vow! Tam saw an unco sight!

Warlocks and witches in a dance:
Nae cotillion, brent new frae France,   *brand*
But hornpipes, jigs, strathspeys, and reels,
Put life and mettle in their heels,
A winnock-bunker in the east,   *window-recess*
120 There sat Auld Nick, in shape o' beast;
A tousie tyke, black, grim, and large,   *shaggy dog*
To gie them music was his charge: *give*
He screw'd the pipes and gart them skirl,   *squeezed the bagpipes; made; squeal*
Till roof and rafters a' did dirl.   *rattle, tremble*
Coffins stood round, like open presses,   *cupboards*
That shaw'd the dead in their last dresses;
And, by some devilish cantraip sleight,   *magic trick*
Each in its cauld hand held a light:
By which heroic Tam was able
130 To note upon the haly table,
A murderer's banes, in gibbet-airns;   *bones; -irons*
Twa span-lang, wee, unchristen'd bairns;   *Two nine-inch-long; children*
A thief new-cutted frae a rape—   *rope*
Wi' his last gasp his gab did gape;   *mouth*
Five tomahawks wi' bluid red-crusted;   *blood*
Five scymitars wi' murder crusted;
A garter which a babe had strangled;
A knife a father's throat had mangled—
Whom his ain son o' life bereft—
140 The grey-hairs yet stack to the heft;   *stuck; handle*
Wi' mair of horrible and awefu',
Which even to name wad be unlawfu'.[6]

---

[6] All earlier versions contain the following four lines, which Burns wisely removed
for the text printed in *Poems, 1793:*

Three Lawyers' tongues, turned inside out,
Wi' lies seamed like a beggar's clout;   *garment*
Three Priests' hearts, rotten black as muck,
Lay stinking, vile, in every neuk."   *corner*

gazed	As Tammie glowr'd, amaz'd, and curious,
	The mirth and fun grew fast and furious;
	The piper loud and louder blew,
	The dancers quick and quicker flew,
took hands	They reel'd, they set, they cross'd, they cleekit,
each old hag sweated and steamed	Till ilka carlin swat, and reekit,
threw off; clothes	And coost her duddies to the wark,
danced; shirt, smock	150 And linket at it in her sark!

these; girls	Now Tam, O Tam! had thae been queans,
	A' plump and strapping in their teens!
greasy flannel	Their sarks, instead o' creeshie flannen,
hundred (i.e., very finely woven)	Been snaw-white seventeen hunder linen!—
These pants	Thir breeks o' mine, my only pair,
	That ance were plush, o' guid blue hair,
buttocks	I wad hae gi'en them off my hurdies
one glance; birds	For ae blink o' the bonie burdies!

old women; odd	But wither'd beldams, auld and droll,
withered; would wean (by causing fright)	160 Rigwoodie hags wad spean a foal,
Jumping; crooked cane	Louping and flinging on a crummock,
	I wonder did na turn thy stomach!

knew; well	But Tam kend what was what fu' brawlie:
pretty; choice	There was ae winsome wench and wawlie,
corps	That night enlisted in the core,
known	Lang after kend on Carrick[7] shore
	(For monie a beast to dead she shot,
caused to perish	An' perish'd monie a bonie boat,
grain; barley	And shook baith meikle corn and bear,
	170 And kept the country-side in fear).
short smock; coarse linen	Her cutty sark, o' Paisley harn,

---

[7] See footnote 4.

That while a lassie she had worn,
In longitude tho' sorely scanty,
It was her best, and she was vauntie. . . .8   *proud of it*
Ah! little kend thy reverend grannie,
That sark she coft for her wee Nannie,   *bought*
Wi' twa pund Scots9 ('twas a' her riches),   *two pounds; all*
Wad ever grac'd a dance of witches!   *Would; have graced*

But here my Muse her wing maun cour,   *must lower*
180 Sic flights are far beyond her power:
To sing how Nannie lap and flang   *leapt; kicked*
(A souple jad she was and strang),   *supple girl*
And how Tam stood like ane bewitch'd,   *one*
And thought his very een enrich'd,   *eyes*
Even Satan glowr'd, and fidg'd fu' fain,   *stared; fidgeted very eagerly*
And hotched and blew wi' might and main;   *jerked*
Till first ae caper, syne anither,   *one; then*
Tam tint his reason a' thegither,   *lost; altogether*
And roars out: "Weel done, Cutty-sark!"
190 And in an instant all was dark;
And scarcely had he Maggie rallied,
When out the hellish legion sallied.

As bees bizz out wi' angry fyke,   *fret*
When plundering herds assail their byke;   *herd-boys; hive*
As open pussie's mortal foes,   *begin the hare's*
When, pop! she starts before their nose;
As eager runs the market-crowd,
When 'Catch the thief!' resounds aloud:
So Maggie runs, the witches follow,
200 Wi' monie an eldritch skriech and hollo.   *unearthly*

---

8 Burns's mark of ellipsis.
9 Equals three shillings and sixpence in English money.

Ah, Tam! Ah, Tam! thou'll get thy
    deserving   fairin!
In hell they'll roast thee like a herrin!
In vain thy Kate awaits thy comin!
Kate soon will be a woefu' woman!
Now, do thy speedy utmost, Meg,
And win the key-stane of the brig;
There, at them thou thy tail may toss,
A running stream they dare na cross!
But ere the key-stane she could make,
The fient a tail she had to shake;
For Nannie, far before the rest,
Hard upon noble Maggie prest,
And flew at Tam wi' furious ettle;
But little wist she Maggie's mettle!
Ae spring brought off her master hale,
But left behind her ain grey tail:
The carlin claught her by the rump,
And left poor Maggie scarce a stump.

Now, wha this tale o' truth shall read,
Ilk man, and mother's son, take heed:
Whene'er to drink you are inclin'd,
Or cutty sarks run in your mind,
Think! ye may buy the joys o'er dear:
Remember Tam o' Shanter's mare.

Margin glosses:

- *deserving* (fairin)
- *-stone; bridge* (key-stane of the brig)
- *No tail had she* 210 (The fient a tail she had to shake)
- *aim, intention* (ettle)
- *knew* (wist)
- *whole* (hale)
- *own* (ain)
- *clutched* (claught)
- 220 (Ilk man, and mother's son)
- *short shirts, smocks* (cutty sarks)

234

SONGS

In the years just before the Romantic period when one of the main literary interests was the recovery of ballads (traditionary verse narratives like those collected by Thomas Percy for *Reliques of Ancient Poetry* and Walter Scott for *Minstrelsy of the Scottish Border*), Burns after the middle of 1787 set about the allied but unprecedented task of collecting all the songs of a nation. And because of his broad knowledge in this area, his enthusiasm, and his creative genius, he succeeded in the brief nine years remaining to him better than anyone else had before or has after him. His main concern was to preserve all the tunes, or "airs" as Burns called them, heard but often unrecorded in Scotland. Many of the old tunes lacked words, because they were purely instrumental dance tunes based on the melodies of old songs whose words were lost except for their titles, or folk songs whose words survived only partially, a few phrases or part of a chorus. Therefore, since Burns correctly believed that a tune could only be preserved as a living part of a broadly-based culture if people could sing it, he completed the fragmentary surviving lyrics for folk songs and composed lyrics for dance tunes. The result is over three-hundred and fifty song lyrics composed in large part or entirely by Burns, a body of song lyrics unparalleled in volume and general excellence and what many critics think constitute his most important literary achievement. Burns is, I believe, unique as a writer of lyrics in another way: he would appear to be the only major poet who wrote lyrics for existing tunes.

The main publication involved in this undertaking was James Johnson's *Scots Musical Museum,* which published six-hundred songs in six volumes between 1787 and 1803, more than half of all Burns's songs among them. Burns met Johnson, an almost illiterate engraver and enthusiast of Scots song, in Edinburgh at a social-singing club called the Crochallan Fencibles, when the latter was about ready to publish the first volume of what he then thought would be a two-volume collection of two-hundred songs with both scores and lyrics. Johnson's project was uncommon, for as Burns's great song editor J. C. Dick estimates, somewhat but not very much too lowly, only some two-hundred Scots tunes with verses had been printed in several collections prior to this projected series.[1] Burns immediately warmed to the idea, convinced Johnson that there was enough material to treble the size of the venture, and in a short time became its real but unacknowledged editor by his gathering of old songs, his original lyrics, advice, and impetus. He proved so energetic, that when he died in 1796 just before the publication of the fifth volume, there was enough of his manuscript to provide almost half the contents of the final one. The *Scots Musical Museum* has remained the "standard collection of Scottish Song"[2] to this day.

Burns brought to this task not only a mind more full of information about Scots song than anyone else alive but a long habit of writing lyrics for folk and dance tunes. As his autobiographical letter shows (see Appendix B), the first verse he ever wrote was of this kind. But he printed only three songs in the first edition of his *Poems,* added only six more in the second, and only one more in the final enlargement of 1793. He seems to have considered his work in song in a radically different way than his work in non-musical poetry. His song writing and collecting was free, for he refused all payment, and it was anonymous, for he forbade almost all printed acknowledgment.

He would not, indeed could not, write a lyric without first being master of the tune for which it was intended.[3] Since Burns in writing lyrics invariably endeavored to fit the poetry to a tune which he could hum with perfect accuracy, it follows that, contrary to almost universal practice, his lyrics must be studied as they are sung to the tunes for which he wrote them. So studied, Burns metrical theories and practice will easily become apparent. In an age which required metrical regularity, he early developed ideas about prosody in relation to music

---

[1] Dick, p. xiii.

[2] *Ibid.,* p. xvi.

[3] *Letters,* II, 200–201.

which were far ahead of his time, going farther than Coleridge's use of
extrasyllabic lines in "Christabel." The difficulties of scansion which
students discover when studying Burns's songs improperly divorced
from music disappear when they study them with a score. Burns wrote
in his Commonplace Book in 1785:

> There is a certain irregularity in the old Scotch Songs, a redundancy of
> syllables with respect to that exactness of Accent & measure that the
> English Poetry requires, but which glides in, most melodiously with the
> respective tunes to which they are set. For instance, the fine old Song of
> "The Mill Mill O," to give it a plain prosaic reading it halts prodigiously
> out of measure; on the other hand, the Song set to the same tune in
> Bremner's collection of Scotch songs which begins "To Fanny fair
> could I impart" &c it is most exact measure, and yet, let them be both
> sung before a real Critic, one above the biasses of prejudice, but a thorough
> Judge of Nature,—how flat & spiritless will the last appear, how trite,
> and lamely methodical, compared with the wild-warbling cadence, the
> heart-moving melody of the first.—This particularly is the case with all
> those airs which end with a hypermetrical syllable.—There is a degree of
> wild irregularity in many of the compositions & Fragments which are
> daily sung to them by my compeers, the common people—a certain happy
> arrangement of old Scotch syllables, & yet, very frequently, nothing,
> not even like rhyme, or sameness of jingle at the ends of the lines.
> This has made me sometimes imagine that perhaps, it might be possible
> for a Scotch Poet, with a nice, judicious ear, to set compositions to many of
> our favorite airs, particularly that class of them mentioned above,
> independent of rhyme altogether.[4]

Although Burns never wrote unrimed lyrics, he did not hesitate to compose quite irregular lines when the music was enhanced by them. In
song he composed by units of length (measures) and matched the
phrasing of the lyric to the phrasing of the music.

---

[4] CW, I, 140-141.

Love

1 BUT WARILY TENT WHEN YE COME TO COURT ME[1]

(1793, 1799)

Lively

TUNE: *Whistle an' I'll come to ye, my lad.*

CHORUS: O, whistle an' I'll come to ye, my lad! O, whistle an' I'll come to ye, my lad! Tho' fa-ther an' mo-ther an' a' should gae mad, O, whistle an' I'll come to ye, my lad! But war-i-ly tent when ye come to court me, And come nae un-less the back-yett be a-jee; Syne up the back-stile, and let nae-bo-dy see, And come as ye were na com-in to me. And come as ye were na com-in to me.

Fine

D.C.

---

[1] The lyrics first appeared in George Thomson's *Select Collection of Original Scotish Airs*, 1799, No. 94. Burns wrote an inferior version for the same tune in *Scots Musical Museum*,

CHORUS

O, whistle an' I'll come to ye, my lad!
O, whistle an' I'll come to ye, my lad!
Tho' father an' mother an' a' should gae mad,
O, whistle an' I'll come to ye, my lad!

– 1 –

But warily tent when ye come to court me,	*take care*
And come nae unless the back-yet be a-jee;	*not; -gate; ajar*
Syne up the back-style, and let naebody see,	*Then*
And come as ye were na comin to me. (*bis*)	*as if*

– 2 –

At kirk, or at market, whene'er ye meet me,	
Gang by me as tho' that ye car'd na a flie;	*Go; fly*
But steal me a blink o' your bonie black e'e,	*glance; eye*
Yet look as ye were na looking to me. (*bis*)	*at me*

– 3 –

Ay vow and protest that ye care na for me,	*Always*
And whiles ye may lightly my beauty awee;	*sometimes; disparage; a bit*
But court na anither, tho' jokin ye be,	*not*
For fear that she wile your fancy frae me. (*bis*)	*beguile*

1788, No. 106, on which the score printed here is based. The chorus is traditional and is found in David Herd's manuscript collection of Scots lyrics, to which Burns probably had access.

2 SIMMER'S A PLEASANT TIME[1]

(ante April 1789, 1790)

Slow

TUNE: *Ay, waukin, O.*

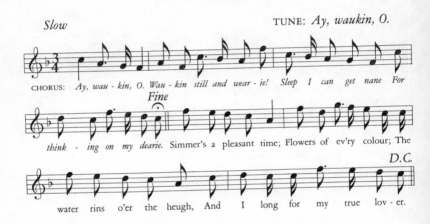

CHORUS: Ay, wau-kin, O. Wau-kin still and wear-ie! Sleep I can get nane For think-ing on my dearie. Simmer's a pleasant time; Flowers of ev'ry colour; The water rins o'er the heugh, And I long for my true lov-er.

---

[1] The lyric is from *Scots Musical Museum*, 1790, No. 213, but Dick thinks (p. 401) that the version of the tune Burns had in mind is from William Napier's *A Selection of Original Scots Songs* published the same year as Burns's lyrics in the *Museum*. Since Dick is usually right about such things, Napier's version is reproduced here. Burns clearly worked from a version of the traditional song, one of which is found in the manuscript collection of David Herd, which Burns probably had access to:

> *wet* O wat, wat and weary,
>   Sleep I can get nane
>   For thinking on my deary.
>   A' the night I wak,
>   A' the night I weary,
>   Sleep I can get nane
>   For thinking on my deary.

CHORUS
Ay, waukin, O.   *awake*
    Waukin still and wearie!
Sleep I can get nane
    For thinking on my dearie.

– 1 –

Simmer's a pleasant time;
    Flowers of ev'ry colour;
The water rins o'er the heugh,   *crag*
    And I long for my true lover.

– 2 –

When I sleep I dream,
    When I wauk I'm eerie,   *troubled*
Sleep I can get nane
    For thinking on my dearie.

– 3 –

Lanely night comes on,
    A' the lave are sleepin,   *rest*
I think on my bonie lad,
    And I blear my een wi' greetin.   *dim; eyes; weeping*

3 JOHN ANDERSON MY JO, JOHN[1]
(*ante* April 1789, 1790)

Slow

TUNE: *John Anderson my jo, John.*

John An - der - son my jo, John, When we were first ac - quent, Your
locks were like the rav - en, Your bon - ie brow was brent; But
now your brow is beld, John, Your locks are like the snaw, But
bless - ings on your fros - ty pow, John An - der - son my jo!

– I –

sweetheart   John Anderson my jo, John,
        When we were first acquent,
        Your locks were like the raven,
straight   Your bonie brow was brent;

---

[1] Burns published this song in *Scots Musical Museum*, 1790, No. 260. Several years later he said, with pointed litotes, "I think it not my worst" (*Letters,* II, 168). He evidently conceived the idea for it from a coarse pornographic song to the same tune which he himself perhaps collected and preserved (*Merry Muses of Caledonia,* ed. James Barke, *et al.;* see Bibliography). The old song records the provocative threats of a lusty wife to her older husband, who is increasingly inactive sexually.

But now your brow is beld, John,   *bald*
   Your locks are like the snaw,
But blessings on your frosty pow,   *pate (poll)*
   John Anderson my jo!

– 2 –

John Anderson my jo, John,
   We clamb the hill thegither;   *climbed*
And mony a cantie day, John,   *happy*
   We've had wi' ane anither:
Now we maun totter down, John,   *must*
   And hand in hand we'll go,
And sleep thegither at the foot,
   John Anderson my jo!

4 MY LOVE IS LIKE A RED, RED ROSE[1]

(? ; 1794, 1796)[2]

Moderate time   TUNE: *Major Graham.*

My luve is like a red, red rose, That's newly sprung in June: My luve is like

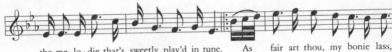

the me-lo-die that's sweetly play'd in tune.   As   fair art thou, my bonie lass,

So deep in luve am I, And I will luve thee still, my dear, Till a' the seas gang dry.

---

[1] This song can be taken as an example of Burns's genius at working together fragments from old songs to create a new one of surpassing beauty. To appreciate how derivative but how superior Burns's song is, one should study the many fragments of unsophisticated lyrics in broadsides earlier than this song to show how these phrases were in the air awaiting Burns's awakening touch (see HH, III, 402–406).

[2] The lyric appeared with a tune Burns had nothing to do with in 1794. The tune for which Burns wrote this song is called "Major Graham" and appeared with this lyric in *Scots Musical Museum,* 1796, No. 402. The popular tune, "Low Down in the Broom" (first printed in 1755), by which the lyric is now known, one which some think is superior to Burns's choice, was first associated with it in 1821 by Robert Archibald Smith, musical editor of *Scotish Minstrel* (Davidson Cook, " 'The Red, Red Rose' and its Tunes," *Burns Chronicle,* 2nd ser., IX, 1934, pp. 66–67).

– 1 –

My luve is like a red, red rose,
    That's newly sprung in June:
My luve is like the melodie,
    That's sweetly play'd in tune.
As fair art thou, my bonie lass,
    So deep in luve am I,
And I will luve thee still, my dear,
    Till a' the seas gang dry.   *80*

– 2 –

Till a' the seas gang dry, my dear,
    And the rocks melt wi' the sun!
And I will luve thee still, my dear,
    While the sands o' life shall run.
And fare-the-weel, my only luve,
    And fare-thee-weel a while!
And I will come again, my luve,
    Tho' it were ten thousand mile.

5 AS I GAED DOWN THE WATER-SIDE[1]

(*ante* April 1789, 1790)

Slow   TUNE: *Ca' the yowes.*

Ca' the yowes to the knowes, Ca' them whare the heath-er grows,

Ca' them whare the bur-nie rowes, My bon-ie dear-ie.

CHORUS

Drive; ewes; knolls   Ca' the yowes to the knowes,
                Ca' them whare the heather grows,
brook; rolls   Ca' them whare the burnie rowes,
                My bonie dearie.

– I –

went   As I gaed down the water-side,
                There I met my shepherd lad:
wrapped (rolled)   He row'd me sweetly in his plaid,
                An' he ca'd me his dearie.

---

[1] Burns preserved this old song from oblivion by recording it from the singing of an acquaintance in about 1787, expanding the old first into the present stanzas 1–2, composing stanzas 5–6 as additions, and printing the result in *Scots Musical Museum*, 1790, No. 264. Burns called it a "beautiful song . . . in the true old Scotch taste" (Dick, p. 389). The chorus and verses are sung to the same tune.

- 2 -

"Will ye gang down the water-side,   *go*
And see the waves sae sweetly glide
Beneath the hazels spreading wide?
   The moon it shines fu' clearly."

- 3 -

"I was bred up in nae sic school,
My shepherd lad to play the fool,
And a' the day to sit in dool,   *sorrow*
   And nae body to see me."

- 4 -

"Ye sall get gowns and ribbons meet,
Cauf-leather shoon upon your feet,   *Calf-*
And in my arms thou'lt lie and sleep,
   An' ay sall be my dearie."

- 5 -

"If ye'll but stand to what ye've said,
I'se gang wi' you my shepherd lad,   *I'll go*
And ye may row me in your plaid,
   And I sall be your dearie."

- 6 -

"While waters wimple to the sea,   *meander*
While day blinks in the lift sae hie,   *shines; sky; high*
Till clay-cauld death sall blin' my e'e,   *blind; eye*
   Ye sall be my dearie."

6 O MARY, AT THY WINDOW BE[1]

(*ante* 1793; 1800, 1903)[2]

Andante   TUNE: *Duncan Davison.*

O, Ma-ry at thy window be, It is the wish'd, the trysted hour! Those
smiles and glances let me see, That make the miser's treasure poor. How
blithely wad I bide the stoure, A weary slave frae sun to sun, Could
I the rich re-ward se-cure The love-ly Ma-ry Mor-i-son.

– I –

O Mary, at thy window be,

appointed   It is the wish'd, the trysted hour!

Those smiles and glances let me see,

That make the miser's treasure poor.

endure the strife   How blithely wad I bide the stoure,

---

[1] The subject of this lyric has not certainly been identified (HH, III, 499–500), but the song was evidently composed for an early sweetheart because he calls it disparagingly "one of my juvenile works" in 1793 (*Letters,* II, 152).

[2] The lyrics were printed by Burns's first editor in 1800 and for the first time with the music assigned by Burns in Dick (p. 58).

A weary slave frae sun to sun,
　　Could I the rich reward secure—
The lovely Mary Morison.

– 2 –

Yestreen, when to the trembling string　　*Last night*
　　The dance gaed thro' the lighted ha',　　*went; hall*
To thee my fancy took its wing,
　　I sat, but neither heard nor saw:
　　Tho' this was fair, and that was braw,　　*fine*
And yon the toast of a' the town,　　*that other one*
　　I sigh'd and said amang them a';—
"Ye are na Mary Morison!"

– 3 –

O Mary, canst thou wreck his peace
　　Wha for thy sake wad gladly die?
Or canst thou break that heart of his
　　Whase only faut is loving thee?　　*fault*
　　If love for love thou wilt na gie,　　*give*
At least be pity to me shown;
　　A thought ungentle canna be
The thought o' Mary Morison.

7 YESTREEN I HAD A PINT O' WINE[1]

(1790?; 1801, 1903)[2]

Merrily

TUNE: *Banks of Banna.*

Yes - treen I had a pint o' wine, A place where bo - dy saw na; Yes - treen lay on this breast o' mine The gow - den locks of An - na. The hun - gry Jew in wil - der - ness Re - joicing o'er his man - na Was naething to my hi - ney bliss Up - on the lips of An - na.

---

[1] Burns wrote this song about sexual intercourse for Anna Parks, niece of the landlady of The Globe Tavern, Dumfries; she bore Burns a daughter in 1791. Burns never intended to publish it in its present form, although in 1793 he called the tune "a Heavenly air" and his song "the best love-song I ever composed in my life" (*Letters,* II, 168).

[2] The lyrics were first published in a chapbook (Egerer, p. 86) and not until Dick with the music that Burns assigned them.

– 1 –

Yestreen I had a pint o' wine,   *Last night*
  A place where body saw na;   *nobody saw*
Yestreen lay on this breast o' mine
  The gowden locks of Anna.   *golden*
The hungry Jew in wilderness
  Rejoicing o'er his manna
Was naething to my hiney bliss   *honey*
  Upon the lips of Anna.

– 2 –

Ye monarchs take the east and west
  Frae Indus to Savannah;
Gie me within my straining grasp   *Give*
  The melting form of Anna:
There I'll despise imperial charms,
  An Empress or Sultana,
While dying raptures in her arms
  I give and take wi' Anna!

– 3 –

Awa, thou flaunting god of day!
  Awa, thou pale Diana!
Ilk star, gae hide thy twinkling ray,
  When I'm to meet my Anna!
Come, in thy raven plumage, Night!
  (Sun, moon, and stars, withdrawn a'),
And bring an angel-pen to write
  My transports with my Anna!

– 4 –

The kirk an' state may join, an' tell
  To do sic things I maunna: *must not*
The kirk an' state may gae to hell,

And I'll gae to my Anna.

eye She is the sunshine o' my e'e

without To live but her I canna:

Had I on earth but wishes three,

The first should be my Anna.

Courtship and Marriage

8 WHAT CAN A YOUNG LASSIE?
(? , 1792)[1]

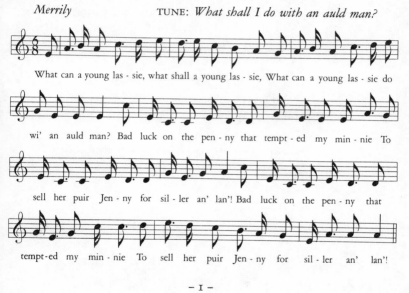

Merrily

TUNE: *What shall I do with an auld man?*

What can a young las-sie, what shall a young las-sie, What can a young las-sie do wi' an auld man? Bad luck on the pen-ny that tempt-ed my min-nie To sell her puir Jen-ny for sil-ler an' lan'! Bad luck on the pen-ny that tempt-ed my min-nie To sell her puir Jen-ny for sil-ler an' lan'!

– I –

What can a young lassie, what shall a young
    lassie,
   What can a young lassie do wi' an auld man?
Bad luck on the penny that tempted my minnie   } *mother*
   To sell her puir Jenny for siller an' lan'! (*bis*)   } *poor; money (silver); land*

---

[1] Published in *Scots Musical Museum*, No. 316. It is evidently entirely original.

– 2 –

He's always compleenin frae mornin to e'enin;
coughs; limps about   He hoasts and he hirples the weary day lang:
stupid; listless   He's doylt and he's dozin; his blude it is frozen, ⎫
O, dreary's the night wi' a crazy auld man! (*bis*) ⎭

– 3 –

grumbles   He hums and he hankers, he frets and he cankers,
I never can please him, do a' that I can:
He's peevish an' jealous of a' the young fellows: ⎫
woe   O, dool on the day I met wi' an auld man! (*bis*) ⎭

– 4 –

My auld auntie Katie upon me taks pity,
I'll do my endeavour to follow her plan:
I'll cross him and wrack him, until I heartbreak
   him, ⎫
And then his auld brass will buy me a new
   pan. (*bis*) ⎭

9 IN SIMMER, WHEN THE HAY WAS MAWN

(? , 1792)[1]

Rather slow

TUNE: *The country lass.*

In sim - mer, when the hay was mawn And corn wav'd green in
il - ka field, While clav - er blooms white o'er the lea, And ro - ses blaw in
il - ka bield, Blythe Bes - sie in the milk - ing shiel, Says
"I'll be wed, come o't what will"; Out spake a dame in
wrinkled eild: — "O' guid ad - vise - ment comes nae ill."

– I –

In simmer, when the hay was mawn
    And corn wav'd green in ilka field,   *every*
    While claver blooms white o'er the lea,   *clover; meadow*
    And roses blaw in ilka bield,   *blow; sheltered place*

---

[1] This original lyric (*Letters,* II, 267) was first printed in *Scots Musical Museum,* No. 366.

shed

Blythe Bessie in the milking shiel,
Says—"I'll be wed, come o't what will";
Out spake a dame in wrinkled eild:—

Some good advice · "O' guid advisement comes nae ill.

- 2 -

many a one · "It's ye hae wooers mony ane,
And lassie, ye're but young, ye ken;
cautiously choose · Then wait a wee, and cannie wale
well-stocked kitchen; parlor · A routhie butt, a routhie ben:
There's Johnie of the Buskie-Glen,
full; cow shed · Fu' is his barn, fu' is his byre:
Take this frae me, my bonie hen:—
kindles · It's plenty beets the luver's fire."

- 3 -

"For Johnie o' the Buskie-Glen
do not; fly · I dinna care a single flie:
crops; cattle (kine) · He lo'es sae weel his craps and kye,
He has nae luve to spare for me:
glance; eye · But blythe's the blink o' Robie's e'e,
know · And weel I wat he lo'es me dear:
One; would not give · Ae blink o' him I wadna gie
wealth · For Buskie-Glen and a' his gear."

- 4 -

fight · "O thoughtless lassie, life's a faught!
quietest way; sore · The canniest gate, the strife is sair;
always full-handed; fighting · But ay fu'-han't is fechtin best;
terrible · A hungry care's an unco care.
But some will spend, and some will spare,
must have · And wilfu' folk maun hae their will.
Syne as ye brew, my maiden fair,
ale · Keep mind that ye maun drink the yill."

"O, gear will buy me rigs o' land,   *strips*
  And gear will buy me sheep and kye!
But the tender heart o' leesome luve   *pleasant, lawful*
  The gowd and siller canna buy: *gold; silver*
  We may be poor, Robie and I;
Light is the burden luve lays on;
  Content and luve brings peace and joy—
What mair hae queens upon a throne?"

10 SHE'S FAIR AND FAUSE THAT CAUSES MY SMART

(1789?, 1792)[1]

Slowly

TUNE: *The lads of Leith.*

She's fair and fause that caus-es my smart; I lo'ed her mei-kle and lang; She's broken her vow, she's broken my heart, And I may e'en gae hang. A coof cam in wi' routh o' gear, And I hae tint my dear-est dear; But wo-man is but warld's gear, Sae let the bon-ie lass gang!

rall. . . . . tempo

---

[1] An unproved but likely story is that Burns wrote this in indignant response to news that the sweetheart of a dear friend had jilted him (HH, II, 371; *Letters,* I, 297–298); written to an old Scots tune and published in *Scots Musical Museum,* No. 398.

– 1 –

She's fair and fause that causes my smart;   *false*
    I lo'ed her meikle and lang;   *a great deal*
She's broken her vow, she's broken my heart,
    And I may e'en gae hang.   *even go*
A coof came in wi' routh o' gear,   *simpleton; plenty of money*
And I hae tint my dearest dear;   *lost*
But Woman is but warld's gear,   *goods*
    Sae let the bonie lass gang!   *go*

– 2 –

Whae'er ye be that woman love,
    To this be never blind;
Nae ferlie 'tis tho' fickle she prove,   *wonder*
    A Woman has't be kind.   *nature*
O Woman lovely, Woman fair,
An angel form's faun to thy share,   *has fallen*
'Twad been o'er meikle to gien thee mair!—   *too (over) much to give; more*
    I mean an angel mind.

11 HAD I THE WYTE[1]

(? , 1796)

Briskly

TUNE: *Come kiss with me.*

Had I the wyte, had I the wyte, Had I the wyte? — she bade me; She watch'd me by the hie-gate side, And up the loan she shaw'd me; And when I wad-na ven-ture in, A cow-ard loon she ca'd me: Had kirk and state been in the gate, I'd light-ed when she bade me.

– I –

blame   Had I the wyte, had I the wyte,

Had I the wyte?—she bade me;

highway   She watch'd me by the hie-gate side,

path; showed   And up the loan she shaw'd me;

---

[1] Burns probably used a fragment of a lyric to this tune which he found in the manuscript collection of David Herd for the general idea of this song and for the first two lines of this and of an indecent song he also wrote (*Merry Muses of Caledonia*, ed. J. Barke, *et al.,* London, 1965, pp. 95–96). The Scots tune goes back to the beginning of the century and is always associated with dirty songs. Burns published this decent version of the old song in *Scots Musical Museum,* No. 415.

And when I wadna venture in,
  A coward loon she ca'd me: *wretch*
Had kirk and state been in the gate, *in opposition*
  I'd lighted when she bade me.   *would have alighted*

– 2 –

Sae craftilie she took me ben   *in*
  And bade me make nae clatter:—
"For our ramgunshoch, glum guidman *surly; husband*
  Is o'er ayont the water:"   *beyond*
Whae'er shall say I wanted grace,   *lacked*
  When I did kiss and dawte her,   *pet*
Let him be planted in my place,
  Syne say I was the fautor!   *Then; offender*

– 3 –

Could I for shame, could I for shame,
  Could I for shame refus'd her?
And wadna manhood been to blame
  Had I unkindly used her?
He claw'd her wi' the ripplin-kame, *flax-comb*
  And blae and bluidy bruised her— *blue*
When sic a husband was frae hame,
  What wife but wad excused her?

– 4 –

I dighted ay her een sae blue,   *wiped; eyes*
  An' bann'd the cruel randy;   *cursed; scoundrel*
And, weel I wat, her willin mou'   *know; mouth*
  Was sweet as sugar-candy.
At gloamin-shot it was, I wot,   *sunset*
  I lighted on the Monday,
But I cam thro' the Tyesday's dew
  To wanton Willie's brandy.

12 GAT YE ME

(? , 1796)[1]

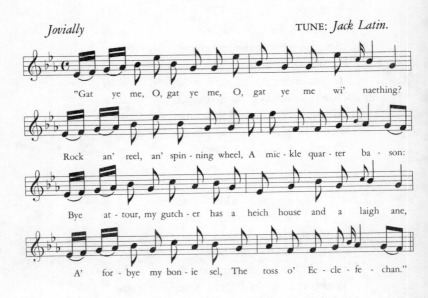

Jovially

TUNE: *Jack Latin.*

"Gat ye me, O, gat ye me, O, gat ye me wi' naething?

Rock an' reel, an' spin-ning wheel, A mic-kle quar-ter ba-son:

Bye at-tour, my gutch-er has a heich house and a laigh ane,

A' for-bye my bon-ie sel, The toss o' Ec-cle-fe-chan."

– I –

Did you get me (as a bride)	"Gat ye me, O, gat ye me,
	O, gat ye me wi' naething?
distaff; spool	Rock an' reel, an' spinning wheel,
large	A mickle quarter bason:[2]
Besides; grandfather	Bye attour, my gutcher has
high; low	A heich house and a laigh ane,[3]

---

[1] This song, which Burns wrote to a bagpipe tune, was published in *Scots Musical Museum*, No. 430; the first two lines are probably from an old song.

[2] A basin for holding meal.

[3] I.e., a house with a porch or a pantry (HH, III, 415).

A' forbye my bonie sel,   *All besides; self*
 The toss o' Ecclefechan."   *toast*

– 2 –

"O, haud your tongue now, Lucky[4] Lang, *hold*
 O, haud your tongue and jauner! *jabbering*
I held the gate till you I met, *kept to the straight and narrow*
 Syne I began to wander:
I tint my whistle and my sang,   *lost*
 I tint my peace and pleasure;
But your green graff, now Lucky Lang, *grave*
 Wad airt me to my treasure." *show*

---

[4] "Lucky" was used of grandmothers, barmaids, and whores.

13 O, WHA MY BABIE-CLOUTS WILL BUY?
(? ; 1790, 1903)[1]

Lively

TUNE: *Whare wad bonie Annie lie.*

O' wha my ba - bie - clouts will buy? Wha will tent me

when I cry? Wha will kiss me where I lie? The ran - tin dog, the

dad - die o't. Wha will own he did the faut?

Wha will buy the groan - in maut? Wha will tell me

how to ca't? The ran - tin dog, the dad - die o't.

[1] The lyric was printed to another tune in *Scots Musical Museum*, 1790, No. 277, but not until Dick's *Songs* to the tune which Burns designated for it in the manuscript-volume of poems which he made for Robert Riddell of Glenriddell (Dick, p. 353). The date of composition is unknown but Burns wrote opposite the song in the interleaved copy of the *Museum:* "I composed this song pretty early in life and sent it to a young girl, a very particular acquaintance of mine, who was at the time under a cloud [that is, of course, pregnant by Burns]."

- 1 -

O, wha my babie-clouts will buy? *-clothes*
Wha will tent me when I cry? *comfort*
Wha will kiss me where I lie?—
 The rantin dog, the daddie o't. *rollicking*

- 2 -

Wha will own he did the faut? *fault*
Wha will buy the groanin maut[2]?
Wha will tell me how to ca't?— *what to call it*
 The rantin dog, the daddie o't.

- 3 -

When I mount the creepie-chair,[3]
Wha will sit beside me there?
Gie me Rob, I'll seek na mair,— *Give*
 The rantin dog, the daddie o't.

- 4 -

Wha will crack to me my lane? *talk; alone*
Wha will make me fidgin fain? *arouse me sexually*
Wha will kiss me o'er again?—
 The rantin dog, the daddie o't.

---

[2] Literally "malt for the lying-in," that is, the traditional ale for the midwives at the birth party.

[3] The stool of repentance in the kirk.

14 O, KEN YE WHAT MEG O' THE MILL HAS GOTTEN?

(*ante* April 1793, 1803)[1]

Moderately

TUNE: *O ken ye what Meg.*

O, ken ye what Meg o' the Mill has got - ten? An' ken ye what Meg o' the

Mill has got - ten? A braw new naig wi' the tail o' a rot - tan, And

that's what Meg o' the Mill has got - ten! O, ken ye what Meg o' the

Mill lo'es dear - ly? An' ken ye what Meg o' the Mill lo'es dear - ly? A

dram o' gude strunt in a morn - ing ear - ly, And

that's what Meg o' the Mill lo'es dear - ly!

---

[1] Published in *Scots Musical Museum*, No. 566; Burns wrote the song for the *Museum* but sent it to an editor of another collection, calling it in the accompanying letter "a Song of considerable merit" (*Letters*, II, 162).

− 1 −

O, ken ye what Meg o' the Mill has gotten?   *know; got*
An' ken ye what Meg o' the Mill has gotten?
A braw new naig wi' the tail o' a rattan,   *fine; horse; rat*
And that's what Meg o' the Mill has gotten!

− 2 −

O, ken ye what Meg o' the Mill lo'es dearly?   *loves*
An' ken ye what Meg o' the Mill lo'es dearly?
A dram o' gude strunt in a morning early,   *liquor*
And that's what Meg o' the Mill lo'es dearly!

− 3 −

O, ken ye how Meg o' the Mill was married?
An' ken ye how Meg o' the Mill was married?
The priest he was oxter'd, the clark he was carried,   *led along by the armpit; clerk*
And that's how Meg o' the Mill was married!

− 4 −

O, ken ye how Meg o' the Mill was bedded?[2]
An' ken ye how Meg o' the Mill was bedded?
The groom gat sae fu', he fell awald beside it,   *drunk; backwards*
And that's how Meg o' the Mill was bedded!

---

[2] I.e., put to bed with the new husband at the end of the wedding party.

15 THERE'S NOUGHT BUT CARE ON EV'RY HAN'
(1784, 1787)[1]

Lively   TUNE: *Green grow the rashes, O.*

CHORUS: Green grow the rash-es, O! Green grow the rash-es, O! The
Fine

sweet-est hours that ere I spend, Are spent a-mang the las-sies, O!

There's nought but care on ev-'ry han', In ev-'ry hour that passes, O; What
D.C.

sig-ni-fies the life o' man, An 'twere na for the las-sies, O?

CHORUS
Green grow the rashes, O!
Green grow the rashes, O!
The sweetest hours that e'er I spend,
Are spent amang the lasses, O!

---

[1] This is the first of Burns's songs which was printed with its music. The lyric first appeared in the Edinburgh edition of 1787 and then the same year with music in the first volume of *Scots Musical Museum*, No. 77. Burns wrote one or two fine bawdy songs to the same tune and with the same traditional title line in the chorus (*Merry Muses of Caledonia*, ed. J. Barke *et al.*, London, 1965, pp. 75–76, 105).

- 1 -

There's nought but care on ev'ry han',
　In ev'ry hour that passes, O;
What signifies the life o' man,
　An' 'twere na for the lasses, O?　　　　*If it*

- 2 -

The warl'y race may riches chase,　　　*worldly*
　An' riches still may fly them, O;
An' tho' at last they catch them fast,
　Their hearts can ne'er enjoy them, O.

- 3 -

But gie me a cannie hour at e'en,　　　*give; quiet; evening*
　My arms about my dearie, O;
An' warl'y cares, an' warl'y men,
　May a' gae tapsalteerie, O!　　　　*topsy-turvy*

- 4 -

For you sae douce, ye sneer at this,　　　*proper, grave*
　Ye're nought but senseless asses, O;
The wisest man[2] the warl' saw,
　He dearly lov'd the lasses, O!

- 5 -

Auld Nature swears, the lovely dears
　Her noblest work she classes, O:
Her prentice han' she tried on man,
　An' then she made the lasses, O.

---

[2] King Solomon.

16 THE BAIRNS GAT OUT WI' AN UNCO SHOUT
(? , 1792)[1]

Merrily.   TUNE: *The deuks dang o'er my daddie.*

The bairns gat out wi' an un - co shout: — "The deuk's dang o'er my

dad-die, O!" "The fien-ma-care," quo' the fei - rie auld wife, "He was but a paid-lin

bo - dy, O! He paid - les out, and he paid - les in, An' he

paid - les late and ear - ly, O! This se - ven lang years I hae

lien by his side, An' he is but a fus - ion - less car - lie, O!"

---

1 Published in *Scots Musical Museum*, No. 396; it uses variations of two lines from an old song (see HH, III, 398–399). The Scots version of the original English tune was many times printed before Burns set these lyrics to it.

- 1 -

The bairns gat out wi' an unco shout:—   *children gave; surprising*
   "The deuk's dang o'er my daddie, O!"   *duck has knocked*
"The fien-ma-care," quo' the feirie auld wife, *fiend-may-; sturdy old*
   "He was but a paidlin body, O!   *hobbling (paddling)*
He paidles out, and he paidles in,
   An he paidles late and early, O!
The seven lang years I hae lien by his side,   *have lain*
   An' he is but a fusionless carlie, O!"   *sapless little man*

- 2 -

"O, haud your tongue, my feirie auld wife,   *hold*
   O, haud your tongue, now Nansie, O!
I've seen the day, and sae hae ye,
   Ye wadna been sae donsie, O!   *would not have been; sassy*
I've seen the day ye butter'd my brose,[2]   *porridge*
   And cuddl'd me late and early, O;
But downa-do's come o'er me now,   *cannot-do has*
   And, och, I find it sairly, O!"   *feel it sorely*

---

[2] The meaning is made even clearer by considering the opening lines to a bawdy song probably by Burns in the *Merry Muses:*

        Put butter in my Donald's brose,
           For weel does Donald fa' that;   *claim, deserve*
        I loe my Donald's tartans weel   *love*
           His naked arse and a' that.

Drinking

17 GANE IS THE DAY
(? , 1792)[1]

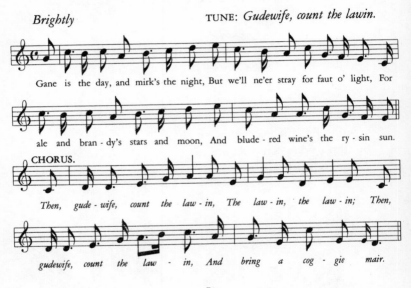

Brightly

TUNE: *Gudewife, count the lawin.*

Gane is the day, and mirk's the night, But we'll ne'er stray for faut o' light, For ale and bran-dy's stars and moon, And blude-red wine's the ry-sin sun.

CHORUS.

Then, gude-wife, count the law-in, The law-in, the law-in; Then, gudewife, count the law-in, And bring a cog-gie mair.

– I –

   dark is   Gane is the day, and mirk's the night,
     lack   But we'll ne'er stray for faut o' light,
       is   For ale and brandy's stars and moon,
             And blude-red wine's the rysin sun.

---

[1] Published in *Scots Musical Museum*, No. 313, opposite which in the interleaved volume Burns wrote: "The chorus of this is part of an old song." He scratched the third stanza with his diamond pen on a window of the Globe Tavern, Dumfries.

GANE IS THE DAY

CHORUS

Then, gudewife, count the lawin,   *landlady; charges*
  The lawin, the lawin;
Then, gudewife, count the lawin,
  And bring a coggie mair.   *wooden cup more*

– 2 –

There's wealth and ease for gentlemen,
And simple folk maun fecht and fen';   *must fight; fend for themselves*
But here we're a' in ae accord,   *all; one*
For ilka man that's drunk's a lord.   *each; is a lord*

– 3 –

My coggie is a haly pool,   *holy*
That heals the wounds o' care and dool,   *sorrow*
And pleasure is a wanton trout:
And ye drink it a', ye'll find him out!   *If; all*

275

18 O, WILLIE BREW'D A PECK O' MAUT
(1789, 1790)[1]

Blythely   TUNE: *Willie brew'd a peck o' maut.*

O, Wil-lie brew'd a peck o' maut, And Rob and Al-lan

cam to see; Three bly-ther hearts that

lee-lang night Ye wad-na found in Chris-ten-die.

CHORUS.

We are na fou, we're nae that fou, But

just a drap-pie in our e'e; The

cock may craw, the day may daw, And

ay we'll taste the bar-ley bree.

[1] Published in *Scots Musical Museum,* No. 291, in the interleaved copy of which Burns
noted that the song was written to celebrate a convivial evening he spent with William

O, WILLIE BREW'D A PECK O' MAUT

– 1 –

O, Willie brew'd a peck o' maut, *a great quantity of malt*
   And Rob and Allan cam to see;
Three blyther hearts that lee-lang night *live-*
   Ye wadna found in Christendie. *would not have; Christiandom*

CHORUS

We are na fou, we're nae that fou, *drunk*
   But just a drappie in our e'e; *little drop; eye*
The cock may craw, the day may daw, *crow; dawn*
   And ay we'll taste the barley bree. *still; brew*

– 2 –

Here are we met three merry boys,
   Three merry boys I trow are we; *believe*
And monie a night we've merry been,
   And monie mae we hope to be! *more*

– 3 –

It is the moon, I ken her horn,
   That's blinkin in the lift sae hie: *shining; sky; high*
She shines sae bright to wyle us hame, *entice*
   But, by my sooth, she'll wait a wee!

– 4 –

Wha first shall rise to gang awa, *go*
   A cuckold, coward loun is he! *rogue*
Wha first beside his chair shall fa', *fall*
   He is the king among us three!

Nicol and Allan Masterton, schoolmasters of Edinburgh, the "Allan" and "Willie"
of the first stanza, and that Masterton composed the tune.

Personal Sentiment

19 O, THAT I HAD NE'ER BEEN MARRIED
(1793?, 1803)

Slowly   TUNE: *Crowdie.*

O, that I had ne'er been mar - ried, I wad ne - ver had nae care!

Now I've got - ten wife an' weans, An' they cry "crow - die" ev - er - mair.

CHORUS: — *Ance crow - die,   twice crow - die,   Three times crow - die   in   a   day;*

Gin ye "crow - die" on - ie mair, Ye'll crow - die a' my meal a - way.

---

¹ Only the second stanza of this song is by Burns, who found the first and the chorus in the manuscript collection of David Herd and sent them with the music (which had apparently not been published before) and his addition to the *Scots Musical Museum*, where it was printed (No. 593). He quoted the old words of the first stanza and the chorus in a letter of 15 December 1793 in relation to his poverty and the illness of his youngest daughter (*Letters*, II, 223-224).

- 1 -

O, that I had ne'er been married,
  I wad never had nae care;
Now I've gotten wife an' weans,   *children*
  An' they cry "crowdie" evermair. *porridge*

CHORUS

Ance crowdie, twice crowdie,   *Once*
  Three times crowdie in a day;
Gin ye "crowdie" onie mair,   *If; any more*
  Ye'll crowdie a' my meal away.

- 2 -

Waefu' want and hunger fley me, *Woeful; scare*
  Glow'rin by the hallan en':   *Scowling; end of the porch*
Sair I fecht them at the door,   *Hard; fight*
  But ay I'm eerie they come ben. *still; frightened; in*

20 IS THERE FOR HONEST POVERTY?[1]
(1794?; 1795, 1805)[2]

Boldly

TUNE: *For a' that.*

Is there for hon-est pov-er-ty That hings his head, an' a' that? The

cow-ard slave, we pass him by — We dare be poor for a' that!

For a' that, an' a' that, Our toils ob-scure, an' a' that, The

rank is but the guinea's stamp, The man's the gowd for a' that.

[1] This song reflects Burns's sympathy with the French Revolution. He wrote the bard's first song in "The Jolly Beggars" (p. 222) and a variation of it (HH, III, 78–79) for this tune some nine years before. An indecent song to the tune probably by Burns appeared in *Merry Muses of Caledonia* in 1799, for which see the modern edition, ed. J. Barke, *et al.,* London, 1965, p. 100. The tune has many old sets, mostly of Jacobite or bawdy sentiment, all with the same variable refrain of lines 5, 6, and 8 in Burns's stanzas. Burns wryly commented on the present version in a letter of January 1795: "A great critic, Aikin on songs, says that love & wine are the exclusive themes for song-writing. —The following is on neither subject, & consequently is no Song; but will be allowed, I think to be two or three pretty good *prose* thoughts, inverted into rhyme. . . . I do not give you the foregoing song for your book, but merely by way of vive la bagatelle; for the piece is not really Poetry" (*Letters,* II, 284).

[2] The lyrics were first published, but for the first stanza, in *The Glasgow Magazine,* August, 1795 (HH, III, 490), and all five stanzas first with the music in Thomson's *Scottish Airs* in 1805.

IS THERE FOR HONEST POVERTY?

– 1 –

Is there for honest poverty
  That hings his head,[3] an' a' that?   *hangs*
The coward slave, we pass him by—
  We dare be poor for a' that!
    For a' that, an' a' that,   *all*
      Our toils obscure, an' a' that,
    The rank is but the guinea's stamp,
      The man's the gowd for a' that.   *gold*

– 2 –

What tho' on hamely fare we dine,
  Wear hodden grey, an' a' that?   *coarse woollen*
Gie fools their silks, and knaves their wine— *Give*
  A man's a man for a' that!
    For a' that, an' a' that,
      Their tinsel show, an' a' that,
    The honest man, tho' e'er sae poor,
      Is king o' men for a' that.

– 3 –

Ye see yon birkie ca'd a lord,   *fellow called*
  Wha struts, and stares, an' a' that;
Tho' hundreds worship at his word,
  He's but a coof for a' that.   *blockhead*
    For a' that, an' a' that,
      His ribband, star, an' a' that,
    The man o' independent mind,
      He looks an' laughs at a' that.

---

[3] I.e., "Is there someone who hangs down his head because of his honest poverty."
An early version reads (HH, III, 490):

      Wha wad for honest poverty
      Hing down his head an' a' that.

- 4 -

A prince can make a belted knight,
A marquis, duke, an' a' that,
above   But an honest man's aboon his might—
must not claim   Gude faith, he mauna fa' that!
     For a' that, an' a' that,
       Their dignities, an' a' that,
       The pith o' sense an' pride o' worth
       Are higher rank than a' that.

- 5 -

Then let us pray that come it may—
As come it will, for a' that—
That sense and worth, o'er a' the earth
bear off the prize   Shall bear the gree, an' a' that;
     For a' that, an' a' that;
       It's comin yet for a' that,
       That man to man the world o'er,
       Shall brothers be for a' that.

21 THERE WAS A LAD WAS BORN IN KYLE

(1784; 1808, 1903)[1]

Brisk

TUNE: *Dainty Davie.*

CHORUS: Ro - bin was   a   ro - vin boy, Ran - tin,   ro - vin,

ran - tin, ro - vin, Ro - bin was   a   ro - vin boy, Ran - tin, ro - vin

Ro - bin!   There   was   a   lad   was   born   in   Kyle,   But

what - na   day   o'   what - na   style,   I   doubt   it's   hard - ly

worth   the   while   To   be   sae   nice   wi'   Ro - bin.

---

[1] Burns set these humorously autobiographical lyrics to a popular Scots tune in his
First Commonplace Book just before an entry dated August 1784. The lyrics appeared
in R. H. Cromek's *Reliques of Robert Burns* and with the music after many years in Dick's
Songs.

CHORUS

Robin was a rovin boy,

roistering   Rantin, rovin, rantin, rovin,

Robin was a rovin boy,

      Rantin, rovin Robin!

– 1 –

There was a lad was born in Kyle,[2]

whatever   But whatna day o' whatna style,

I doubt it's hardly worth the while

fastidious   To be sae nice wi' Robin.

– 2 –

one   Our monarch's[3] hindmost year but ane

Was five-and-twenty days begun,

January wind 'Twas then a blast o' Janwar win'

an inaugurative   Blew hansel in on Robin.
luck-gift

– 3 –

peeked; palm   The gossip keekit in his loof,

said she   Quo' scho "wha lives will see the proof,

strapping; fool This waly boy will be nae coof;

call   I think we'll ca' him Robin.

– 4 –

small   "He'll hae misfortunes great an' sma',

always; above; all But ay a heart aboon them a';

to   He'll be a credit till us a';

    We'll a' be proud o' Robin.

---

[2] The section of Ayrshire where Burns was born.

[3] George II died in 1760; Burns's manuscript note to these two lines: "Jan. 25th, 1795, the date of my Bardship's vital existence."

– 5 –

"But sure as three times three mak nine,
I see by ilka score and line,   *every*
This chap will dearly like our kin',   *kind*
   So leeze me on thee, Robin.   *blessings*

– 6 –

"Guid faith," quo' scho, "I doubt you, sir,   *suspect*
Ye gar the lasses lie aspar,   *will make; aspread*
But twenty fauts ye may hae waur,—   *faults; worse*
   So blessins on thee, Robin!"

Bawdry

22 YE JOVIAL BOYS WHO LOVE THE JOYS
(1784?; 1799, 1957)[1]

Lively

TUNE: *Clout the caudron.*

Ye jo-vial boys who love the joys, The bliss-ful joys of lov-ers, Yet dare a-vow, with daunt-less brow, When bo-ny lass dis-co-vers, I pray draw near, and lend an ear, And wel-come in a Fra-ter, For, I've late-ly been in quar-an-tine, A pro-ven for-ni-ca-tor.

---

[1] Burns probably wrote this song to celebrate his affair with Elizabeth ("Betsy" of stanza 2 and 3) Paton, who gave birth to his child in Nov. 1784 and with whom he underwent public penance for fornication in front of the congregation in the kirk (the "buttock-hire," stanza 3, line 2). He used the tune the next year for the caird's song in "The Jolly Beggars" (p. 220). The first four stanzas were published in *Merry Muses of Caledonia* (1799) and all six stanzas from Burns' manuscript (Honresfeld Collection) in the scholarly *Merry Muses* (ed. J. Barke, *et al.* London, 1965, pp. 67–68), on which the present text is based. The song first appeared with its music in Robert D. Norton, *The Tuneful Flame* (1957).

- 1 -

Ye jovial boys who love the joys,
  The blissful joys of Lovers,
Yet dare avow, with dauntless brow,
  When the bony lass discovers,
I pray draw near, and lend an ear,
  And welcome in a Frater,
For I've lately been on quarantine,
  A proven Fornicator.

- 2 -

Before the Congregation wide,
  I passed the muster fairly,
My handsome Betsy by my side,
  We gat our ditty rarely;
But my downcast eye did chance to spy
  What made my lips to water,
Those limbs so clean where I between
  Commenc'd a Fornicator.

- 3 -

With rueful face and signs of grace
  I pay'd the buttock-hire,
But the night was dark and thro' the park
  I could not but convoy her;
A parting kiss, I could not less,
  My vows began to scatter,
My Betsy fell—lal de dal lal lal,
  I am a Fornicator.

- 4 -

But for her sake this vow I make,
  And solemnly I swear it,

That while I own a single crown
  She's welcome for to share it;
And my roguish boy his Mother's joy
  And the darling of his Pater,
For him I boast my pains and cost,
  Although a Fornicator.

– 5 –

Ye wenching blades whose hireling jades
  Have tipt you off blue-joram,[2]
I tell you plain, I do disdain
  To rank you in the Quorum;[3]
But a bony lass upon the grass
  To teach her esse Mater,[4]
And no reward but fond regard,
  O that's a Fornicator.

– 6 –

Your warlike Kings and Heros bold,
  Great Captains and Commanders;
Your mighty Caesars fam'd of old,
  And conquering Alexanders;
In fields they fought and laurels bought,
  And bulwarks strong did batter,
But still they grac'd our noble list,
  And ranked Fornicator!!!

---

[2] The precise meaning of this bawdy phrase has escaped the search of the editor; it is, of course, a service performed by professional prostitutes ("hireling jades") for paying customers.

[3] I.e., the Company.

[4] To be a mother.

23 O, I HAE TINT MY ROSY CHEEK

(? ; 1800?, 1967)[1]

Slow

TUNE: *Comin thro' the rye.*

O I hae tint my ro-sy cheek, Like-wise my waist sae sma'; O wae gae by the sod-ger lown, The sod-ger did it a'. O wha'll mow me now, my jo, An' wha'll mow me now: A sod-ger wi' his band-i-leers Has banged my bel-ly fu'.

– 1 –

O, I hae tint my rosy cheek,   *lost*
    Likewise my waste sae sma';   *waist; small*
O wae gae by the sodger lown,   *woe betide; soldier fellow*
    The sodger did it a'.   *all*

---

[1] This song, universally attributed to Burns by scholars, first appeared in the original *Merry Muses of Caledonia* (1799) and now for the first time with the tune that Dick assigns it (p. 406), a variant of the popular tune of Burns's "Auld Lang Syne." The text is based on that in the scholarly *Merry Muses,* ed. J. Barke, *et al.,* London, 1965, pp. 93–94.

CHORUS

who'll lay; sweetheart   O wha'll mow[2] me now, my jo,
         An' wha'll mow me now:
         A sodger wi' his bandileers
full   Has bang'd my belly fu'.

– 2 –

must endure   Now I maun thole the scornfu' sneer
girl   O' mony a saucy quine;
         When, curse upon her godly face!
         Her cunt's as merry's mine.

– 3 –

holds   Our dame hauds up her wanton tail,
Whenever; lies down   As due as she gaes lie;
abuse   An' yet misca' [a] young thing,
         The trade if she but try.

– 4 –

lay; own husband   Our dame can lae her ain gudeman,
         An' mow for glutton greed;
         An' yet misca' a poor thing,
         That's mowin' for its bread.

– 5 –

         Alake! sae sweet a tree as love,
         Sic bitter fruit should bear!
         Alake, that e'er a merry arse,
cause; salty   Should draw a sa'tty tear.

---

[2] Pronounced to rime with the American pronunciation of *cow;* from *to moll* (to amble, ride, copulate)

But deevil damn the lousy loon,   *fellow*
  Denies the bairn he got!   *child*
Or lea's the merry arse he lo'ed,   *leaves*
  To wear a ragged coat!

Humorous Fancy

24 WILLIE WASTLE DWALT ON TWEED
(? , 1792)[1]

Moderate time   TUNE: *Sic a wife as Willie had.*

Wil - lie Was - tle dwalt on Tweed, The spot they ca'd it
Lin - kum - dod - die; Wil - lie was a wabs - ter gude Could stoun a clue wi'
o - ny bod - ie: He had a wife was dour and din, O,
Tink - ler Maid - gie was her mith - er; Sic a wife as
Wil - lie had, I wad - na gie a but - ton for her.

---

[1] There is a seventeenth-century song called "Sike a wife as Willy had," but the music is different from that for which Burns set this original song (Dick, p. 426), which first appeared with the first printing of this tune in *Scots Musical Museum,* No. 376.

- 1 -

Willie Wastle dwalt on Tweed,	*dwelt*
The spot they ca'd it Linkumdoddie;	*called*
Willie was a wabster gude	*weaver*
Could stoun a clue wi' ony bodie:	*have stolen; ball of thread*
He had a wife was dour and din,	*sulky; ill-colored*
O, Tinkler Maidgie was her mither;	*Tinker*
Sic a wife as Willie had,	
I wadna gie a button for her.	*would not give*

- 2 -

She has an e'e—she has but ane,—	*eye; one*
The cat has twa the very colour,	
Five rusty teeth, forbye a stump,	*besides*
A clapper tongue wad deave a miller;	*deafen*
A whiskin beard about her mou',	*sweeping; mouth*
Her nose and chin they threaten ither:	*one another*
Sic a wife as Willie had,	
I wadna gie a button for her.	

- 3 -

She's bow-hough'd, she's hem-shinn'd,[2]	*bow-legged*
Ae limpin leg a hand-breed shorter;	*One; -breadth*
She's twisted right, she's twisted left,	
To balance fair in ilka quarter:	*every*
She has a hump upon her breast,	
The twin o' that upon her shouther:	*shoulder*
Sic a wife as Willie had,	
I wadna gie a button for her.	

---

[2] Shins shaped like the wooden haims of a horse's collar, that is curved like an elongated letter-S: the lower part of Willie's wife's bow-legs bend outward!

293

— 4 —

Old pussy; fireplace   Auld baudrans by the ingle sits,
paw   An' wi' her loof her face a-washin;
neat   But Willie's wife is nae sae trig,
wipes; snout; old stocking   She dights her grunzie wi' a hushion;
large fists; manure-baskets   Her walie nieves like midden-creels,
would defile   Her face wad fyle the Logan Water:
Sic a wife as Willie had,
   I wadna gie a button for her.

25 THE DEIL CAM FIDDLIN THRO' THE TOWN
(1792, 1792)[1]

Merrily

TUNE: *The Hemp-dresser.*

The deil cam fidd - lin thro' the town, And danc'd a - wa wi' the Excise - man, And il - ka wife cries: "Auld Ma - houn, I wish you luck o' the prize, man!" *The deil's a - wa, the deil's a - wa, The deil's a - wa wi' the Exciseman! He's danc'd a - wa, he's danc'd a - wa, He's danc'd a - wa wi' the Excise - man!*

— I —

The deil cam fiddlin thro' the town,   *devil*
　　And danc'd awa wi' the Exciseman,   *away; Tax Collector*
And ilka wife cries:—"Auld Mahoun,   *every; Old Satan (Mahomet)*
　　I wish you luck o' the prize, man!"

[1] Burns sang this song, which he composed for the occasion, at a dinner for local tax collectors in Dumfries (*Letters*, II, 113); it appeared in *Scots Musical Museum*, No. 399.

CHORUS
The deil's awa, the deil's awa,
   The deil's awa wi' the Exciseman!
He's danc'd awa, he's danc'd awa,
   He's danc'd awa wi' the Exciseman!

– 2 –

malt   "We'll mak our maut, and we'll brew our drink,
   We'll laugh, sing, and rejoice, man,
fine; great   And monie braw thanks to the meikle black deil,
   That danc'd awa wi' the Exciseman.

– 3 –

"There's threesome reels, there's foursome reels,
   There's hornpipes and strathspeys, man,
very (one)   But the ae best dance e'er came to the land,
   Was *The deil's awa wi' the Exciseman!*"

Jacobite

26 OUR THRISSLES FLOURISH'D FRESH AND FAIR

(1789?, 1790)[1]

Moderate   TUNE: *Awa, Whigs, awa!*

CHORUS: A - wa, Whigs, a - wa! A - wa, Whigs, a - wa! Ye're

but a pack o' trai - tor louns, Ye'll do nae gude at a'.

Our thris - sles flour - ish'd fresh and fair, And

bon - ie bloom'd our ros - es; But Whigs cam like a

frost in June, An' with - er'd a' our pos - ies.

---

[1] Taking the chorus almost verbatim and the general idea from a fragment of an old song in the manuscript collection of David Herd (HH, III, 350), Burns composed this fierce song against the Union of England and Scotland and published it in *Scots Musical Museum*, No. 263.

CHORUS

Away   Awa, Whigs, awa!
       Awa, Whigs, awa!
wretches   Ye're but a pack o' traitor louns,
       Ye'll do nae gude at a'.

– 1 –

thistles   Our thrissles flourish'd fresh and fair,
       And bonie bloom'd our roses;
       But Whigs cam like a frost in June,
       An' wither'd a' our posies.

– 2 –

has fallen   Our ancient crown's fa'en in the dust—
Devil blind; dust cloud of it   Deil blin' them wi' the stoure o't,
       And write their names in his black beuk,
gave   Wha gae the Whigs the power o't!

– 3 –

       Our sad decay in Church and State
describing   Surpasses my descriving:
       The Whigs cam o'er us for a curse,
       An' we hae done wi' thriving.

– 4 –

       Grim Vengeance lang has taen a nap,
waking   But we may see him waukin;
       Gude help the day when royal heads
rabbit   Are hunted like a maukin!

27 THE LOVELY LASS OF INVERNESS

(? , 1796)[1]

Slow

TUNE: *The lovely lass of Inverness.*

The love - ly lass of In - ver - ness, Nae joy nor pleasure
can she see; For e'en to morn she cries "a - las!" And
ay the saut tear blin's her e'e:—"Dru-moss - ie Moor, Dru - moss - ie day—A
wae - fu' day it was to me! For there I lost my
fa - ther dear, My fa - ther dear and breth - ren three."

– 1 –

The lovely lass of Inverness,
  Nae joy nor pleasure can she see;
For e'en to morn she cries, "alas!"
  And ay the saut tear blin's her e'e:— *salt*

---

[1] Published in *Scots Musical Museum*, No. 401; original lyrics set to a tune by James Oswald (published 1743).

"Drumossie Moor, Drumossie day[2]—
  woeful   A waefu' day it was to me!
For there I lost my father dear,
  My father dear and brethern three.

– 2 –

"Their winding-sheet the bluidy clay,
  Their graves are growin green to see,
And by them lies the dearest lad
  That ever blest a woman's e'e.
Now wae to thee, thou cruel lord,[3]
  A bluidy man I trow thou be,
  sore   For monie a heart thou hast made sair
  That ne'er did wrang to thine or thee."

---

[2] The Jacobite forces of the last Stuart pretender, Charles Edward, were defeated at the battle of Culloden on Drumossie Moor, April 16, 1746.

[3] William, Duke of Cumberland, the bloody and hated commander of the Government forces at Culloden.

28 IT WAS A' FOR OUR RIGHTFU' KING

(? , 1796)[1]

TUNE: *Mally Stuart.*

It was a' for our right - fu' king We left fair Scot - land's
strand; It was a' for our right - fu' king, We
e'er saw I - rish land, my dear — We e'er saw I - rish land.

– I –

It was a' for our rightfu' king
　　We left fair Scotland's strand;
It was a' for our rightfu' king,
　　We e'er saw Irish land, my dear—
　　We e'er saw Irish land.

---

[1] The song was published in *Scots Musical Museum*, No. 497, but only when Burns's manuscript was produced in 1877 was it known to be by him. Burns got stanza 3 from a street ballad. The song is symmetrical: stanzas 1–2 give the words of the soldier who has to flee after the defeat of the forces of his "rightfu' king," Charles Edward Stuart, at Culloden (1746); stanza 3 describes him exiled in Ireland; stanzas 4–5 give the words of the girl he has left behind in Scotland.

– 2 –

Now a' is done that men can do,
    And a' is done in vain,
My Love and native land fareweel,
must   For I maun cross the main, my dear—
    For I maun cross the main.

– 3 –

He turn'd him right and round about
    Upon the Irish shore,
gave   And gae his bridle reins a shake,
    With Adieu for evermore, my dear,
    With adieu for evermore!

– 4 –

soldier   The soger frae the wars returns,
    The sailor frae the main,
But I hae parted frae my love
    Never to meet again, my dear—
    Never to meet again.

– 5 –

When day is gane, and night is come,
    And a' folk bound to sleep,
I think on him that's far awa
live-long   The lee-lang night and weep, my dear—
    The lee-long night and weep.

29 SCOTS, WHA HAE WI' WALLACE BLED[1]

(1793, 1801)[2]

Boldly

TUNE: *Hey, tutti taitie.*

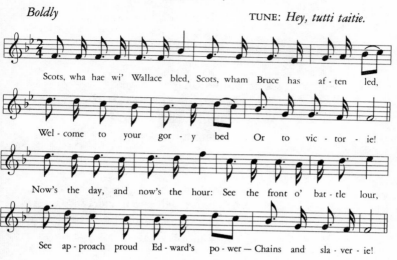

Scots, wha hae wi' Wallace bled, Scots, wham Bruce has af-ten led,

Wel-come to your gor-y bed Or to vic-tor-ie!

Now's the day, and now's the hour: See the front o' bat-tle lour,

See ap-proach proud Ed-ward's po-wer — Chains and sla-ver-ie!

— I —

Scots, wha hae wi' Wallace bled,   *who have*
Scots, wham Bruce has aften led,
Welcome to your gory bed
    Or to victorie!

---

[1] Burns wrote this famous revolutionary song to the title of "Robert Bruce's march to Bannockburn—To its ain tune," or, as in another version "Robert Bruce's Address to his Army," which he cast, as he wrote, "into a kind of Scots Ode," fitted to the tune which he believed (erroneously) was the march to which Bruce took his men into battle (*Letters*, II, 195-197). Robert, the Bruce (Robert I of Scotland), won independence from England by defeating the army of Edward II at Bannockburn. Burns admitted in a letter that he wrote the song because he associated the struggle of Scotland for freedom with that of the French Republic (*ibid.*, p. 196). He was very partial to the song: "in my best manner" (*ibid.*, p. 231). For Wallace, see p. 25, note 6.

[2] George Tomson published a revised version of the song to the wrong tune in *Scotish Airs* in 1799, and only when forced by public opinion, the original words to the tune which Burns had designated.

— 2 —

Now's the day, and now's the hour:
See the front o' battle lour,
See approach proud Edward's power—
    Chains and slaverie!

— 3 —

Wha will be a traitor knave?
Wha can fill a coward's grave?
Wha sae base as be a slave?—
    Let him turn, and flee!

— 4 —

Wha for Scotland's king and law
Freedom's sword will strongly draw,
Freeman stand or freeman fa',
    Let him follow me!

— 5 —

By Oppression's woes and pains,
By your sons in servile chains,
We will drain our dearest veins
    But they shall be free!

— 6 —

Lay the proud usurpers low!
Tyrants fall in every foe!
Liberty's in every blow!
    Let us do, or die![3]

---

[3] Since the last syllables in the short fourth lines of the other stanzas rime, this word is to be pronounced as Scots: *dee*. There are other suggestions of Scots in this song, intended to be international and thus, perhaps, largely in the English manner (compare the Bard's second song in "The Jolly Beggars," p. 224). The "Marseillaise" was, as Dick points out (p. 449), written only seventeen months before this song.

APPENDIXES

Appendix A: Burns's "Preface" to the Kilmarnock Edition of *Poems Chiefly in the Scottish Dialect* (1786)

The following trifles are not the production of the Poet, who, with all the advantages of learned art, and perhaps amid the elegancies and idlenesses of upper life, looks down for a rural theme, with an eye to Theocrites or Virgil. To the Author of this, these and other celebrated names their countrymen are, in their original languages, "A fountain shut up, and a "book sealed." Unacquainted with the necessary requisites for commencing Poet by rule, he sings the sentiments and manners, he felt and saw in himself and his rustic compeers around him, in his and their native language. Though a Rhymer from his earliest impulses of the softer passions, it was not till very lately, that the applause, perhaps the partiality, of Friendship, wakened his vanity so far as to make him think any thing of his was worth showing; and none of the following works were ever composed with a view to the press. To amuse himself with the little creations of his own fancy, amid the toil and fatigues of a laborious life; to transcribe the various feelings, the loves, the griefs, the hopes, the fears, in his own breast; to find some kind of counterpoise to the struggles of a world, always an alien scene, a task uncouth to the poetical mind; these were his motives for courting the Muses, and in these he found Poetry to be its own reward.

It is an observation of the celebrated Poet [Shenstone], whose divine Elegies do honor to our language, our nation, and our species, that "Humility has depressed many a genius to a hermit, but never raised one to fame." If any Critic catches at the word *genius,* the Author tells him, once for all, that he certainly looks upon himself as possest of some poetic abilities, otherwise his publishing in the manner he has done, would be a manoeuvre below the worst character, which, he hopes, his worst enemy will ever give him: but to the genius of a Ramsay, or the glorious dawnings of the poor, unfortunate Fergusson, he, with equal unaffected sincerity, declares, that, even in his highest pulse of vanity, he has not the most distant pretensions. These two justly admired Scotch Poets he has often had in his eye in the following pieces; but rather with a view to kindle at their flame, than for servile imitation.

To his Subscribers, the Author returns his most sincere thanks. Not the mercenary bow over a counter, but the heart-throbbing gratitude of the Bard, conscious how much he is indebted to Benevolence and Friendship, for gratifying him, if he deserves it, in that dearest wish of every poetic bosom—to be distinguished. He begs his readers, particularly the Learned and the Polite, who may honor him with a perusal, that they will make every allowance for Education and Circumstances of Life: but, if after a fair, candid, and impartial criticism, he shall stand convicted of Dulness and Nonsense, let him be done by, as he would in that case do by others—let him be condemned, without mercy, to contempt and oblivion.

Appendix B: Burns's Autobiographical Letter to Dr. John Moore, 2 August 1787.

After seeing the second edition of the *Poems* published, Burns's business in Edinburgh was finished. He took a tour of the Border country and then of the south-west Highlands. Undecided and troubled about his future, he settled for a short period into his old habits in Mauchline. During this still time between decisions, he wrote a long letter about his life to an Anglicized Scottish medical doctor, an insignificant writer of travel books and a novel, who evidently had earned Burns's respect by his success and his high connections, and who wanted Burns to abandon Scots for English poetry. The letter is designed more as a summing-up of his life for himself and for his friends, to whom he showed his copy, than for the particular edification of Moore, who by accident is remembered today only as the addressee of Burns's letter. The text which follows is from *Letters*, I, 105–115, and includes a version of Delancey Ferguson's footnotes (with permission of the Clarendon Press). Brief portions at the beginning and the end are omitted as irrelevant. If the student finds Burns's chronology in the letter difficult, Burns's biographers have found it maddening.

I have not the most distant pretensions to what the pyecoated guardians of escutcheons call, A Gentleman.—When at Edin^r last winter, I got acquainted in the Herald's Office, and looking through that granary of Honors I there found almost every name in the kingdom; but for me,

> "—*My ancient but ignoble blood*
> *Has crept thro' Scoundrels ever since the flood*"—[1]

Gules, Purpure, Argent, &c. quite disowned me.—My Fathers rented land of the noble Kieths of Marshal, and had the honor to share their fate.—I do not use the word, Honor, with any reference to Political principles; loyal and disloyal I take to be merely relative terms in that ancient and formidable court known in this Country by the name of CLUB-LAW.—Those who dare welcome Ruin and shake hands with Infamy for what they sincerely believe to be the

---

[1] Pope, *Essay on Man*, IV, 211.

cause of their God or their King—"Brutus and Cassius are honorable men."—[2] I mention this circumstance because it threw my father on the world at large; where after many years' wanderings and sojournings, he pickt up a pretty large quantity of Observation and Experience, to which I am indebted for most of my little pretensions to wisdom.—I have met with few who understood "Men, their manners and their ways"[3] equal to him; but stubborn, ungainly Integrity, and headlong, ungovernable Irrascibillity are disqualifying circumstances: consequently I was born a very poor man's son. —For the first six or seven years of my life, my father was gardiner to a worthy gentleman of small estate in the neighbourhood of Ayr.—Had my father continued in that situation, I must have marched off to be one of the little underlings about a farm-house; but it was his dearest wish and prayer to have it in his power to keep his children under his own eye till they could discern between good and evil; so with the assistance of his generous Master my father ventured on a small farm in his estate.—At these years I was by no means a favorite with any body.—I was a good deal noted for a retentive memory, a stubborn, sturdy something in my disposition, and an enthusiastic, idiot piety.—I say idiot piety, because I was then but a child.—Though I cost the schoolmaster some thrashings, I made an excellent English scholar; and against the years of ten or eleven, I was absolutely a Critic in substantives, verbs and particles.—In my infant and boyish days too, I owed much to an old Maid of my Mother's, remarkable for her ignorance, credulity and superstition.—She had, I suppose, the largest collection in the county of tales and songs concerning devils, ghosts, fairies, brownies, witches, warlocks, spunkies, kelpies, elf-candles, dead-lights, wraiths, apparitions, cantraips, giants, inchanted towers, dragons and other trumpery.—This cultivated the latent seeds of Poesy; but had so strong an effect on my imagination, that to this hour, in my nocturnal rambles, I sometimes keep a sharp look-out in suspicious places; and though nobody can be more sceptical in these matters than I, yet it often takes an effort of Philosophy to shake off these idle terrors. —The earliest thing of Composition that I recollect taking pleasure in was, The vision of Mirza and a hymn of Addison's beginning—"How are Thy servants blest, O Lord!" I particularly remember one half-stanza which was music to my boyish ear—

---

2 Shakespeare, *Julius Caesar*, III, ii.
3 Pope, *January and May*, line 157.

For though in dreadful whirls we hung,
High on the broken wave—

I met with these pieces in Mas[s]on's English Collection, one of my school-books.—The two first books I ever read in private, and which gave me more pleasure than any two books I ever read again, were, the life of Hannibal and the history of Sir William Wallace.—Hannibal gave my young ideas such a turn that I used to strut in raptures up and down after the recruiting drum and bagpipe, and wish myself tall enough to be a soldier; while the story of Wallace poured a Scotish prejudice in my veins which will boil along there till the flood-gates of life shut in eternal rest.—Polemical divinity about this time was putting the country half-mad; and I, ambitious of shining in conver-sation parties on Sundays between sermons, funerals, &c. used in a few years more to puzzle Calvinism with so much heat and indiscretion that I raised a hue and cry of heresy against me which has not ceased to this hour.—

My vicinity to Ayr was of great advantage to me.—My social disposition, when not checked by some modification of spited pride, like our catechism definition of Infinitude, was "without bounds or limits."—I formed many connections with other Youngkers who possessed superiour advantages; the youngling Actors who were busy with the rehearsal of PARTS in which they were shortly to appear on that STAGE where, Alas! I was destined to drudge behind the SCENES.—It is not commonly at these green years that the young Noblesse and Gentry have a just sense of the immense distance between them and their ragged Playfellows.—It takes a few dashes into the world to give the young Great man that proper, decent, unnoticing disregard for the poor, insignificant, stupid devils, the mechanics and peasantry around him; who perhaps were born in the same village.—My young Superiours never insulted the clouterly appearance of my ploughboy carcase, the two extremes of which were often exposed to all the inclemencies of all the seasons.—They would give me stray volumes of books; among them, even then, I could pick up some observations; and ONE, whose heart I am sure not even the MUNNY BEGUM'S scenes have tainted, helped me to a little French.—Parting with these, my young friends and benefactors, as they dropped off for the east or west Indies, was often to me a sore affliction; but I was soon called to more serious evils.—My father's generous Master died; the farm proved a ruinous bargain; and, to clench the curse, we fell into the hands of a Factor who sat for the picture I have drawn of one in my Tale of two dogs.—My father was advanced in life when he married; I was the eldest of seven children; and he, worn out by early hardship, was unfit for labour.—My father's spirit was soon irritated, but not easily broken.—There was a freedom in his lease in two years more, and to weather these two years we retrenched expences.—We lived very poorly; I was a dextrous Ploughman for my years; and the next eldest to me was a brother, who could drive the plough very well and help me to thrash.—A Novel-Writer might perhaps have viewed these scenes with some satisfaction, but so did not I: my indignation yet boils at the recollection of the scoundrel tyrant's insolent, threatening epistles, which used to set us all in tears.—

This kind of life, the chearless gloom of a hermit with the unceasing moil of a galley-slave, brought me to my sixteenth year; a little before which period I first committed the sin of RHYME.—You know our country custom of coupling a man and woman together as Partners in the labors of Harvest.—In my fifteenth autumn, my Partner was a bewitching creature who just counted an autumn less.—My scarcity of English denies me the power of doing her justice in that language; but you know the Scotch idiom, She was a bonie, sweet, sonsie lass.—In short, she altogether unwittingly to herself, initiated me in a certain delicious Passion, which in spite of acid Disappointment, gin-horse Prudence and bookworm Philosophy, I hold to be the first of human joys, our dearest pleasure here below.—How she caught the contagion I can't say; you medical folks talk much of infection by breathing the same air, the touch, &c. but I never expressly told her that I loved her.—Indeed I did not well know myself, why I liked so much to loiter behind with her, when returning in the evening from our labors; why the tones of her voice made my heartstrings thrill like an Eolian harp; and particularly, why my pulse beat such a furious ratann when I looked and fingered over her hand, to pick out the nettle-stings and thistles.—Among her other love-inspiring qualifications, she sung sweetly; and 'twas her favorite reel to which I attempted giving an embodied vehicle in rhyme.—I was not so presumtive as to imagine that I could make verses like printed ones, composed by men who had Greek and Latin; but my girl sung a song which was said to be composed by a small country laird's son, on one of his father's maids, with whom he was in love; and I saw no reason why I might not rhyme as well as he, for excepting smearing sheep and casting peats, his father living in the moors, he had no more Scholarcraft than I had.—

Thus with me began Love and Poesy; which at times have been my only, and till within this last twelvemonth have been my highest enjoyment.—My father struggled on till he reached the freedom in his lease, when he entered on a larger farm about ten miles farther in the country.—The nature of the bargain was such as to throw a little ready money in his hand at the commencement, otherwise the affair would have been impractible.—For four years we lived comfortably here; but a lawsuit between him and his Landlord commencing, after three years tossing and whirling in the vortex of Litigation, my father was just saved from absorption in a jail by phthisical consumption, which after two years promises, kindly stept in and snatch'd him away—"To where the wicked cease from troubling, and where the weary be at rest."[4]

It is during this climacterick that my little story is most eventful.—I was, at the beginning of this period, perhaps the most ungainly, aukward being in the parish.—No Solitaire was less acquainted with the ways of the world.— My knowledge of ancient story was gathered from Salmon's and Guthrie's geographical grammars; my knowledge of modern manners, and of literature and criticism, I got from the Spectator.—These, with Pope's works, some plays of Shakespear, Tull and Dickson on Agriculture. The Pantheon, Locke's Essay on the human understanding, Stackhouse's history of the bible, Justice's British Gardiner's directory, Boyle's lectures, Allan Ramsay's works, Taylor's scripture doctrine of original sin, a select Collection of English songs, and Hervey's meditations had been the extent of my reading.—The Collection of Songs was my vade mecum.—I pored over them, driving my cart or walking to labor, song by song, verse by verse; carefully noting the true tender or sublime from affectation and fustian.—I am convinced I owe much to this for my critic-craft such at it is.—

In my seventeenth year, to give my manners a brush, I went to a country dancing school.—My father had an unaccountable antipathy [to (*deleted*)] against these meetings; and my going was, what to this hour I repent, in absolute defiance of his commands.—My father, as I said before, was the sport of strong passions: from that instance of rebellion he took a kind of dislike to me, which, I believe was one cause of that dissipation which marked my future years.—I only say, Dissipation, comparative with the strictness and sobriety of Presbyterean country life; for though the will-o'-wisp meteors of thoughtless Whim were almost the sole lights of my path, yet early ingrained

---

[4] Job 3:17.

313

Piety and Virtue never failed to point me out the line of Innocence.—The great misfortune of my life was, never to have AN AIM.—I had felt early some stirrings of Ambition, but they were the blind gropins of Homer's Cyclops round the walls of his cave: I saw my father's situation entailed on me perpetual labor.—The only two doors by which I could enter the fields of fortune were, the most niggardly economy, or the little chicaning art of bargain-making: the first is so contracted an aperture, I never could squeeze myself into it; the last, I always hated the contamination of the threshold.—Thus, abandoned of [every (*deleted*)] aim or view in life; with a strong appetite for sociability, as well from native hilarity as from a pride of observation and remark; a constitutional hypochondriac taint which made me fly solitude; add to all these incentives to social life, my reputation for bookish knowledge, a certain wild, logical talent, and a strength of thought something like the rudiments of good sense, made me generally a welcome guest; so 'tis no great wonder that always "where two or three were met together, there was I in the midst of them."[5]—But far beyond all the other impulses of my heart was, un penchant á l'adorable moitiée du genre humain.—My heart was compleatly tinder, and was eternally lighted up by some Goddess or other: and like every warfare in this world, I was sometimes crowned with success, and sometimes mortified with defeat.—At the plough, scythe or reap-hook I feared no competitor, and set Want at defiance; and as I never cared farther for my labors than while I was in actual exercise, I spent the evening in the way after my own heart.—A country lad rarely carries on an amour without an assisting confident.—I possessed a curiosity, zeal and intrepid dexterity in these matters which recommended me a proper Second in duels of that kind; and I dare say, I felt as much pleasure at being in the secret of half the amours in the parish, as ever did Premier at knowing the intrigues of half the courts of Europe.—

The very goosefeather in my hand seems instinctively to know the well-worn path of my imagination, the favorite theme of my song; and is with difficulty restrained from giving you a couple of paragraphs on the amours of my Compeers, the humble Inmates of the farm-house and cottage; but the grave sons of Science, Ambition or Avarice baptize these things by the name of Follies.—To the sons and daughters of labor and poverty they are matters of the most serious nature: to them, the ardent hope, the stolen interview,

---

5 Matthew 18:20.

the tender farewell, are the greatest and most delicious part of their enjoyments.—

Another circumstance in my life which made very considerable alterations in my mind and manners was, I spent my seventeenth[6] summer on a smuggling [coast] a good distance from home at a noted school, to learn Mensuration, Surveying, Dialling, &c. in which I made a pretty good progress.— But I made greater progress in the knowledge of mankind.—The contraband trade was at that time very successful; scenes of swaggering riot and roaring dissipation were as yet new to me; and I was no enemy to social life.—Here, though I learned to look unconcernedly on a large tavern-bill, and mix without fear in a drunken squabble, yet I went on with a high hand in my Geometry; till the sun entered Virgo, a month which is always a carnival in my bosom, a charming Fillette who lived next door to the school overset my Trigonomertry, and set me off in a tangent from the sphere of my studies.— I struggled on with my Sines and Co-sines for a few days more; but stepping out to the garden one charming noon, to take the sun's altitude, I met with my Angel,

> —*Like Proserpine gathering flowers,*
> *Herself a fairer flower*—[7]

It was vain to think of doing any more good at school.—The remaining week I staid, I did nothing but craze the faculties of my soul about her, or steal out to meet with her; and the two last nights of my stay in the country, had sleep been a mortal sin, I was innocent.—

I returned home very considerably improved.—My reading was enlarged with the very important addition of Thomson's and Shenstone's works; I had seen mankind in a new phasis; and I engaged several of my schoolfellows to keep up a literary correspondence with me.—This last helped me much on in composition.—I had met with a collection of letters by the Wits of Queen Ann's reign, and I pored over them most devoutly.—I kept copies of any of my own letters that pleased me, and a comparison between them and the composition of most of my correspondents flattered my vanity.—I carried this whim so far that though I had not three farthings worth of business in

---

[6] "Seventeenth" has been deleted, and "nineteenth or twentieth" written above it in another hand.

[7] Milton, *Paradise Lost*, IV, 269.

the world, yet every post brought me as many letters as if I had been a broad, plodding son of Day-book & Ledger.—

My life flowed on much in the same tenor till my twenty third year.—Vive l'amour et vive la bagatelle, were my sole principles of action.—The addition of two more Authors to my library gave me great pleasure; Sterne and Mckenzie.—Tristram Shandy and the Man of Feeling were my bosom favorites.—Poesy was still a darling walk for my mind, but 'twas only the humour of the hour.—I had usually half a dozen or more pieces on hand; I took up one or other as it suited the momentary tone of the mind, and dismissed it as it bordered on fatigue.—My Passions when once they were lighted up, raged like so many devils, till they got vent in rhyme; and then conning over my verses, like a spell, soothed all into quiet.—None of the rhymes of those days are in print, except, Winter, a dirge, the eldest of my printed pieces; The death of Poor Mailie, John Barleycorn, And songs first, second and third: song second was the ebullition of that passion which ended the forementioned school-business.—

My twenty third year was to me an important era.—Partly thro' whim, and partly that I wished to set about doing something in life, I joined with a flax-dresser in a neighbouring town, to learn his trade and carry on the business of manufacturing and retailing flax.—This turned out a sadly unlucky affair.— My Partner was a scoundrel of the first water who made money by the mystery of thieving; and to finish the whole, while we were giving a welcoming carousal to the New year, our shop, by the drunken carelessness of my Partner's wife, took fire and was burnt to ashes; and left me like a true Poet, not worth sixpence.—I was obliged to give up business; the clouds of misfortune were gathering thick round my father's head, the darkest of which was, he was visibly far gone in a consumption; and to crown all, a belle-fille whom I adored and who had pledged her soul to meet me in the field of matrimony, jilted me with peculiar circumstances of mortification.—The finishing evil that brought up the rear of this infernal file was my hypochondriac complaint being irritated to such a degree, that for three months I was in [a] diseased state of body and mind, scarcely to be envied by the hopeless wretches who have just got their mittimus, "Depart from me, ye Cursed."—[8]

From this adventure I learned something of a town-life.—But the principal thing which gave my mind a turn was, I formed a bosom-friendship with a young fellow, the first created being I had ever seen, but a hapless son of

[8] Matthew 25:41.

misfortune.—He was the son of a plain mechanic; but a great Man in the neighbourhood taking him under his patronage gave him a genteel education with a view to bettering his situation in life.—The Patron dieing just as he was ready to launch forth into the world, the poor fellow in despair went to sea; where after a variety of good and bad fortune, a little before I was acquainted with him, he had been set ashore by an American Privateer on the wild coast of Connaught, stript of every thing.—I cannot quit this poor fellow's story without adding that he is at this moment Captain of a large westindiaman belonging to the Thames.—

This gentleman's mind was fraught with courage, independance, Magnanimity, and every noble, manly virtue.—I loved him, I admired him, to a degree of enthusiasm; and I strove to imitate him.—In some measure I succeeded: I had the pride before, but he taught it to flow in proper channels.—His knowledge of the world was vastly superiour to mine, and I was all attention to learn.—He was the only man I ever saw who was a greater fool than myself when WOMAN was the presiding star; but he spoke of a certain fashionable failing with levity, which hitherto I had regarded with horror.—Here his friendship did me a mischief; and the consequence was, that soon after I resumed the plough, I wrote the WELCOME inclosed.—My reading was only encreased by two stray volumes of Pamela, and one of Ferdinand Count Fathom, which gave me some idea of Novels.—Rhyme, except some religious pieces which are in print, I had given up; but meeting with Fergusson's Scotch Poems, I strung anew my wildly-sounding, rustic lyre with emulating vigour.—When my father died, his all went among the rapacious hell-hounds that growl in the kennel of justice; but we made a shift to scrape a little money in the family amongst us, with which, to keep us together, my brother and I took a neighbouring farm.—My brother wanted my harebrained imagination as well as my social and amorous madness, but in good sense and every sober qualification he was far my superiour.—

I entered on this farm with a full resolution, "Come, go to, I will be wise!" —I read farming books; I calculated crops; I attended markets; and in short, in spite of "The devil, the world and the flesh," I believe I would have been a wise man; but the first year from unfortunately buying in bad seed, the second from a late harvest, we lost half of both our crops: this overset all my wisdom, and I returned "Like the dog to his vomit, and the sow that was washed to her wallowing in the mire.—"9

9 Peter 2:22.

I now began to be known in the neighbourhood as a maker of rhymes.— The first of my poetic offspring that saw the light was a burlesque lamentation on a quarrel between two rev^d Calvinists, both of them dramatis person in my Holy Fair.—I had an idea myself that the piece had some merit; but to prevent the worst, I gave a copy of it to a friend who was very fond of these things, and told him I could not guess who was the Author of it, but that I thought it pretty clever.—With a certain side of both clergy and laity it met with a roar of applause.—Holy Willie's Prayer next made its appearance, and alarmed the kirk-Session so much that they held three several meetings to look over their holy artillery, if any of it was pointed against profane Rhymers. Unluckily for me, my idle wanderings led me, on another side, point-blank within the reach of their heaviest metal.—This is the unfortunate story alluded to in my printed poem, The Lament.—'Twas a shocking affair, which I cannot yet bear to recollect; and had very nearly given [me] one or two of the principal qualifications for a place among those who have lost the chart and mistake the reckoning of Rationality.—I gave up my part of the farm to my brother, as in truth it was only nominally mine; and made what little preparation was in my power for Jamaica.—Before leaving my native country for ever, I resolved to publish my Poems.—I weighed my productions as impartially as in my power; I thought they had merit; and 'twas a delicious idea that I would be called a clever fellow, even though it should never reach my ears a poor Negro-driver, or perhaps a victim to that inhospitable clime gone to the world of Spirits.—I can truly say that pauvre Inconnu as I then was, I had pretty nearly as high an idea of myself and my works as I have at this moment.—It [is] ever my opinion that the great, unhappy mistakes and blunders, both in a rational and religious point of view, of which we see thousands daily guilty, are owing to their ignorance, or mistaken notions of themselves.—To know myself had been all along my constant study.—I weighed myself alone; I balanced myself with others; I watched every means of information how much ground I occupied both as a Man and as a Poet: I studied assiduously Nature's DESIGN where she seem'd to have intended the various LIGHTS and SHADES in my character.—I was pretty sure my Poems would meet with some applause; but at the worst, the roar of the Atlantic would deafen the voice of Censure, and the novelty of west-Indian scenes make me forget Neglect.—

I threw off six hundred copies, of which I had got subscriptions for about three hundred and fifty.—My vanity was highly gratified by the reception I met with from the Publick; besides pocketing, all expences deducted, near twenty pounds.—This last came very seasonable, as I was about to indent myself for want of money to pay my freight.—So soon as I was master of nine guineas, the price of wafting me to the torrid zone, I bespoke a passage in the very first ship that was to sail, for

> *Hungry wind {ruin} had me in the wind—*[10]

I had for some time been sculking from covert to covert under all the terrors of a Jail; as some ill-advised, ungrateful people had uncoupled the merciless legal Pack at my heels.—I had taken the last farewel of my few friends; my chest was on the road to Greenock; I had composed my last song I should ever measure in Caledonia, "The gloomy night is gathering fast," when a letter from Dr Blacklock to a friend of mine overthrew all my schemes by rousing my poetic ambition.—The Doctor belonged to a set of Critics for whose applause I had not even dared to hope.—His idea that I would meet with every encouragement for a second edition fired me so much that away I posted to Edinburgh without a single acquaintance in town, or a single letter of introduction in my pocket.—The baneful Star that had so long shed its blasting influence in my Zenith, for once made a revolution to the Nadir; and the providential care of a good God placed me under the patronage of one of his noblest creatures, the Earl of Glencairn: "Oublie moi, Grand Dieu, si jamais je l'oublie!"—

I need relate no farther.—At Edin^r I was in a new world: I mingled among many classes of men, but all of them new to me; and I was all attention "to catch the manners living as they rise."—

You can now, Sir, form a pretty near guess what sort of a Wight he is whom for some time you have honored with your correspondence.—That Fancy & Whim, keen Sensibility and riotous Passions may still make him zig-zag in his future path of life, is far from being improbable; but come what will, I shall answer for him the most determinate integrity and honor; and though his evil star should again blaze in his meridian with ten-fold more direful influence, he may reluctantly tax Friendship with Pity but no more.—

---

[10] Not identified.

Appendix C:
Guide to the Pronunciation of Scots

Burns wrote his best poems in the Scots language, which like American derives from Anglo-Saxon. He did not write in dialect using Ayrshire speech but in a selection from all the Scots dialects he knew or had read in Scots vernacular literature. To appreciate Burns's poems, one must pronounce them, except for those written in pure English, in a Scots way. Even those poems or passages written in Scots-English, that is, those that look like English but which have occasional vernacular words or occasional rime words of non-English sound in spite of English spelling, should be so pronounced.

Considerable progress can be made toward learning to pronounce Scots by unsystematic effort. One can simply trill "r," pronounce "a" as *ah,* "ow" or "ou" (*cow, house*) as *oo,* medial or terminal "gh" and "ch" (*night, nicht*) with the German velar sound in *ach.* One can pick up a great deal by carefully listening to Burns's rimes. And one can also listen to native Scots folk singers, like Ewan MacColl, on records of Scots songs (being careful, however, to avoid the welter of sentimental and arty renditions of Burns's songs not true to his language at all).

But those who wish to augment these methods with a more systematic approach should use the following Guide, which is based on (1) the relationship between Central Scots and American sounds and (2) the sounds indicated by Burns's spelling (unfortunately very inconsistent). The learner can thus use his knowledge of his own speech to determine Scots and as an additional benefit be able to determine the meaning of many Scots words by now recognizing the English counterpart (example: if we know that the English medial *v* is generally not found in Scots, then we recognize Scots *siller* as English *silver*). The Guide is simplified drastically by equating wide ranges of real Scots sounds to a relatively few sounds almost all familiar to American ears. To use it, the student need not have training in linguistics but should be familiar with the International Phonetic Alphabet, a description of which can be found in any good dictionary. Those who wish to be even more accurate in pronunciation than the degree of accuracy this Guide is designed to teach should study James Wilson's *The Dialect of Robert Burns* (see Bibliography) and William Grant's Introduction in the first volume of the *Scottish National Dictionary*.

I wish to acknowledge with gratitude the use I have made of an unpublished, very complete guide to the pronunciation of Central Scots compiled by Mr. Trevor Hill of the Linguistic Survey of Scotland.

I. SCOTS SOUNDS

A. *Vowels* (the only vowel sound distinctively different from most American speech is marked by an asterisk; there is no [æ] as in American *man* nor [ʊ] as in American *took* in Scots)

sound	American equivalent
[ə]	b*u*tter, *a*bout
[i]	*see*
[ɪ]	s*i*t
[e]	s*ay*, ch*a*otic
[ɛ]	s*e*t
[a]	f*a*ther, n*o*t
[ɔ]	s*aw*
[o]	s*o*, n*o*tation
[u]	t*oo*
[ai]	b*uy*
[au]	c*ow*
[əɪ]*	similar to the diphthong of Brooklynese *voice* and *verse* [vəɪs]; not the vowel of American *joy* [dʒɔɪ], it is formed near the front of the mouth and does not have lip-rounding.

B. CONSONANTS UNLIKE AMERICAN ENGLISH

x as in German *ach,* that is, further back (velar) than German *ich* (palatal).

r always a trill, i.e. tapping the tip of the tongue above the front teeth even if only a single tap; the General American retroflex sound (the tongue curled back) when pronouncing an *r* after a vowel is to be avoided. And natives of Eastern New England and the South should be careful to pronounce all written *r*'s.

II. CORRESPONDENCE OF AMERICAN AND SCOTS SOUNDS

A. *Stressed vowels*

(General Note: unlike American speech, Scots vowels preceding *r* are not changed in quality except for those instances explicity described below)

American	Scots
[i]	generally the same
[ɪ]	generally the same
[e]	generally the same, but often [əɪ], especially terminally: *aye* (always), *clay, hay, May, pay, stay, way, rein, jail, tailor;* and sometimes [a] when indicated by spelling: *outspak, tak, cam*
[ɛ]	generally the same; [i] in most "ea"-spellings: *thread, breast* [θrid, brist]; but sometimes [e], especially in "ear"-spellings: *learn, earth, verse* [lern, erθ, vers]
[æ]	generally [a]: *cat, bag* [kat, bag]; but sometimes [ɔ] when required by rime or spelling "au" or "aw"; and [e] when followed by an unstressed syllable other than an inflectional ending: *master, jacket* [mestər, dʒekət]
[a] spelled "a"	generally same, but [ɔ] when before silent *l*: *small, salt* [smɔ, sɔt], and usually [e] before *r* plus a consonant: *arm, carter, charms* [erm, kertər, tʃerms]
[a] spelled "o"	[ɔ]: *lot, knock, bodies* [lɔt, nɔk, bɔdiz]
[ɔ]	same, but [a] before *ng*, as indicated spelling: *sang* (song), *thrang* (throng) [saŋ, θraŋ]
[o]	commonly the same, but often [e] as indicated by rime or spelling; and often [ɔ] when terminal: *lade* (load), *blaw* (blow) [led, blɔ]
[ə] and [ʊ] spelled "u"	with some exceptions [ə]; *but, bull* [bət, bəl]; but [u] when final *l* is absent: *full, pull* [fu, pu]
[ə] spelled otherwise	generally [ɪ]: *blood, trouble* [blɪd, trɪbəl]
[u] or [ju] spelled "ew" or "ue"	same (*blew, dew, view, true*)

[ʊ], [u], [ju] spelled otherwise	(1.) very often [ɪ], especially when spelled "oo": *good, roof, school, tune, fruit* [gɪd, rɪf, skɪl, tɪn, frɪt]
	(2.) [e] or [je] finally and before *r* or the voiced fricatives ([z], [ʒ], [v], [ð]): *do, to use, poor* [de, jez, per]
	(3.) [jə] before [k], [x]: *book, sheuk* (shook), *teuch* (tough) [bjək, ʃjək, tjəx]
[au]	almost always [u]: *loud, out, round, down* [lud, ut, rund, dun]
[ai] and [oi]	always [əɪ] in American [oi]-words; and in American [ai]-words when final and before voiced fricatives ([z], [ʒ], [v], [ð]): *spoil, join, lie* (down), *five, despise, noise* [spəɪl, dʒəɪn, ləɪ, fəɪv, dɛspəɪz, nəɪz]; in other American [ai]-words the Scots for the diphthong is the same; but in some common ones [i]: *thy, e'e* (eye), *die, lie* (prevaricate) [ði, i, di, li]; and [ɪ] before [x]: *night* [nɪxt]

B. *Unstressed vowels*

Generally like American, but with more of their full value, less of a tendency to reduce all unstressed vowels to [ə]: *correct* [korɛk] instead of [kərɛkt], and *allow* [alu] instead of [əlau]. Unstressed final American [o] in polysyllabic words is Scots [ɔ]: *fellow, sorrow, tobacco* [fɛlɔ, sorɔ, tobakɔ].

C. *Consonant changes* (where the consonant feature is not listed, it remains the same)

1. Consonants at the end of or between syllables

American sound	Scots sound
[tʃ], [dʒ]	generally in words of Germanic origin [k] and [g] respectively: *sic* (such), *brig* (bridge) [sək, brɪg]
[kt]	[k]: *fact, distracted* [fak, dɪstrakət]
[mbl], [mbr], [ndl], [ndr]	the middle consonant absent in these clusters: *rumble, timber, candle, wonder, thunder* [rəml, tɪmər, kanl, wɪnər, θənər]
[nd], [ld]	[d] absent: *land, child* [lan, tʃil]
[l], [lt], [ld], [lk]	[l] is usually absent after the back vowels ([u], [o], [ɔ]): *wall, fault, fa'* (fall), *a'* (all), *fu'* (full), *soldier* [wɔ, fɔt, fɔ, ɔ, fu, sodʒər]

| [v] | very often absent: *owre* (over), *o't* (of it), *e'en* (even), *gies* (gives), *ne'er* (never) [or, oɪt, in, giz, nir] |
| (silent "gh" spelling) | generally [x]: *weight* [wext] |

2. Consonants at the beginning of syllables

American sound	*Scots sound*
[tʃ]	commonly [k] in Germanic words: *chaff, churn* [kaf, kirn]
[tj] or [tʃ]	[t]: *creature, natural* [kretər, netərəl]

3. Consonants in inflectional endings:

| -[əd] or -[d] or -[t] for -"ed" | -[ət] or -[t] after [t], [d], [p], [k] or where rime requires: *blinket* (blinked), *hookit* (hooked), *painted, crowded, stopped, cracked, speckled* [blinkət, hjəkət, pentət, krudət, stɔpət, krakət, spɛkəlt] |
| -[ɪŋ] for -"ing" | -[ən]: *seeing, waiting* [siən, wetən] |

III. BURN'S SCOTS SPELLING

Phonetic equivalents of uniquely Scots words and of Scots-English words sometimes spelled differently from their Standard English counterparts

Spelling	*Sound*
ei, ee, e'e, ie	[i]: *breist, neebors, e'e, skiegh* (breast, neighbors, eye, skittish)
a-e, ai, -ae	[e]: *hame, ain, caird, sae* (home, own, tinker, so)
a, a'	[a]: *lang, ca', vera* (long, call, very)
aw, au	[ɔ]: *snaw, auld, cauld* (snow, old, cold)
ou, u'	[u]: *fou, fu'* (full)
ow	[au]: *pow, cowte* (poll, colt)
ui, u-e	[ɪ]: *guid, gude* (good or god)
eu	[jə]: *sheuk, leuk* (shook, look)
ch, gh	[x]: *nicht, teuch* (night, tough)

The Library of Literature